Photography Wisdom

www.thedigitalimagemaker.com

www.dimagemaker.com

Photography Wisdom

A Practical Guide
To
Successful Photography
and
Self Expression

Wayne J. Cosshall

TechnoMagickal Press

An imprint of
TechnoMagickal Pty Ltd
Melbourne, Australia

www.TechnoMagickal.com

TechnoMagickal Press
Published by
TechnoMagickal Pty Ltd
26 Kathleen Street, Preston, VIC 3072 Australia
www.TechnoMagickal.com

Copyright 2010 © Wayne J. Cosshall

The moral right of the author has been asserted.

All rights reserved. No part of this publication may be reproduced or transmitted in any form or by any means, electronic or mechanical, including scanning, recording, scanning or by any information storage and retrieval system, without permission in writing from TechnoMagickal Press. Reviewers may quote brief passages.

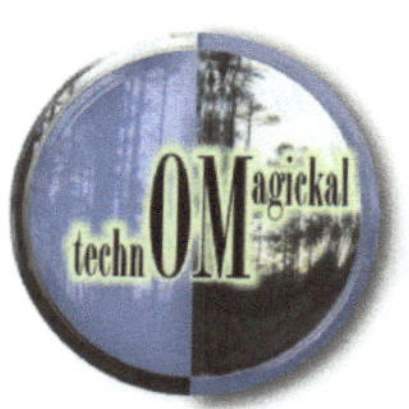

ISBN: 978-0-9807500-1-0

Printed in the United States of America and in the United Kingdom.

For Bruno

About the book

Photography Wisdom came about from my desire to take a series of tips for better photography I have been publishing on www.dimagemaker.com, expand on them and publish them in book form. Some people like and use online resources but others do not, and it seemed a shame to miss out on reaching such people. Plus the printed form (and even e-books) offers a different look and design layout options than a website does.

The tips come from my 35+ years of photography experience, from my passions of landscape, macro, collage and infrared photography to portraits, weddings, product shots and the odd bit of fashion. They also draw from my varied other interests and activities: helping people overcome creative blocks, teaching photography, art and computers at all levels of adult education, a passion for science, philosophy, spirituality and history, and much more. I find it constantly amazing that interests in one area will often yield insights in a completely different field.

Photography Wisdom is designed to be used in many ways. You can read it through sequentially, dive into it at random or go find the specific tip relevant to whatever you are dealing with at the time. I took particular time over the index to ensure you can access the book directly to what you need.

As with all books, I provide only information. What you do with it is your responsibility. So the author and publishers accept no responsibility for any damage, costs, loses or missed opportunities that you incur.

Dedication

I dedicate this book to by late brother-in-law, Bruno. He was a deeply sensitive and creative man who hid both well, though not well for him as it turned out. While my wife and I were working slowly to help him to find an expression for his creativity, sadly his sensitivity caught up with him first. If ever there was a perfect example of how critical it is for creative people to get in touch with this aspect of themselves, Bruno was it.

We love you and miss you Bruno.

About the author

Wayne J. Cosshall has been a photographer since he turned 14 and was given his first SLR by his parents to take pictures through his telescopes. Since then his photography has come more down to earth, though his wife claims he never has.

While growing in his photographic practice, Wayne shaped an academic career in Computer Science, specialising in computer graphics and imaging. After close on 20 years Wayne left the university system for awhile and started writing full time. Later Wayne came back to teaching through workshops, teaching and running the photography department at a number of private universities, consulting with others on digital photography course design and consulting with other education providers. Through this period Wayne's photography broadened and he brought his professional computer skills across into his imaging, working first with his own software to do image manipulation and later becoming expert with software like Photoshop and Painter, as well as many 3D graphics programs.

Wayne has exhibited his photography and digital art pieces both within Australia and internationally. For many years he co-directed the International Digital Art Awards with his friend and IDAA founder Steve Danzig. Wayne has been involved in organising several photography conferences, has curated a number of photography and digital art exhibitions and is active with a local photography biennale.

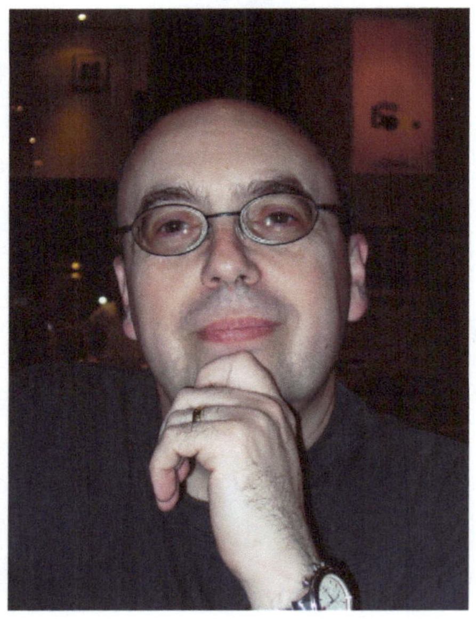

Acknowledgements

Many people have helped to shape this book and I would like to thank them.

Firstly I want to thank for wife, Adriana, and my daughter, Lauren, for putting up with me and for being guinea pigs. Adriana has also been a great proof reader and an excellent sounding board.

Secondly, I want to thank my best friend Steve Danzig, with whom I have shared many great discussions about photography and art, and also for involving me in his pet project, the IDAA, for many years.

Thirdly, my friends Tony Dimmock and John Pollard who have shared many great discussions of photography over beer and excellent food.

Lastly I want to thank all my students over the years. Writing a book is very much like teaching and the questions and issues we have discussed over the years has informed the writing of this book.

Contents

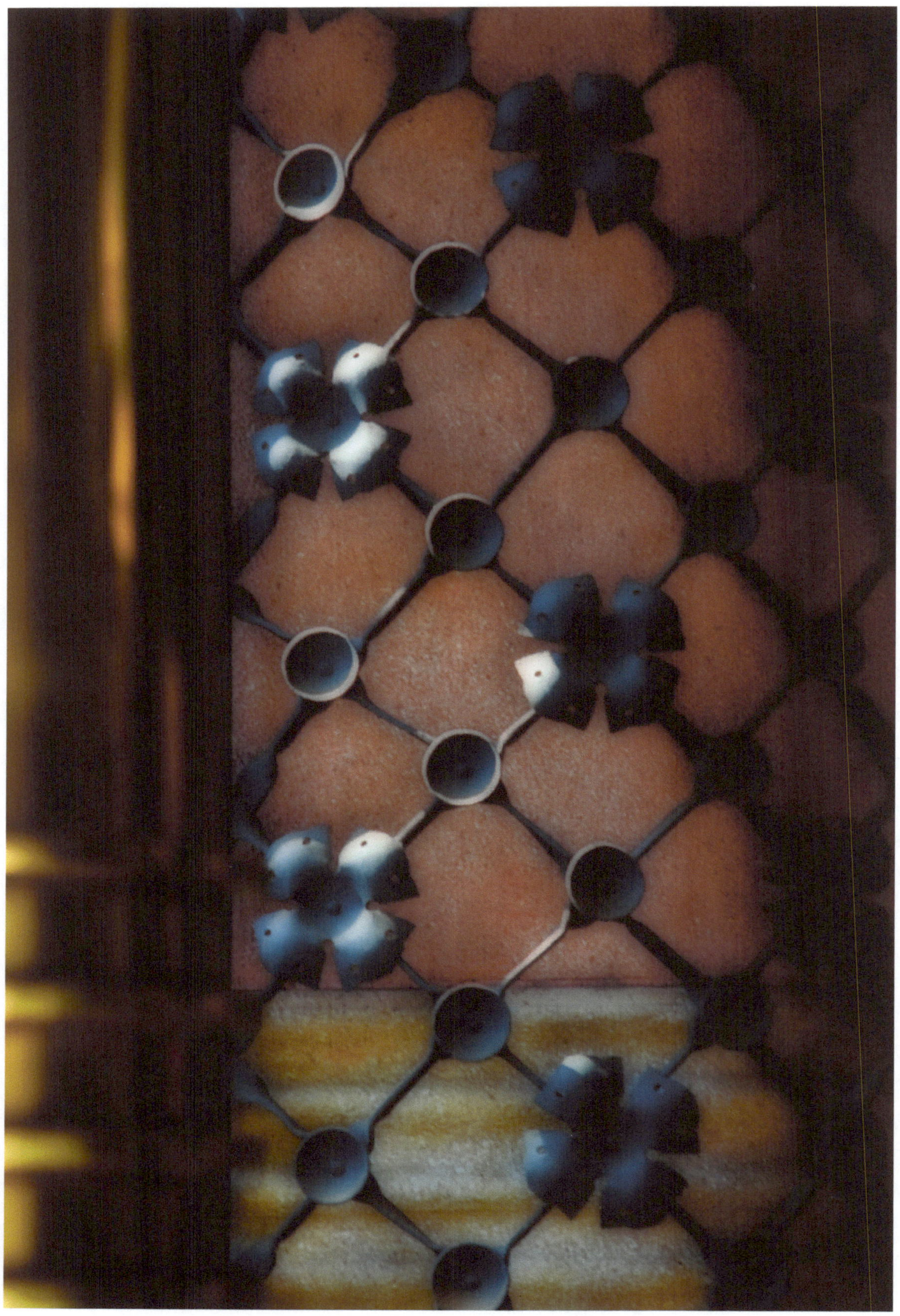

Introduction

There are so many ways to get stuck in our photographic practice. It is human nature to fall into ruts, to become habitual or unthinking about what we do, or to just plain get bored. It is also natural for the rest of our life to intrude, diverting us and sometimes causing us to forget what we were once passionate about. Thankfully there are so many ways to overcome this, reawaken our passion and to help us to extend and grow in our photographic practice that it need not be a lasting disconnection.

In this book we explore proven ways to extend ourselves as photographers and artists, from changing the way we think to adding to the techniques we use.

You can read and do one lecture a week, one a month, read them all at once, dive into the book at random as needed or use it any way you like. I've divided the book into sections, with each section grouping together a number of related ideas, lectures or action plans, whatever you wish to call them. For the sake of discussion in this book, I'll call them lectures. Each lecture has some associated images to stimulate you and some activities to help you make the subject of the lesson real and help you make the ideas your own.

The contents of this book have evolved over about ten years, from topics I have covered with my photography students and workshop participants, to short tips published on www.dimagemaker.com and now to the present form. As such they represent a distillation of my thinking about photography and the photographic process.

There are many more I could have included, and so a volume two will follow at some point soon. Putting this book together has also been an interesting exercise in looking at my photography. Since all the images in the book are mine, it prompted me to go through my catalogue of images and choose which ones would illustrate which point, and to also go out and shoot some more specifically for this book. In that process it has given me a new appreciate of some of my older images and caused me to rework some of them in line with my present thinking.

Photography is a wonderful, fluid, living thing and it is a great source of joy in my life. I hope it is in yours too.

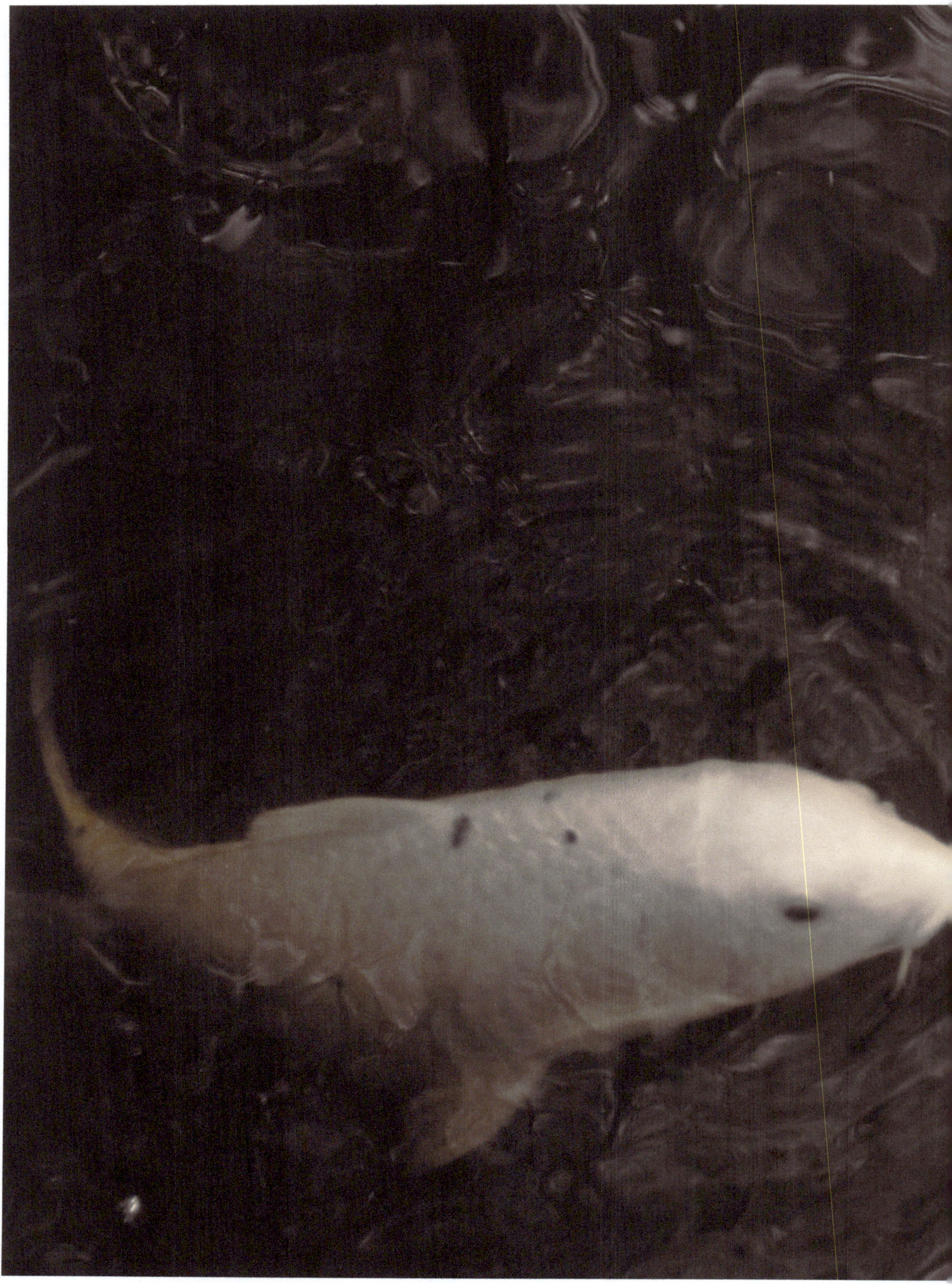

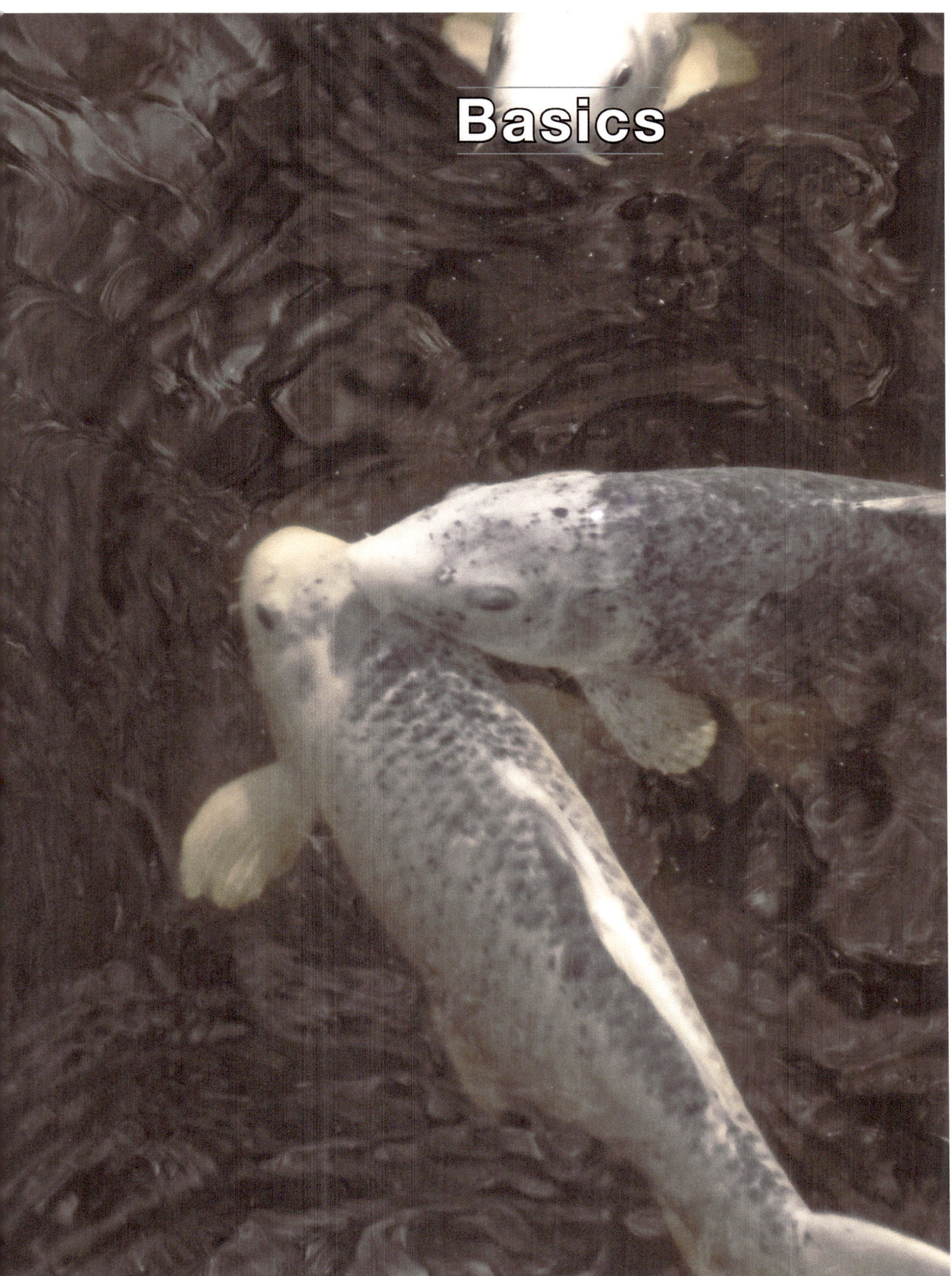

Basics

1. Composition

Composition is a far from simple topic, yet also not impossibly difficult. The main reason it is not simple is that there are no rules to simply follow. Yes, that's what I said: no rules. There are some principles of composition, but they are not rules because often the great shot requires that you break them.

The average photographer follows the rules. The outstanding photographer knows when to break them and how to make their own up.

A snap-shooter records what they are presented with, generally with little or no thought to the arrangement of subjects within the frame, while a professional crafts the position of and relationships between the objects in the scene.

What we are looking for with composition is a successful arrangement and inter-relationship between the main elements of the image and with the shape of the image. But successful in what way? Not some rules imposed by someone else, like a judge, but rather in what you want to say

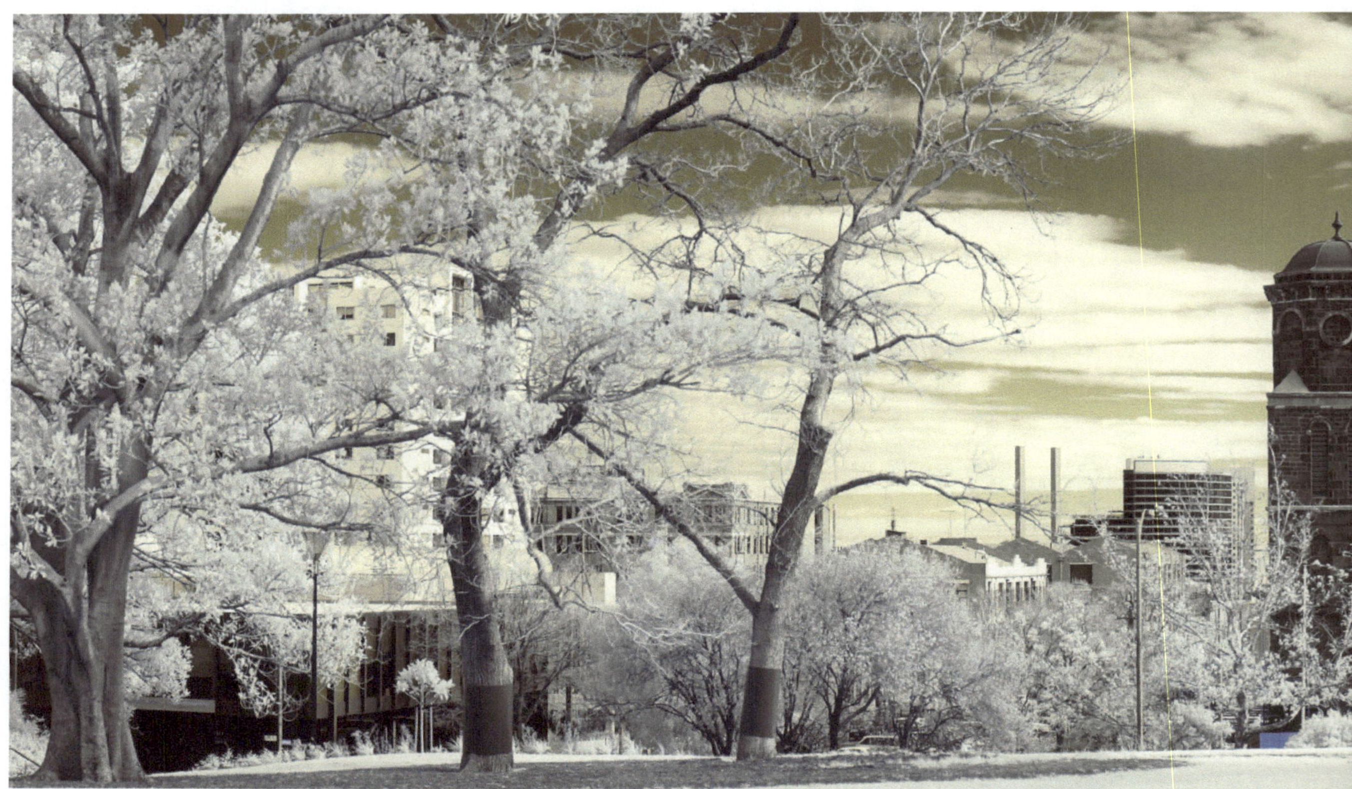

with the image. Everything that is in the image should contribute to this message and their placements within the frame and with respect to each other should all serve to enhance your vision.

In composition, you have the following design concepts to work with:

- Point
- Line
- Shape
- Negative Space
- Volume
- Value (brightness)
- Colour
- Texture
- Placement
- Repetition
- Rhythm
- Contrast or Variety
- Sharpness
- Balance

Furthermore, there are ideas about the placement of key elements in the image, such as the Rule of Thirds, static vs. dynamic arrangements, the Golden Section and more that can all be worked with.

A common thing we hear is that you should not put your main subject in the

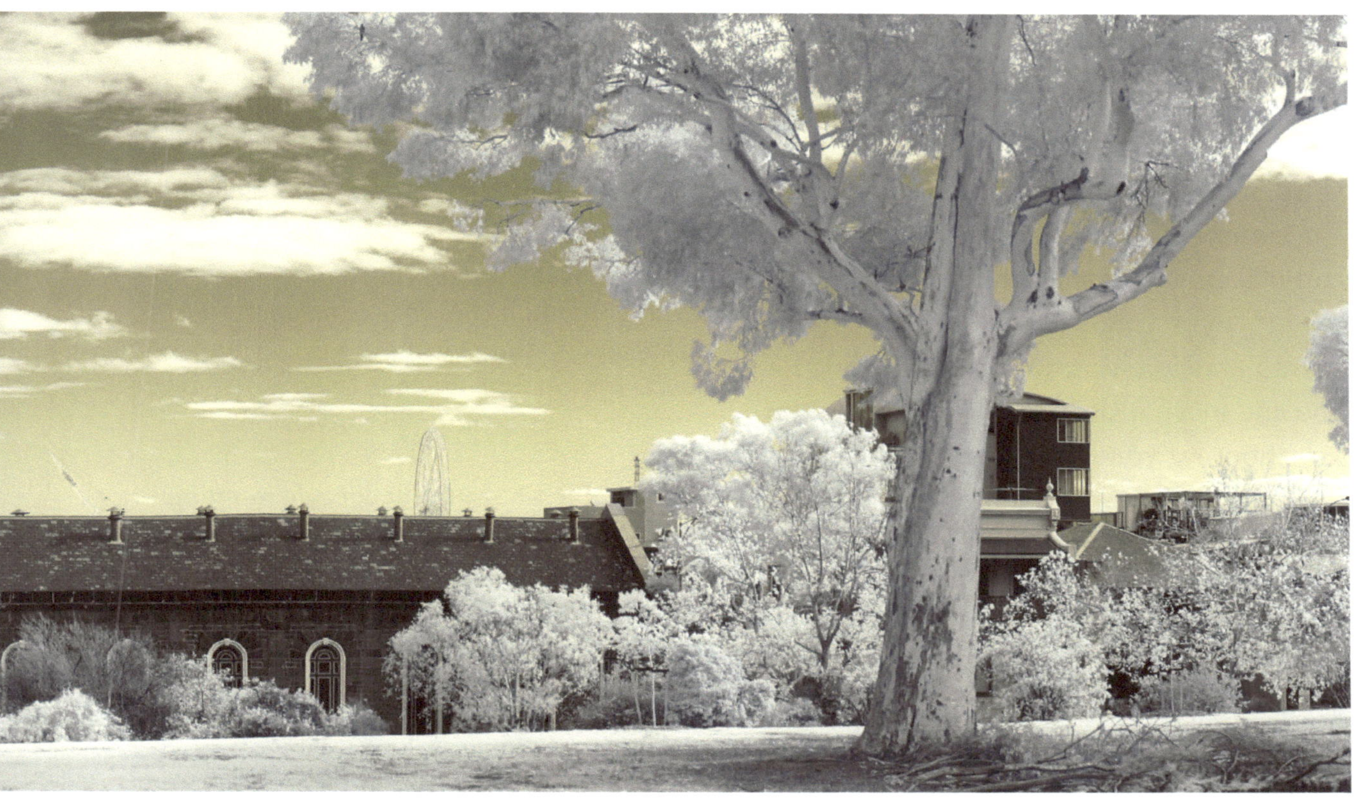

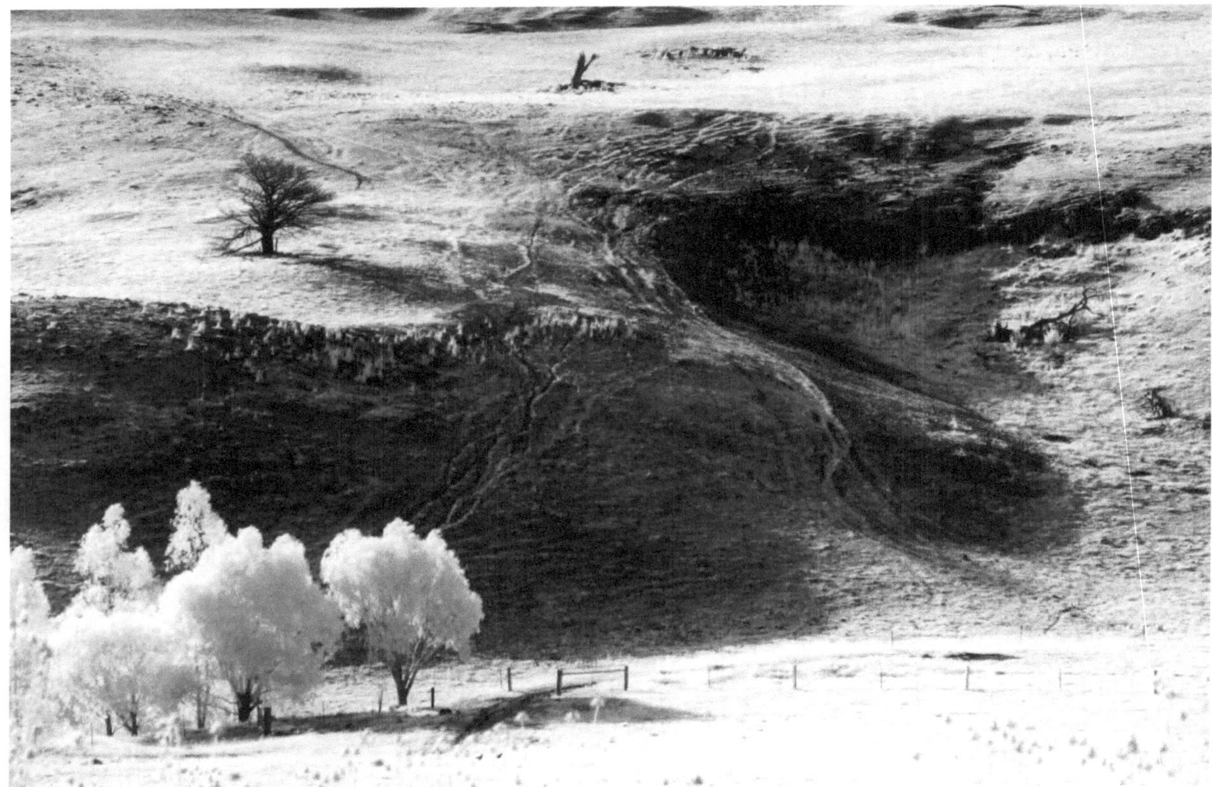

centre of the image. This is often good advice and placement on one of the one-third intersections works better much of the time. But there are times when a central placement is perfect. How can you tell when? By trying various subject placements and learning which ones work for you and in what situations. Then when you are shooting you listen to your intuition, which has been informed and trained by the prior practice.

There are also situations where the image works best if the main subject or subjects are put almost on the edge of the frame, moving them even further from the centre. This can be the case when you need to create a strong sense of space or sparseness in the image. Sometimes it is also best to substantially crop the main subject.

In the image above the strong, dark depression in the ground on the right is balanced by the single dark tree and the the group of white trees on the left. Seeking balance in an image is an important consideration in composition.

On the right we see an image where multiple elements come together to lead the viewer's eye deep into the background. The red curved rail with the line of the bridge serves to move you to the tower middle left, while the shadow of the bridge in the water does the same, making for a very strong pull. The red lamp top serves as a nice balance to this tower as well.

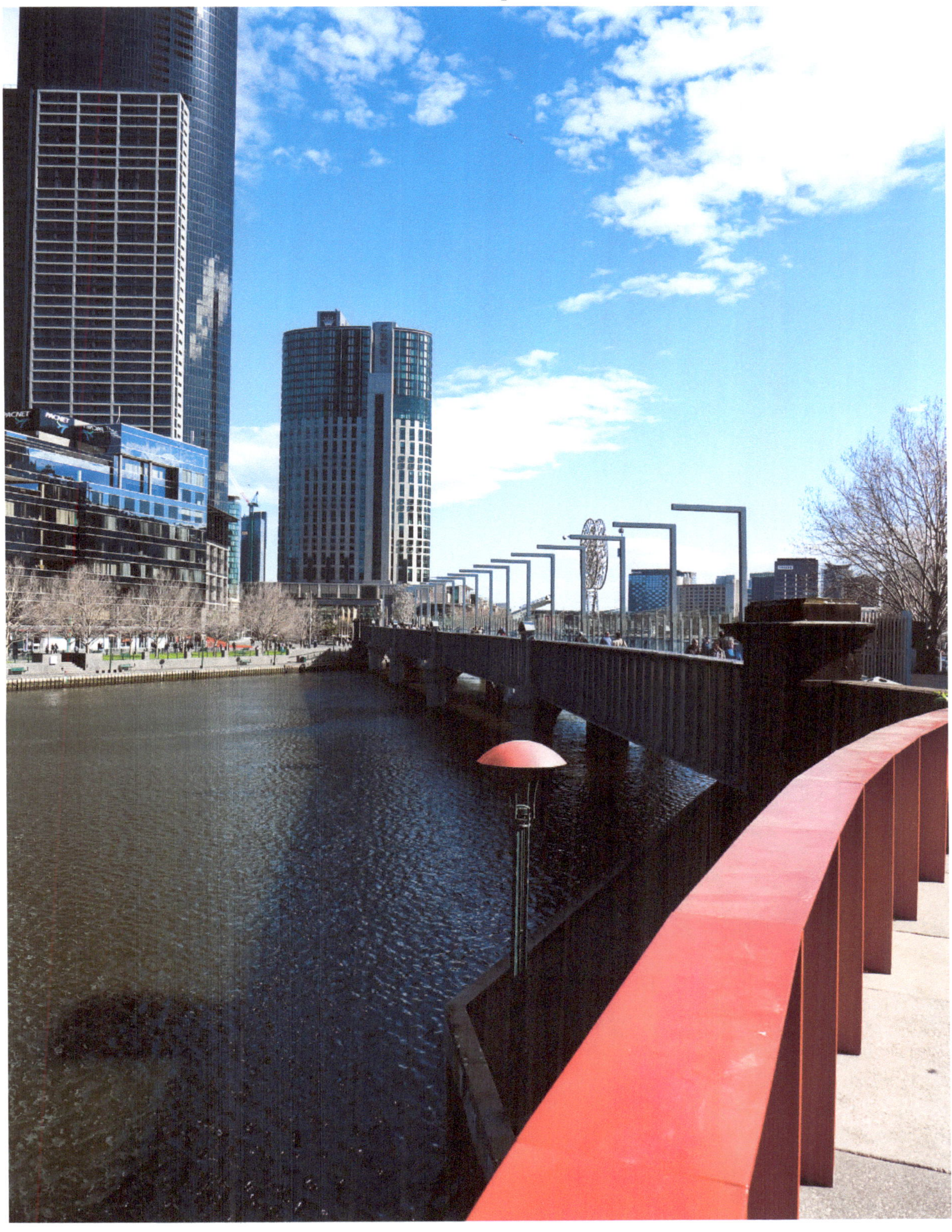

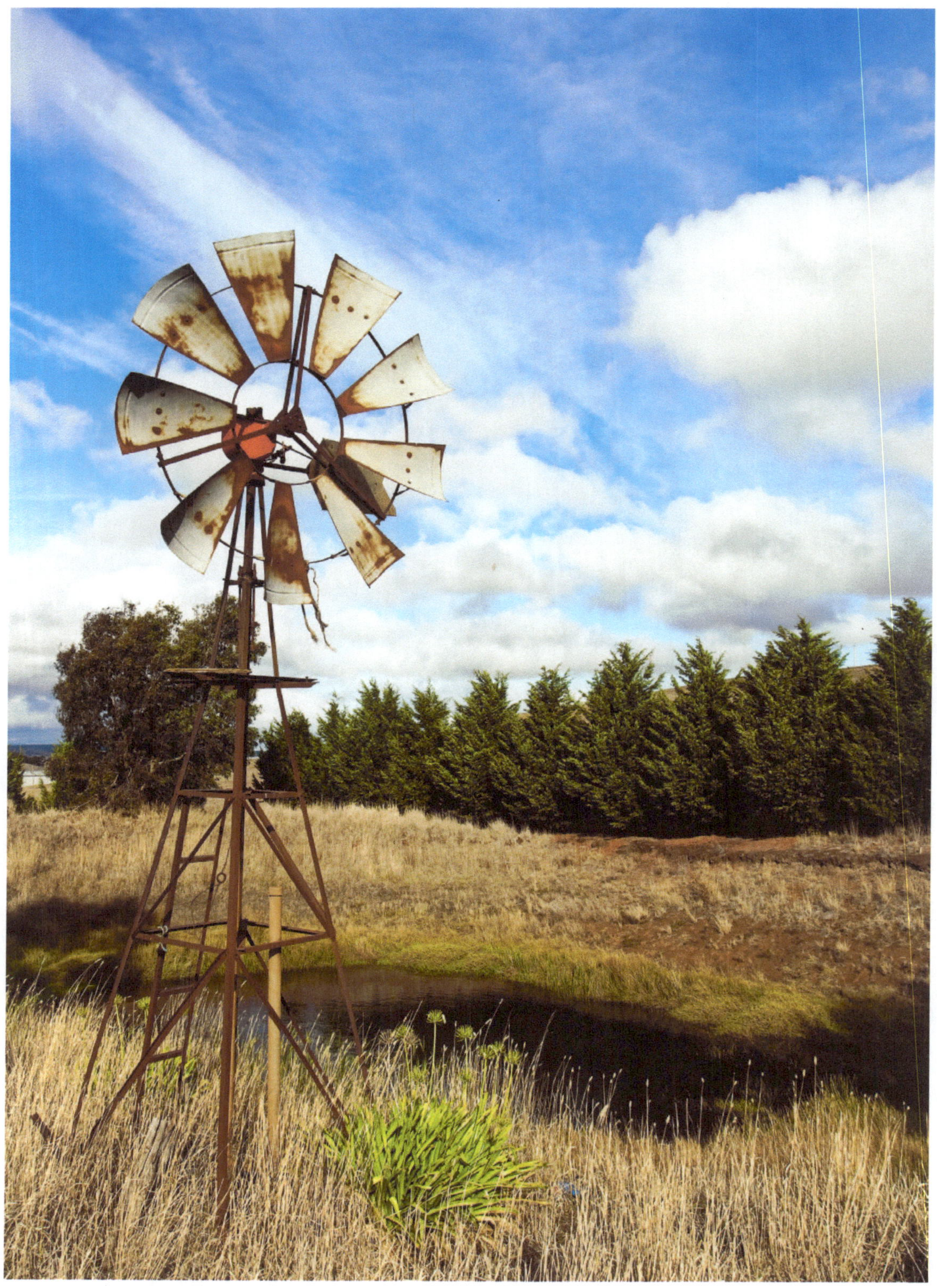

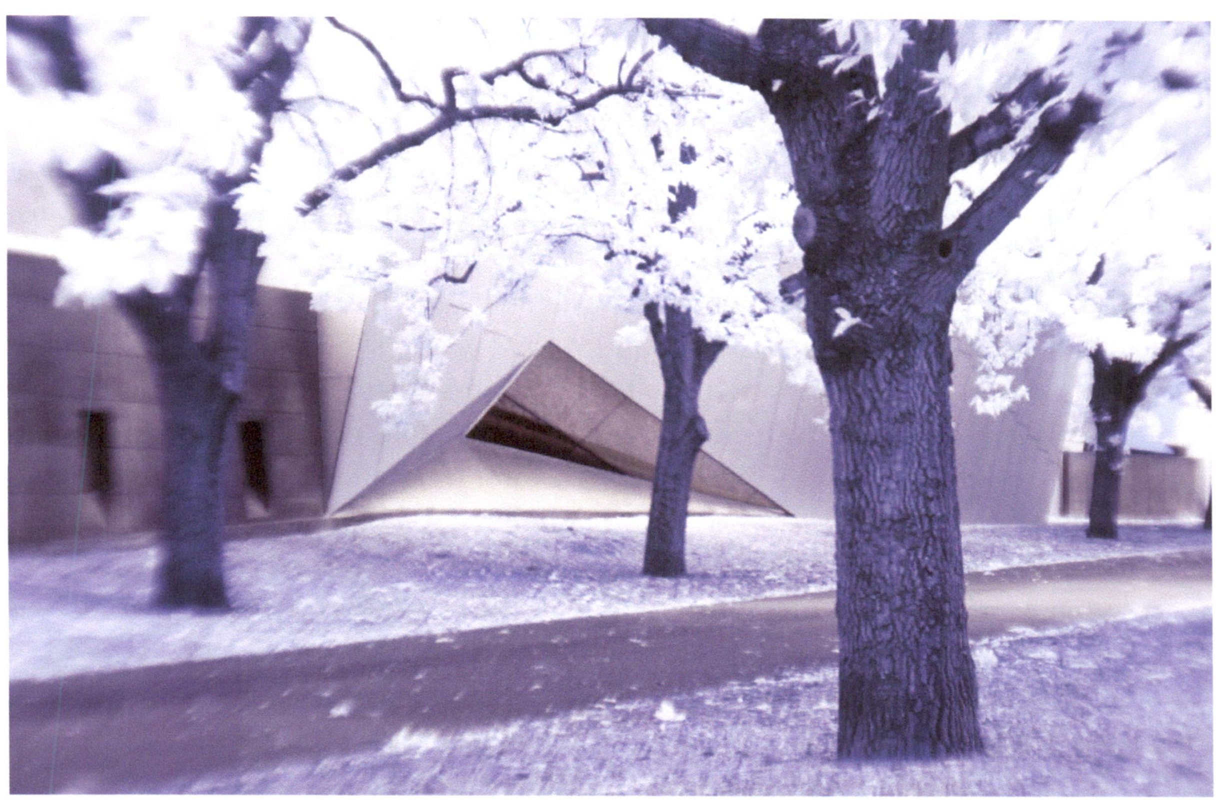

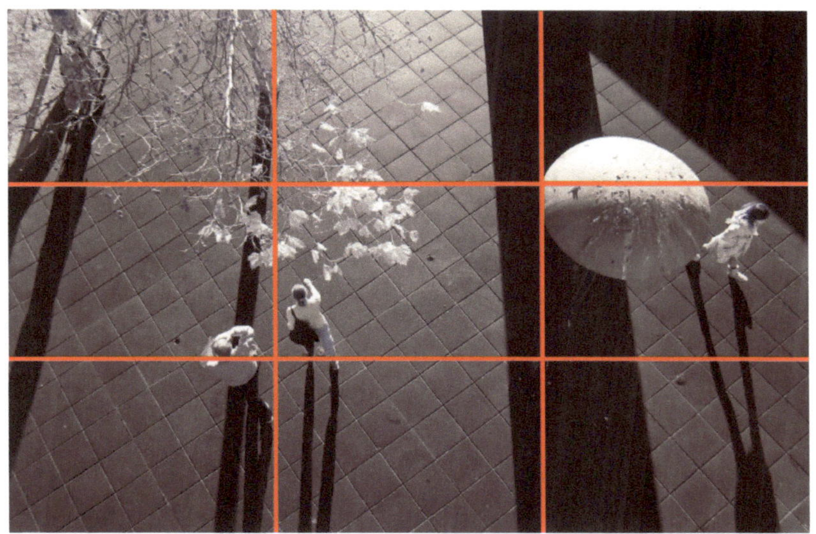

The rule of thirds divides the image up into thirds and recommends object placement on these divisions. Some cameras can project such a grid on the screen or in the viewfinder. While not universally appropriate, it has the benefit of being easy to visualise and use. It also often creates a pleasant arrangement.

2. Exposure

Exposure is what photography is all about: using light in the way you want to create the image that you intend or visualise.

With film, one has to expose appropriately for the characteristics of the film and, in the case of black and white, how it will be processed. Slide or transparency film does not tolerate over exposure very well, so many of us would under expose by half a stop to provide not only a bit of extra security but also to increase colour saturation. I say used to because I haven't really shot film in over 8 years. Colour negative film doesn't handle under exposure well, and so was often better over-exposed slightly.

Most of us are now shooting digital, and photography is all the better for it. Digital offers so many advantages over film that I fail to understand really why anyone is still using film in the smaller camera sizes, like 35mm. Digital does not tolerate both over and under exposure of an extreme, as pixels lock at either 0 on the under exposure side or the maximum value of 255 or 65,636 or something in between if the camera only uses 10, 12 or 14 bits in RAW mode.

Where digital cameras excel is in giving us the tools to properly handle exposure. The histogram display which most digital SLRs and many compacts can display either before or more usually after a shot is taken is the key to good exposure. A histogram shows the distribution of brightness levels that has been or will be captured, from darkest to brightest. It is this immediate feedback that makes digital the best tool for learning photography ever. The only thing that came close was Polaroid, but the cost was a killer for students.

Since noise is ever present with digital cameras, even if you can only see it as the ISO is raised, it is smart to expose to allow you to minimize this. Since you can always adjust brightness later in Photoshop using Levels, you should expose to make the image as bright as possible without blocking up the highlights. This may result in an image that looks too bright on screen but that is perfect for processing. So long as you have not clipped the highlights, you can always pull the brightness down later.

In a low contrast image you will have a curve that does not use the full range on the histogram. By over exposing the image when shooting, you then require only that the black point be adjusted in Levels, effectively pulling a grey down and making it black. This pulling down process compresses the noise further and may drop it below the threshold that you can perceive. When we under expose the image the opposite is required, pulling up a grey to be white and this actually magnifies the noise. This might make the noise more obvious or raise it above the perception threshold.

One tricky aspect to this is how the histogram displayed on your camera works. Even when shooting in RAW, the on camera histogram is produced from a JPEG version of your image. The camera captures a greater range of tones than JPEG can handle, so in the processing the range is reduced to fit within what JPEG can cope with. This reduction also seems to clip a greater amount of highlight and shadow that the camera has captured. The proof of this is when you shoot in RAW (which might be called NEF on a Nikon, etc). Shooting in RAW allows all the information your camera captures to be written to the file. Later you use RAW processing software, such as Adobe Camera RAW, to process this information into a form that you can work on. In RAW processing the data from the camera is processed to compensate for the way the camera captures colour, etc and give us a normal image file to work with in Photoshop or whatever software we are using. At this stage we can choose to produce a so-called 16-bit image (which shows the full tonal range of the image) or an 8-bit one with reduced tonal separation. Most RAW software gives you significant ability to pull back clipped highlights and recover clipped shadows compared to what you see on the camera histogram. This means that you can't always judge an image well from the camera display. What you need to learn, from a simple process of experimentation, is just how over exposed an image can look on the camera and still pull it back to a great image in RAW processing. This will vary from camera model to model and so is best determined by you.

In tough lighting conditions (very high contrast with very bright highlights and very dark shadows) using the exposure bracketing capability of the camera is a huge plus. This will give you a number of images with different exposures, maximising your chance of finding an image that shows well the range you require. If you shoot this sequence at high speed or with the camera tripod mounted it also offers the possibility of High Dynamic Range Imaging or HDRi for short, an advanced technique where the sequence of images is combined in software to produce an image that contains a huge tonal range that you can then choose to use as required. HDR is worth exploring.

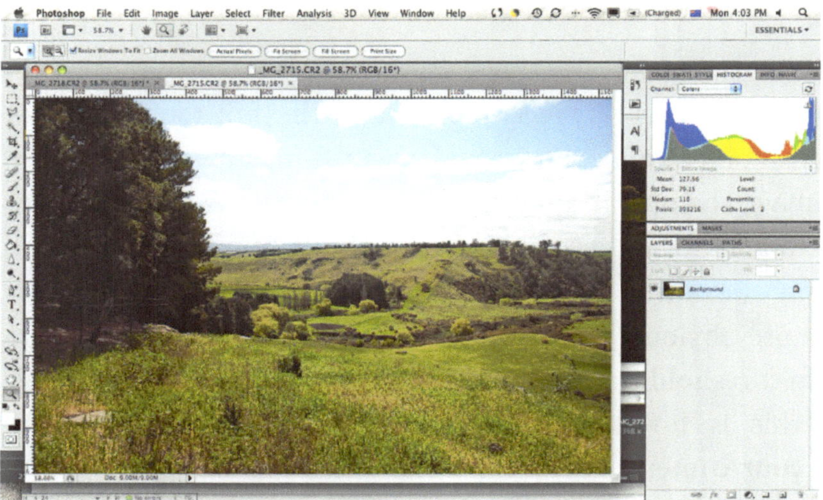

This image is correctly exposed for the foreground but over exposes the sky somewhat. This is a straight RAW conversion with no adjustment in the RAW conversion.

This under-exposed image might look like a better bet for adjustment because of the full range of tones in the sky.

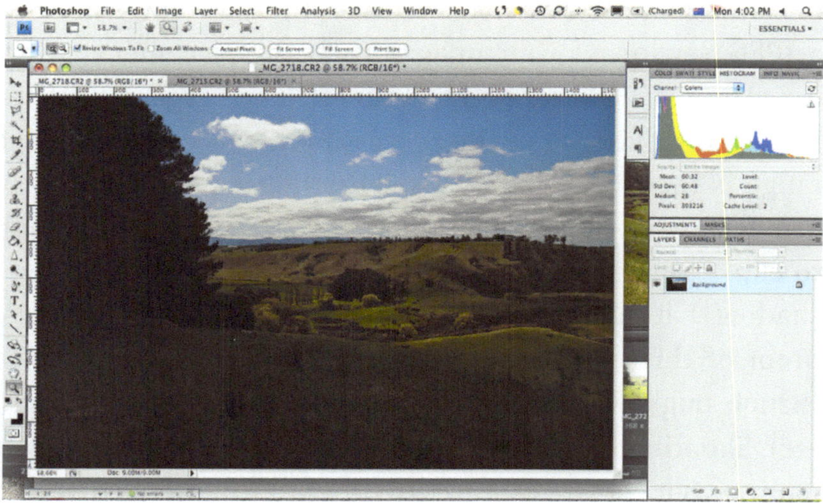

Below are closeups of the correctly exposed (left) and under exposed (right image after a Levels adjustment to get the foreground into the correct range. It would still need a local contrast curve to bring it up. But look at the noise which is now clearly visible in the 1000ISO shot.

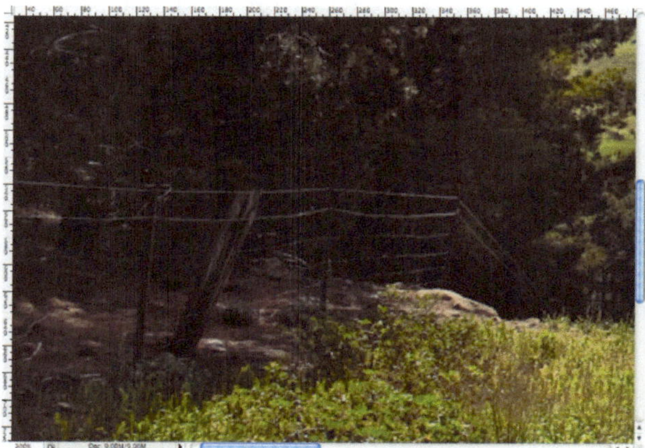

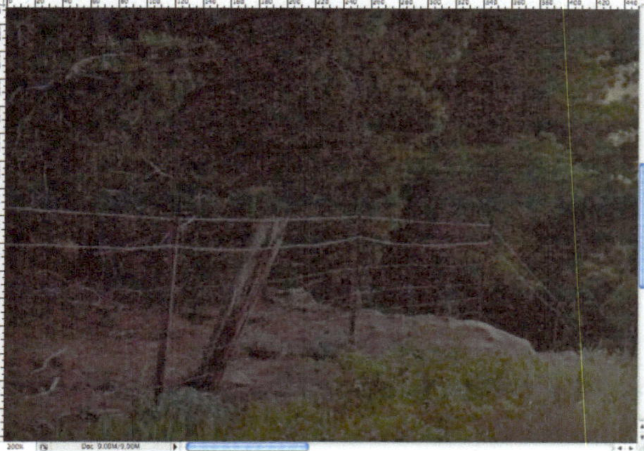

Taking the first image back into the RAW conversion software (Adobe Camera RAW) we can recover the highlights to bring the sky back to a point that has no clipping without increasing the noise in the image at all. All these shots were taken with a Canon 5D.

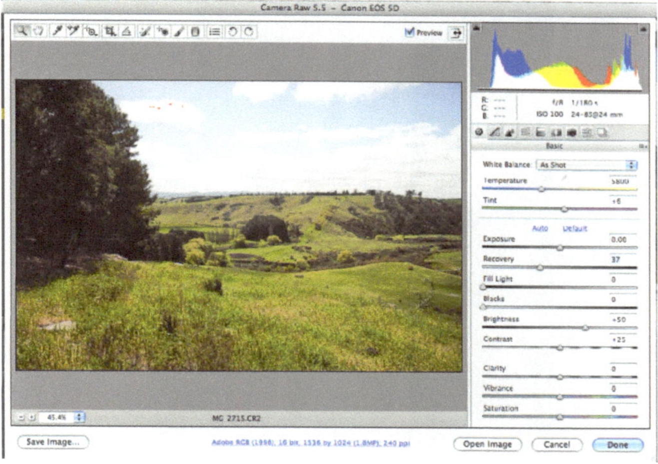

Night shots can be very tricky because of the extreme lighting contrast. This is San Gimignano in Italy. Bracketing is definitely a desirable practice in such situations as it opens up more options later on. Don't let people tell you bracketing is for the lazy or stupid, it is just another technique and if it works for you that is great. As an alternative use the in-camera or a handheld spot meter.

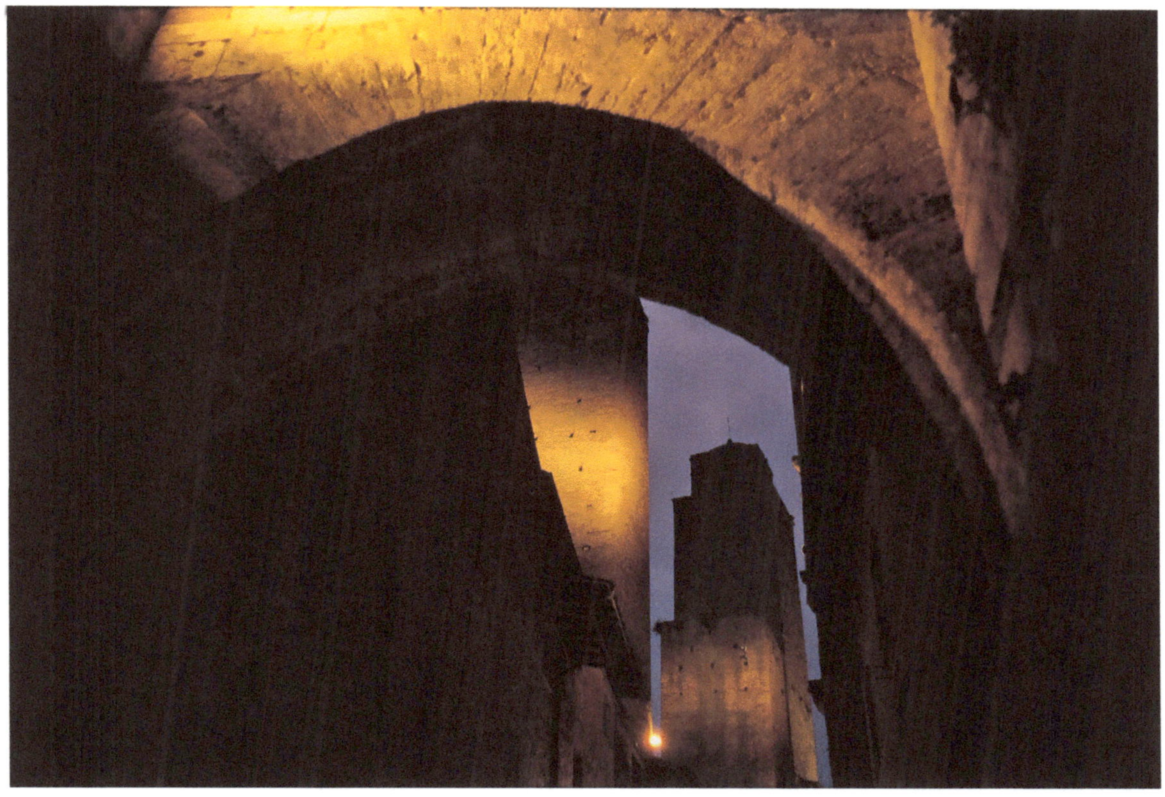

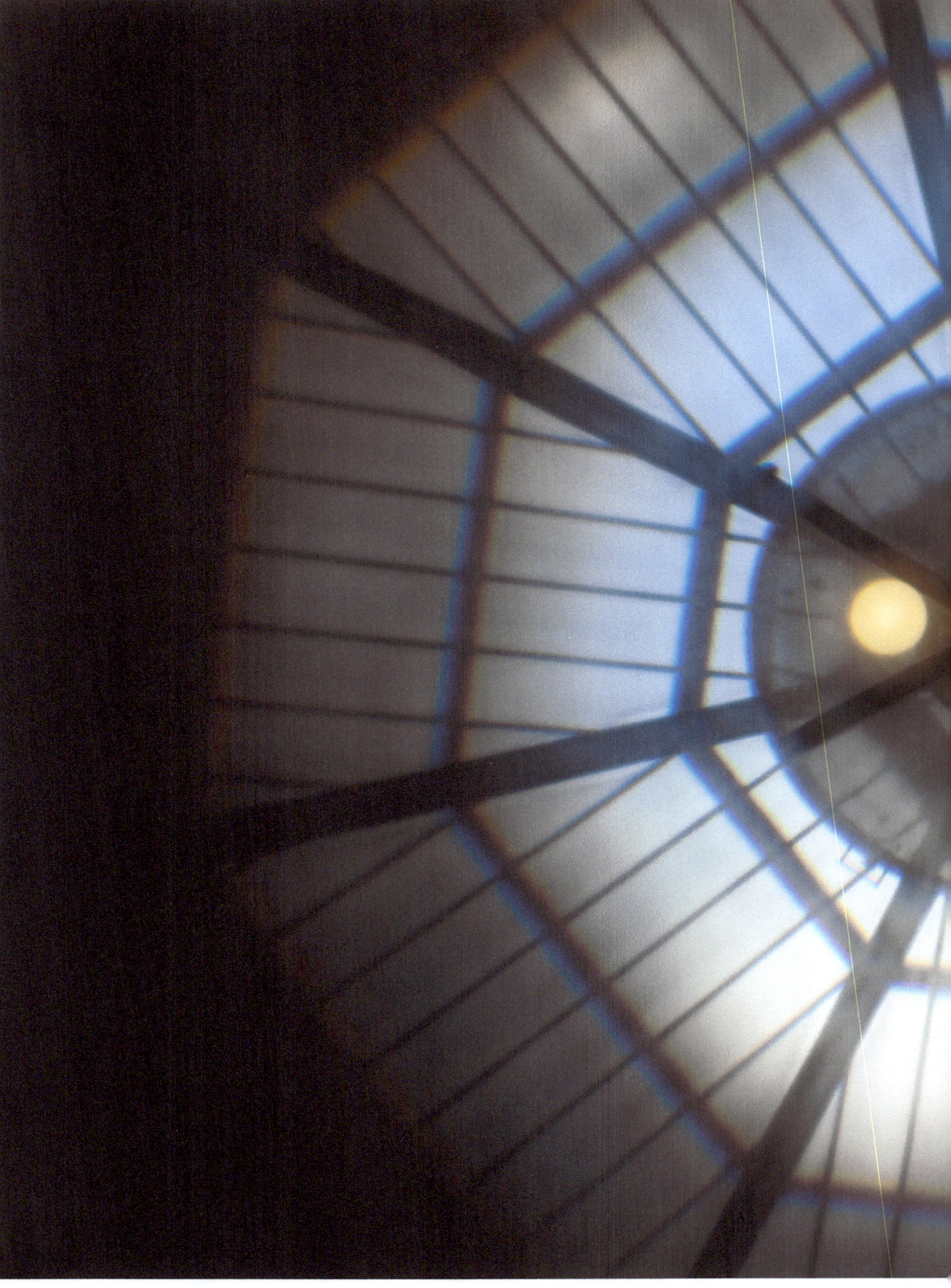

Technique

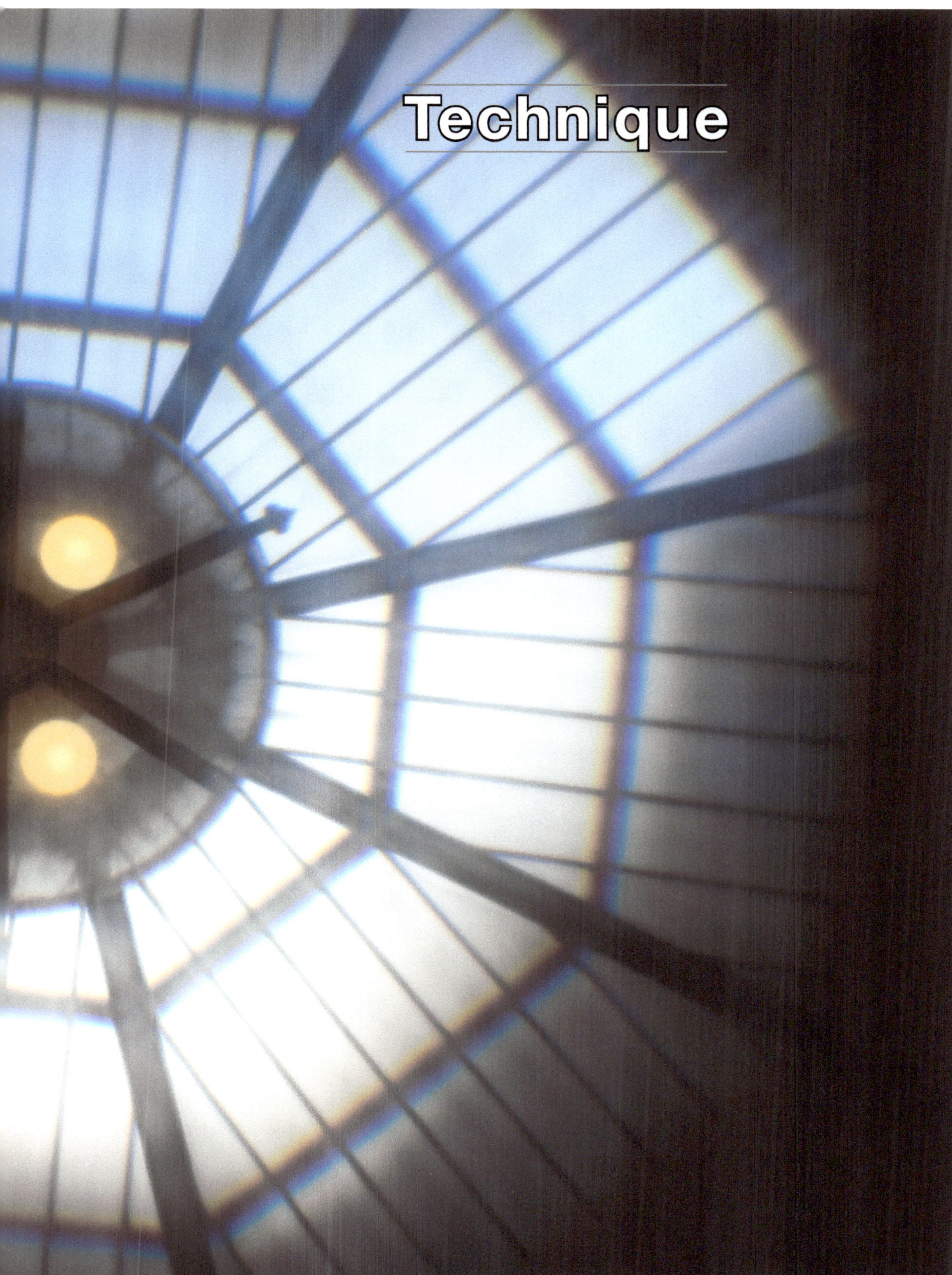

3. Support Your Camera Properly

Most of us do not use a tripod anywhere near as often as we should. But this oversight is easy to correct.

Tripods have other benefits than just supporting the camera in very low light. They can help to make images sharper, even if your shutter speed seems fast enough to hand hold, take some pressure off of your arms and aid with controlled motions, like panning.

One of the biggest benefits of using a tripod is that it slows your shooting down and allows you to setup a shot, step back and consider the camera in context with the scene and then shoot with consideration. The fact that you can lock the exact position and then consider, adjust, reconsider, and so on as much as you want gives you a huge benefit. Getting things right when you shoot gives you the best starting point for later work, again with careful consideration, on the computer.

I know many of us put ball heads on our tripods. I know I do. They are excellent for so many shooting situations, quick to use, more compact and often lighter than the alternative. But there is also a lot of value in a two or ideally three-axis tilt pan head. This allows you to readily adjust the camera position and view one axis at a time.

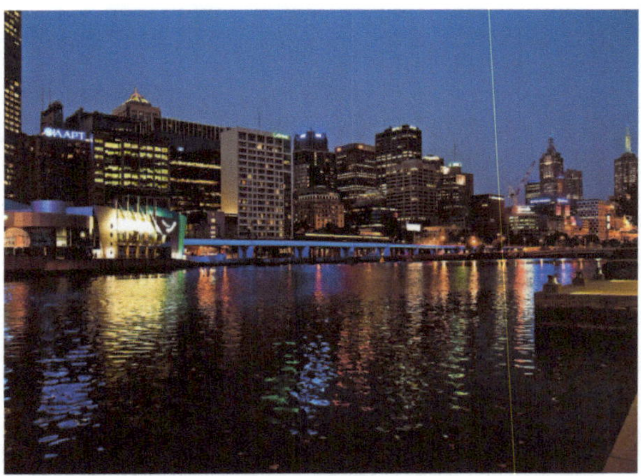

Sometimes you have to slow down to be in the flow.

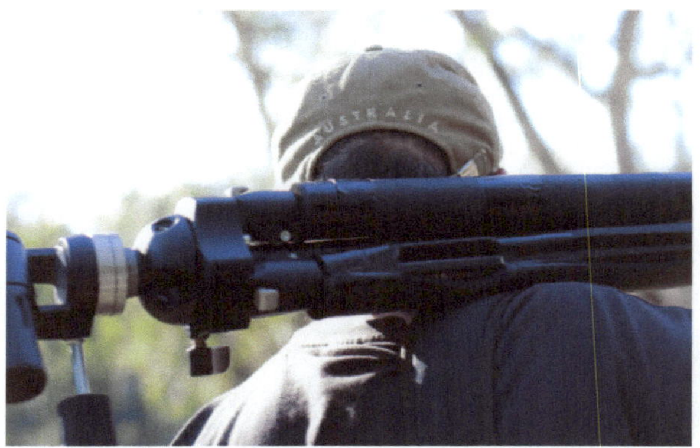

Tripods are essential for low light shots, like the night image above, but also for carefully considered images such as that on the right, where waiting for the cloud pattern to align correctly was necessary.

Adding padding to the tripod legs, as in the shot immediately above, not only makes the tripod safer to handling in extreme cold but also makes carrying the tripod much easier. For short moves I keep the tripod legs extended and balanced on my shoulder.

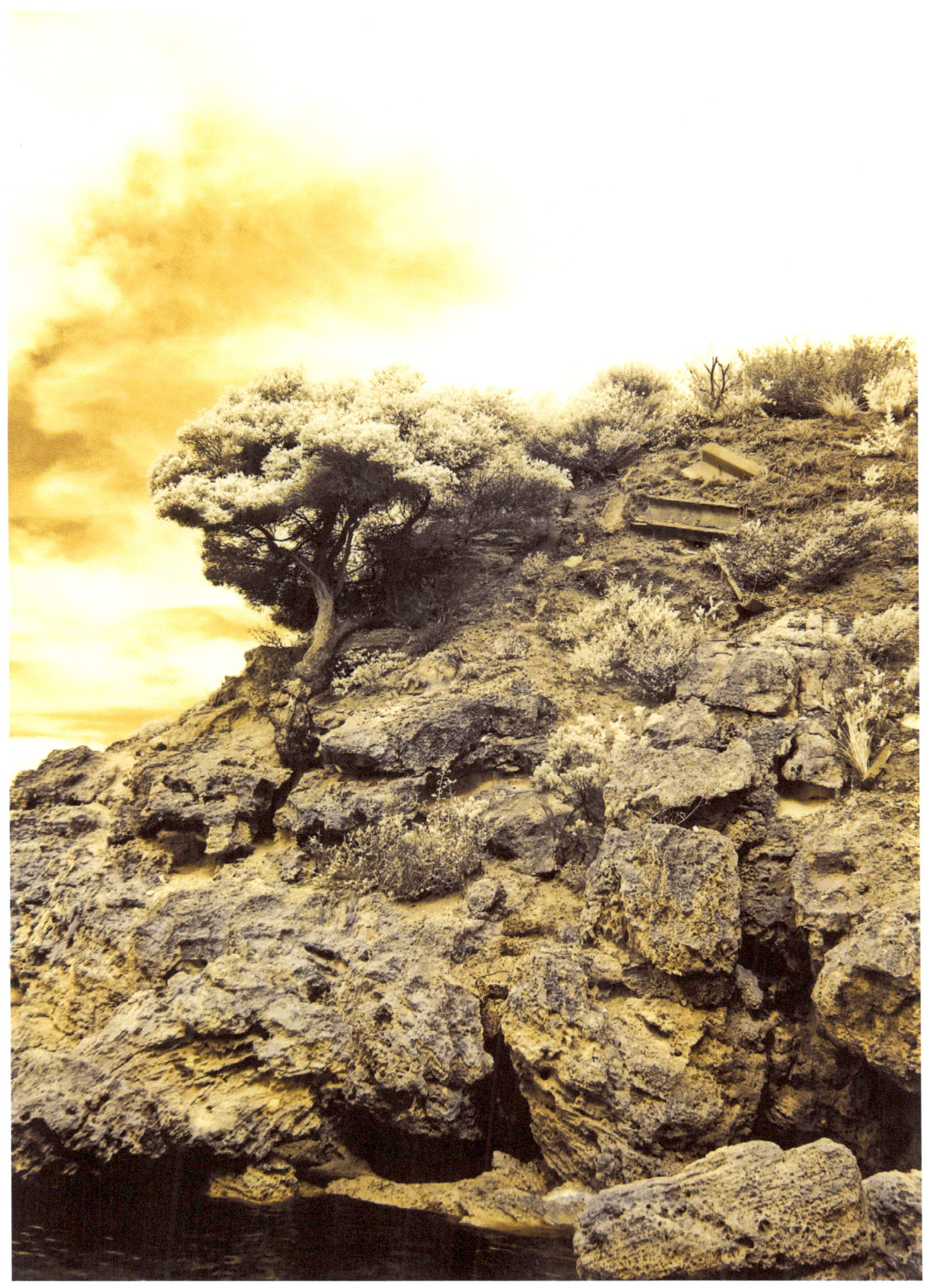

4. Get Back to Basics

Today when you buy an SLR, whether analog or digital, it either is a body only or it comes with a zoom lens. Kits zooms are usually ok lenses but with one major limitation, a fairly small widest aperture. When I started in photography the lens that came with a 35mm SLR was a 50mm, usually f1.8 lens.

Digital cameras are, in general, prone to making it hard to use one of the great techniques of photography, shallow depth of field. While the field of view may be narrower by the multiplication factor if the sensor is smaller than the 35mm frame, the depth of field is a function of the actual lens focal length and the aperture. So that f5.6 zoom at 50mm might make a great portrait lens with an effective focal length of around 80mm, the shallowest depth of field you can get is what you get at 50mm and f5.6. This is not very shallow.

Indeed many photographers of the digital age have never experienced what a really shallow depth of field can give you. So the tip is to go get a 50mm lens of at least f1.8 maximum aperture and preferably f1.4. The 50mm f1.8's are very cheap either new or second hand and 50mm f1.4's can also be picked up very cheap second hand. On most digital SLRs this will give you the equivalent of a 75 or 80mm f1.4 or f1.8 lens, perfect for portraiture. With a lens like this you have real control over your depth of field, from getting only one eye sharp to the whole face.

So if you have never experienced the joy of a prime lens, give one a go.

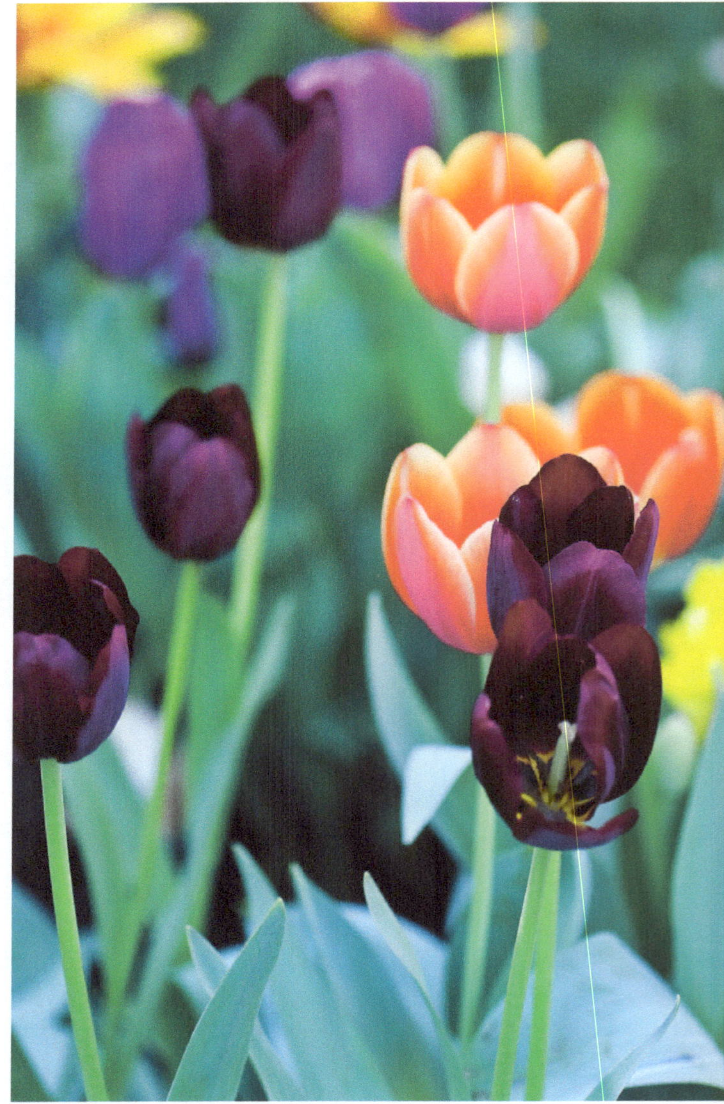

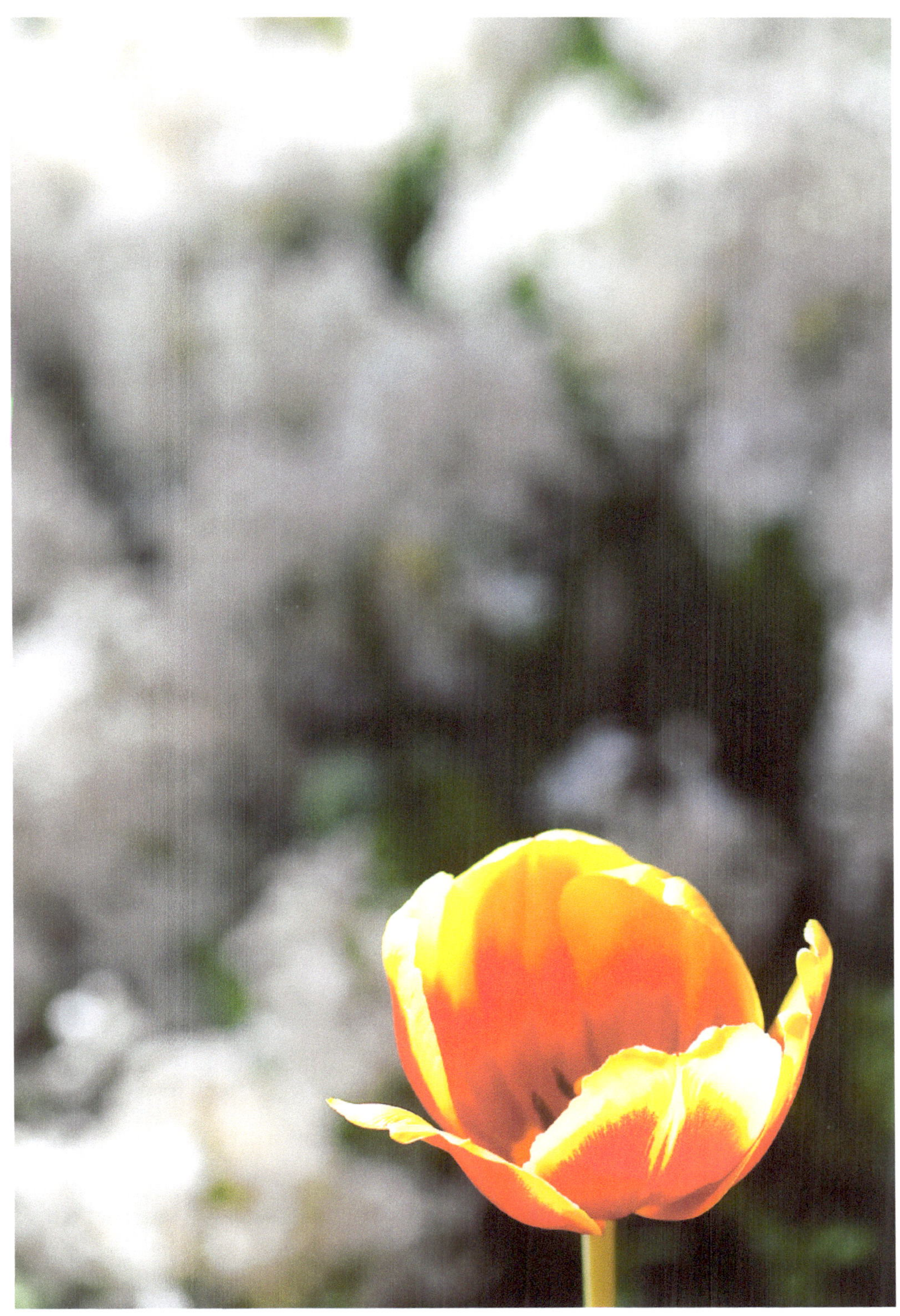

5. The Importance of the Eyepiece Shutter

Lately I have been doing a lot of long exposure photography, both digital infrared and visible light.

In the process of doing this work I have had shots that have been spoilt by flares, fogging and other artefacts. It turns out that these effects were caused because I did not have my eye blocking the viewfinder and had not used the eyepiece blind that most cameras offer.

In the shot below I was using a Nikon D3 with a Hoya R72 filter to shoot digital infrared. With a 15 second exposure there was plenty of time for moving objects, in this case water and clouds, to produce movement. With the eyepiece shutter activated (the Nikon D3 has a lever next to the viewfinder that activates a proper blind), the result in a smooth image that can be

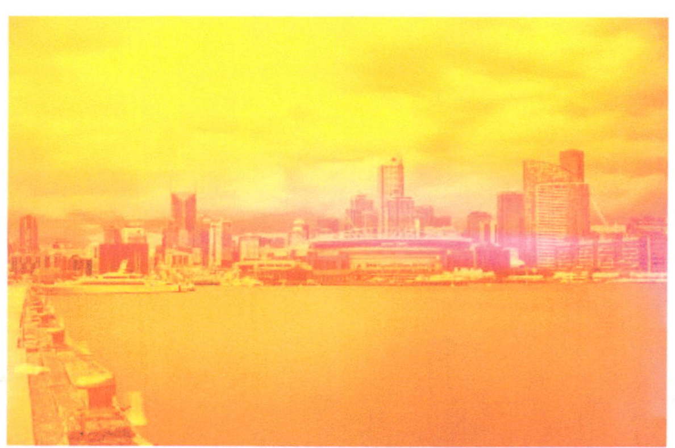

converted to monochrome using one of the channels.

With the eyepiece blind open the result is very different. Light has leaked in and fogged not only across the centre of the image but also down one side. You can see this even more clearly when you examine the three channels individually and see the strong fogging in the blue (the difference in exposure is typical of unmodified digital

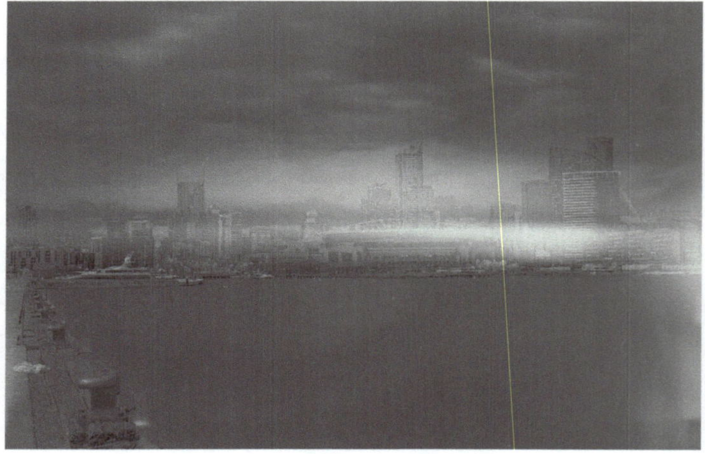

cameras when shooting in infrared).

All cameras can be affected. My Canon 400D had the artefact on the right of the image when the klutzy eyepiece shield on the camera strap was not used.

Some cameras make closing off the eyepiece hard and others make it easy. But on every camera it is important to do this when taking longer exposures. On some cameras I have seen no image artefacts but rather the exposure has been way off. So get in the habit.

An eyepiece shutter or cover is important even if you do not do long exposure photography. If you have taken the advice in the tip on supporting your camera properly, you will be using a tripod more often to allow you to step back and consider while maintaining your framing. When you shoot with a camera on a tripod you will often not have your eye right up to the eyepiece. On some cameras light leaking into the eyepiece can interfere with the auto exposure system, causing the resulting image to usually be under exposed.

Some cameras, usually the high end ones, have a built-in eyepiece blind activated by a lever next to the eyepiece. Lower end cameras usually provide a separate blink that lives on the camera strap and can be slipped over the eyepiece if the rubber eyecup is removed first. As you can tell, this is frankly a pain and is probably why people used the eyepiece blind far less than they should.

If you are shopping for a new camera and intend to do much long exposure or infrared photography, or shoot carefully on a tripod a lot, then having a convenient eyepiece blind needs to be up there on your selection criteria.

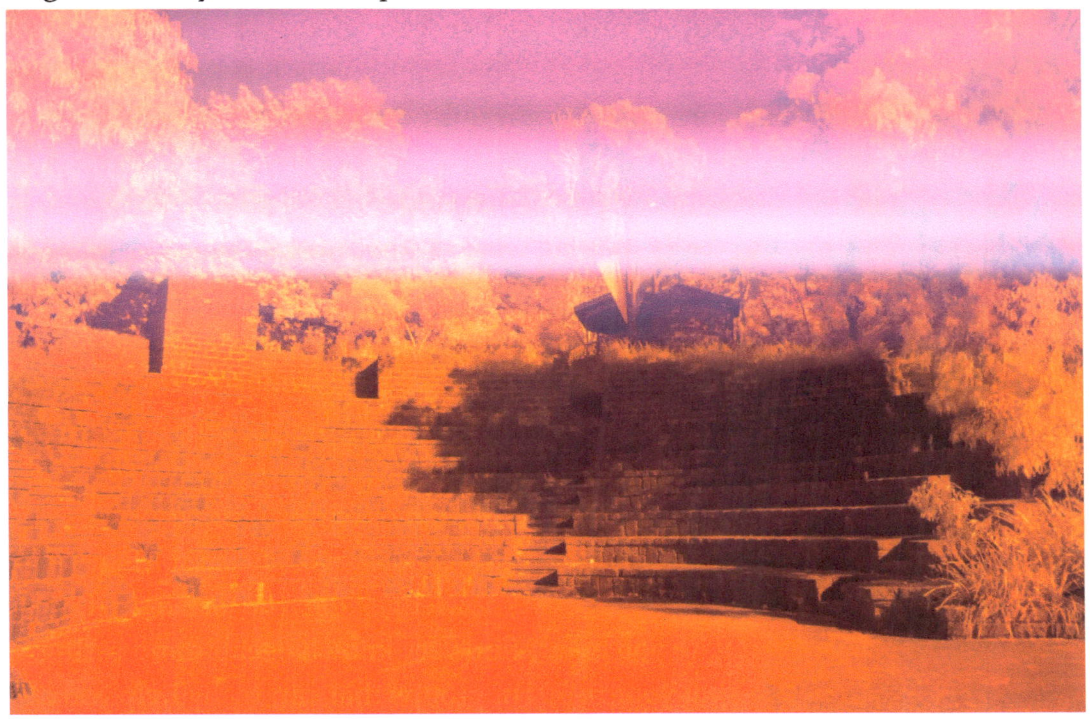

6. Analyse More

The process that should go hand-in-hand with shooting more, is analysing more. Analyse more means to bring more conscious consideration to all the images you look at, both yours and other people's, and to setting aside the time to actually go through your own work with a careful eye.

This ties in with another tip on Reconsideration is Good about the value in going through your old images and reconsidering your reactions to them, but extends it to ensure that you not only shoot a lot but sit down and have a good look at what you have done. This allows you time to examine your results, see what is working and what is not and to determine directions you might want to explore further.

Without this analysis, taking images becomes only a learning process at the time of shooting. This has its own benefits in training your eye to see possibilities, etc, but you are missing out on a lot of the learning potential if you do not follow this up with carefully examining the results.

One of the benefits of shooting digitally is the EXIF data the camera stores along with the image. This can help you greatly in your analysis. Just what was the aperture and focal length that gave you exactly the depth of field in that shot your really like, for example?

Some people like a formal analysis approach, with checklists and rating sheets (or a rating system in your software, as in Aperture), while others prefer a less formal approach. Either way, make sure it is thorough. Check exposure and sharpness, composition and colour, positioning of elements, expressions, and eye lines. Look for cropping options, areas you can improve with processing, aspects you need to reshoot for and things you really need to watch for when you shoot. For example an analysis of your beach shots may show you have an issue with keeping the horizon level. Note this and become more aware when you shoot. After time this will become automatic but you need to practice it until it does. Of put in a focusing screen with a grid or activate it if your camera has that option.

Sometimes as part of your analysis you may wish to seek the opinion of others. Just be careful whom you ask. Family may not know enough to offer meaningful advice and groups whether online or camera clubs may have people who are prone to the big fish in a small pond syndrome and whose ego is larger than their real knowledge. On the other hand you can find very knowledgeable and caring people in groups that can really help you along. A very valuable thing is to participate in a folio evaluation group, where you get together a small and select group of people with similar interests so you can learn together.

Analysis closes the circle with taking your images. It is necessary. Find ways to make it enjoyable.

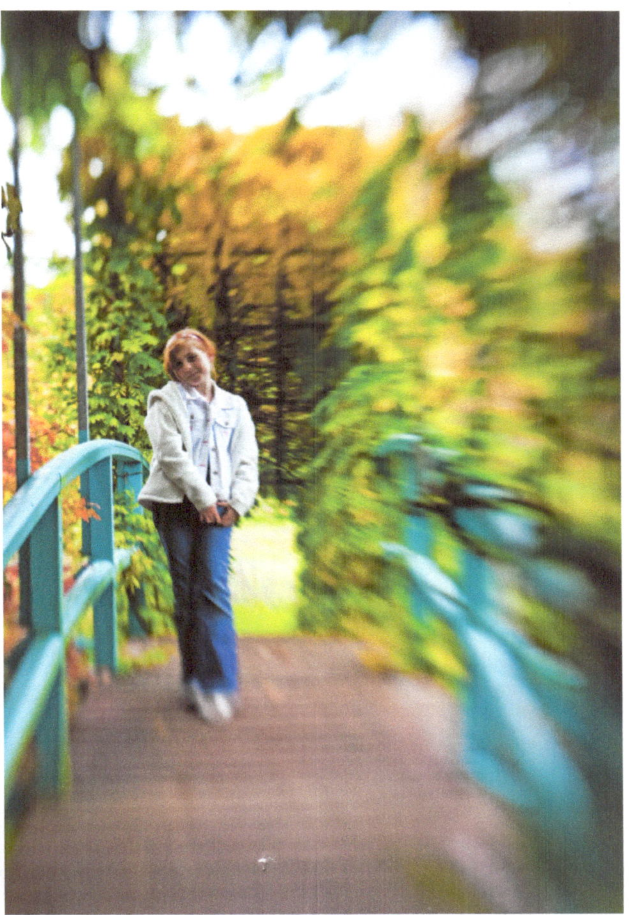

Remember that your imaging software contains tools to help you analyse your images, from a grid, rulers and guides to look after positioning to measuring tools and careful rotation aids. Use all the support you have.

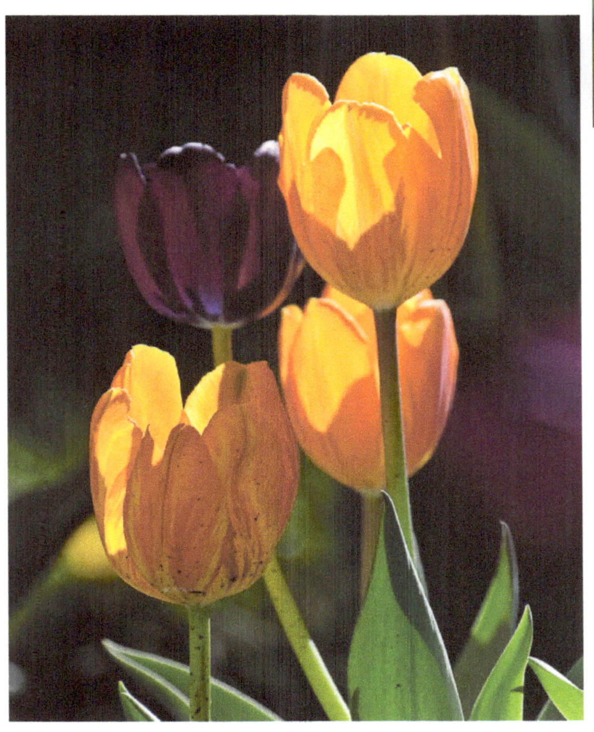

Family member feedback of shots involving other members of the family are rarely likely to be objective. With such images it is best to just show them to family for fun and show them to other people for critical feedback.

In fact, family feedback can be a big negative for most photographers. Firstly such people are rarely visually educated, such as art trained, and so their feedback is largely meaningless except as a possible consumer audience opinion. Secondly you never know when family issues, such as jealousy or fear that you may run off to be a photographer may be impacting on their advice.

7. Watch the Eye Line

We are very sensitive to where people are looking. Consider how disturbing it is when you are talking to someone and they look away from you. We are very keyed into people's eyes and we can use this in our photography.

One of the things we can try to control with an image is how the viewer's eyes travel around the image (we'll cover this in a much longer article on the site soon). If you shoot people then where they are looking is very important. A subject looking straight at the camera can be very striking.

When the subject (or subjects) is not looking at the camera but elsewhere, the direction they are looking creates a major line in the image that the viewer will probably explore. You should exploit this. If the subject is looking straight out of the frame it makes a very definite statement. Sometimes this is what you want and sometimes it is not, so you need to be conscious of this in crafting your image. If it is a grab shot you may have little control beyond cropping or later darkroom or digital manipulations. If you are posing the shot then you have full control.

When the subject (or one of the subjects) is looking at another person or object within the image you create a relationship between the two. You can exploit this to build the message you wish to convey. We have probably all seen the movie poster (can't remember the film) where the bride is looking at the groom but the groom is looking at someone else. We can be obvious (as in this example) or we can be either more subtle or more intriguing. Why is that person looking at that object that, on first glance, seems so unrelated? What is going on here?

Photography and art uses a visual language to communicate with the viewer. Make sure you are making full use of the language.

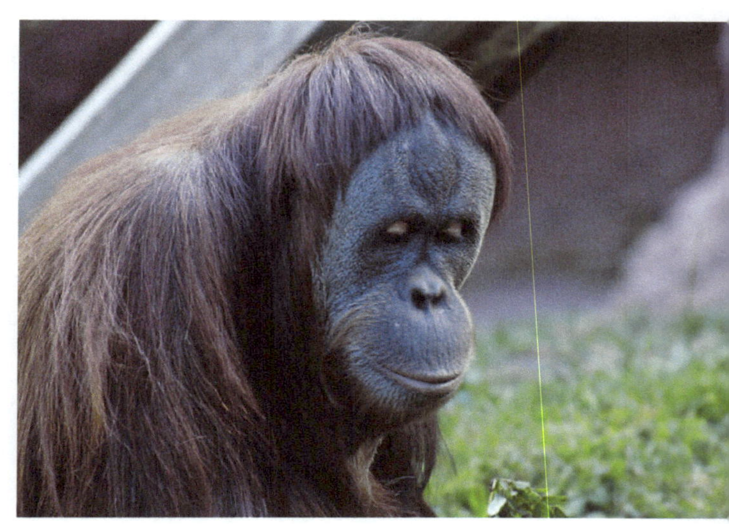

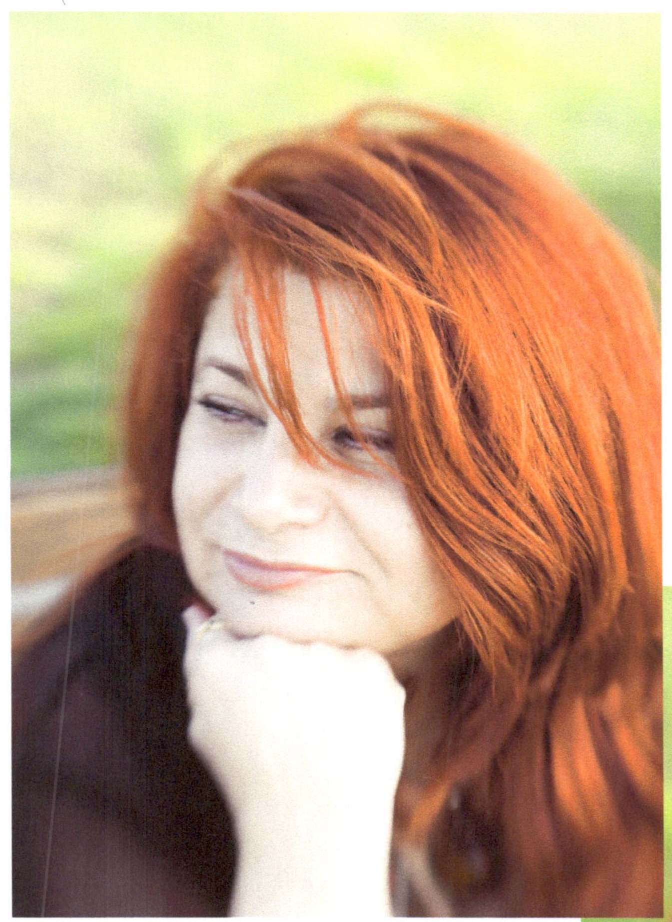

In posed portraits you should direct you subject exactly where to look for the effect you want. There is an advantage in working on a tripod, since you can setup the shot, determine what you want, leave the camera and direct or position the model/ subject the way you want and then return to the camera in the same position.

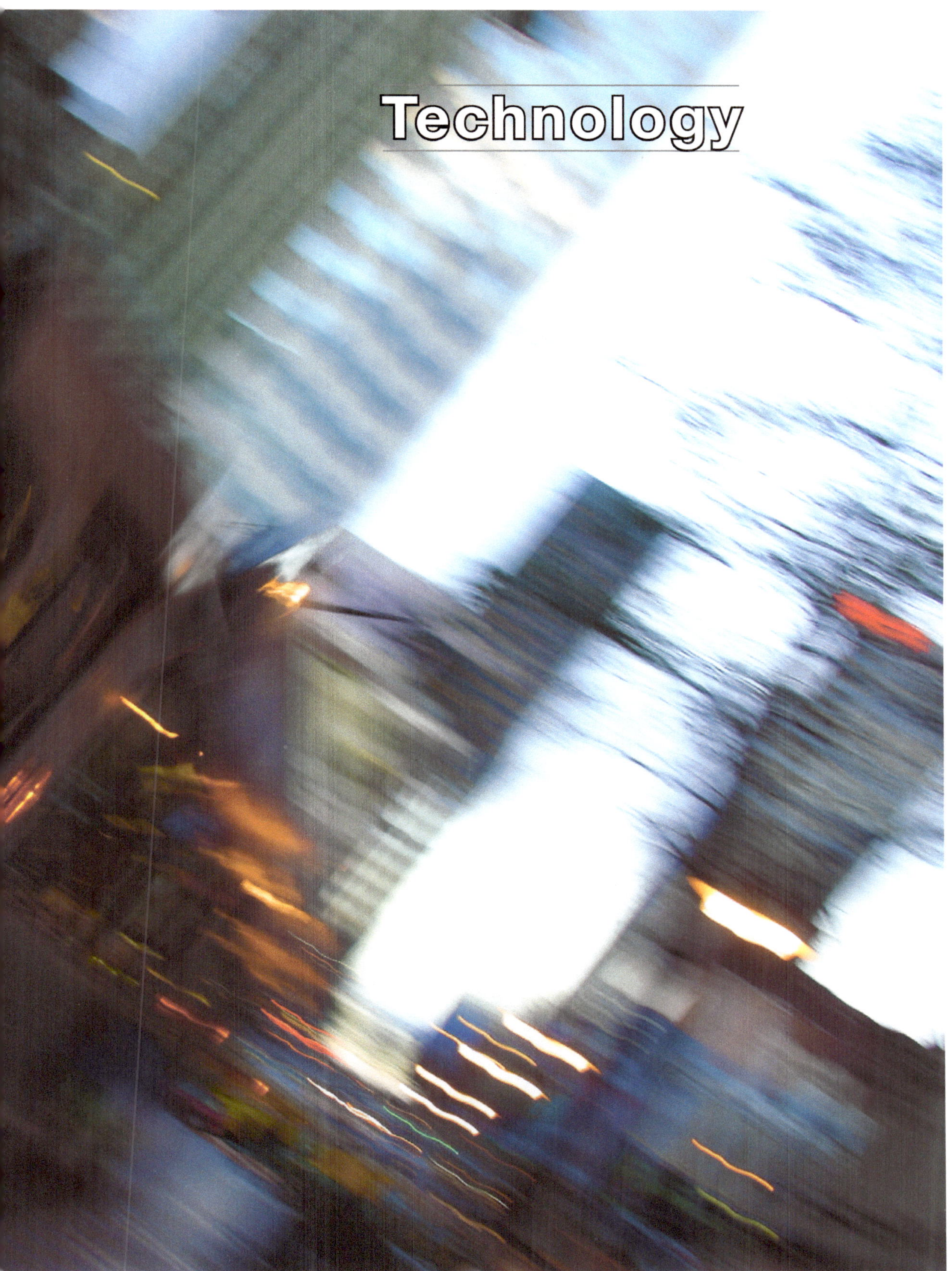

Technology

8. Test Your Own Gear

Reading the manuals is only the first step of getting the most from your camera gear, you have to become familiar with how it actual works in practice. This means playing with it every chance you get. That's right, play. Life should be enjoyable and photography in particular. Here, the value of play is getting to know your gear and making your interactions with it and its controls automatic.

You must test your gear for yourself so that you get to know all its idiosyncratic aspects. Make sure you test the following aspects:

- What ISO setting becomes too noisy for your general shooting?
- What ISO setting is ok in a pinch?
- At what shutter speed does the mirror slap produce the worse vibration?
- For each lens, which apertures are most and least sharp?
- For each lens, which focal lengths produce the most distortion?
- What coverage does each of your flash units have and how do these correspond with your lenses?

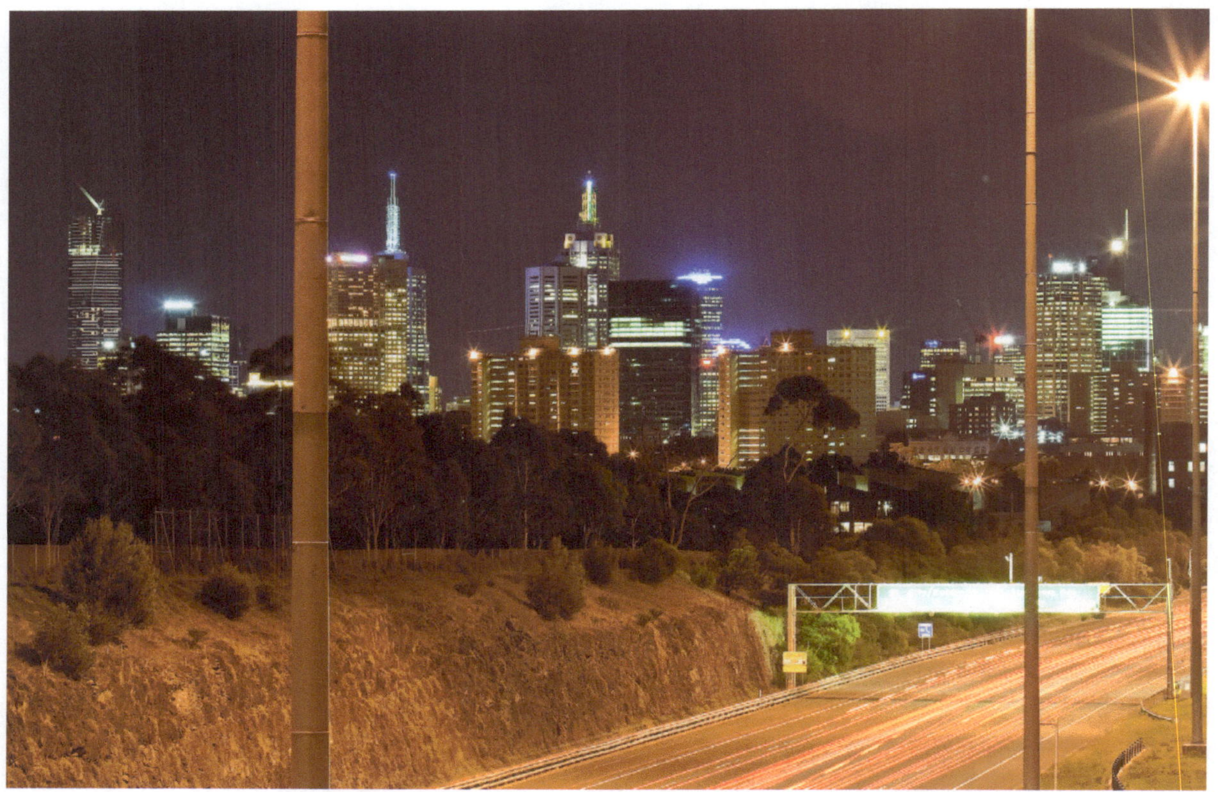

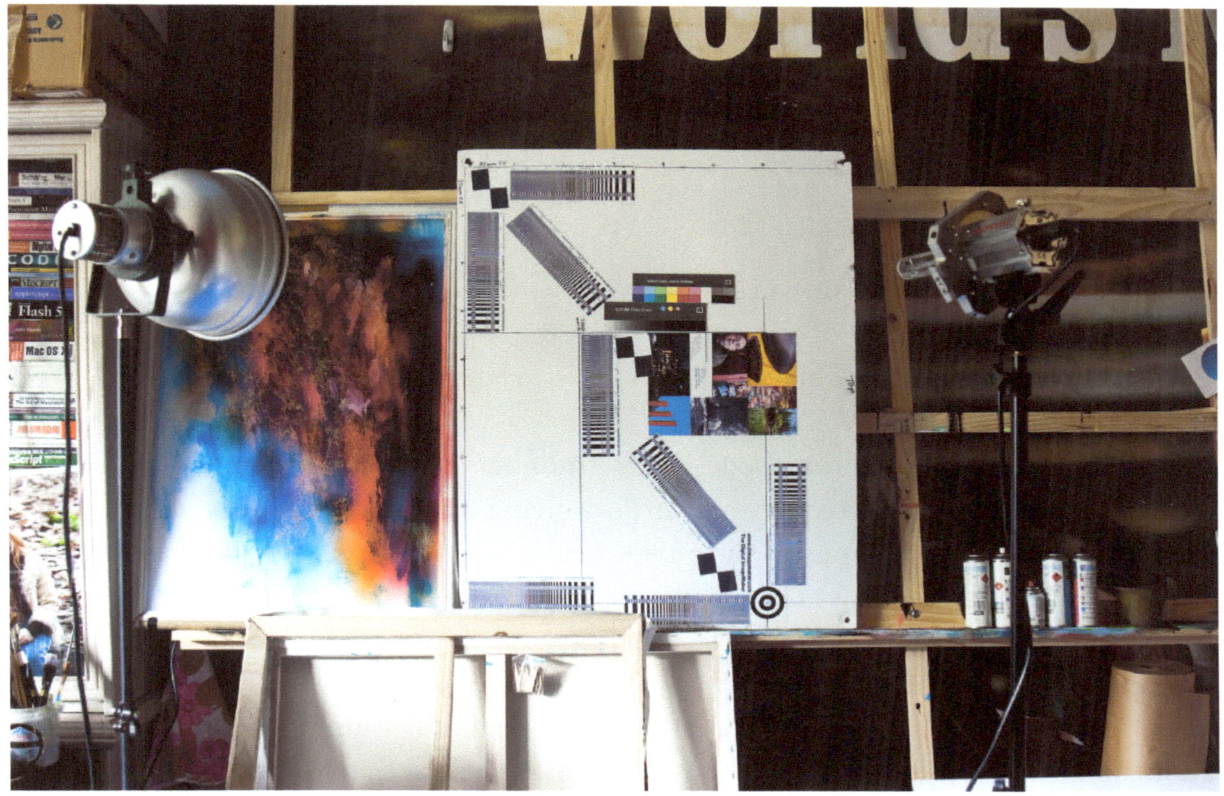

Pick some favourite locations that you can use over and over again with fairly consistent lighting. Such a place is great to visit many times over to test cameras, lens sharpness and more (left).

You can also test at home, either with a test rig like that above or with just a standard object or arrangement of objects that you can shoot for the same purposes.

The other thing to remember is that all equipment is subject to manufacturing tolerances. That means that your particular lens can vary significantly in performance from whatever lens a reviewer tested. This is also true of other gear than lenses.

Real familiarity with your own gear lets you fully exploit what it can do. Know yourself an know your gear.

Activity

Plan out a program of testing for your camera gear. In this sense try to view yourself as an independent reviewer of your gear.

When you test take extensive notes and then analyse your results.

Workout for yourself the best and worse settings for your gear.

9. The Numbers Have Meaning

A recent trip away to test a couple of cameras, and the shooting of one scene in particular, really brought home the meaning of those camera numbers.

Recently I combined the need to get away with the need to test a couple of cameras, specifically the Olympus E-3 and the Pentax K20D. The shooting of one particular scene really brought home to me the meaning of a couple of numbers.

The two images below were shot about a minute apart from roughly the same position (I was dodging waves, so there was some movement). One was with the Pentax K20D fitted with the Sigma 10-20mm zoom, shot at 10mm. The other was taken with the Olympus E-3 and the Zuiko 12-60mm zoom, at 12mm.

Now when you get to the wide-angle end of the focal length range, 2mm of focal length can make a significant difference to the field of view. On a 35mm film camera a 10mm lens has a field of view of 130 degrees, while the 12mm covers 122 degrees.

But another number that makes a huge difference here is the focal length multiplication factor. The Olympus has a 2.0x multiplication factor, whilst the Pentax has a 1.5x factor. That means the 12mm on the Olympus is effectively 24mm, while the 10mm on the Pentax is effectively 15mm, in 35mm terms. The field of view (FOV) of a 24mm is 84 degrees with the 15mm covering 110 degrees, a huge difference.

So what does all this mean? Well, firstly you have to pay attention to the numbers when making any decisions involving cameras. Secondly system choices, especially sensor size, have huge implications for your actual picture taking. What should be an amazingly wide lens becomes only a moderately wide one on the Olympus system because of the tiny sensor. Of course sensor size has other implications.

F Stop	Light intensity
1	100.00%
1.4	50.00%
2	25.00%
2.8	12.50%
4	6.25%
5.6	3.13%
8	1.56%
11	0.78%
16	0.39%
22	0.20%
32	0.10%
45	0.05%
64	0.02%
90	0.01%
128	0.01%

Depth of Field for 35mm format in metres									
	24mm Lens			**50mm Lens**			**100mm Lens**		
		Focused at 5m			**Focused at 5m**			**Focused at 5m**	
Aperture	**Hyperfocal distance**	**Near Focus**	**Far Focus**	**Hyperfocal distance**	**Near Focus**	**Far Focus**	**Hyperfocal distance**	**Near Focus**	**Far Focus**
2.8	7.09	2.93	16.94	30.79	4.30	5.97	123.15	4.80	5.21
4	4.97	2.49	infinity	21.55	4.06	6.51	86.21	4.73	5.31
5.6	3.55	2.07	infinity	15.39	3.77	7.41	61.58	4.62	5.44
8	2.48	1.66	infinity	10.78	3.42	9.33	43.10	4.48	5.66
11	1.81	1.33	infinity	7.84	3.05	13.81	31.35	4.31	5.95
16	1.24	0.99	infinity	5.39	2.59	69.44	21.55	4.06	6.51
22	0.90	0.76	infinity	3.92	2.20	infinity	15.67	3.79	7.34
32	0.62	0.55	infinity	2.69	1.75	infinity	10.78	3.42	9.33

Depth of Field for 35mm format in feet									
	24mm Lens			50mm Lens			100mm Lens		
		Focused at 16.4 ft			Focused at 16.4 ft			Focused at 16.4 ft	
Aperture	Hyperfocal distance	Near Focus	Far Focus	Hyperfocal distance	Near Focus	Far Focus	Hyperfocal distance	Near Focus	Far Focus
2.8	23.27	9.62	55.53	101.01	14.11	19.58	404.04	15.76	17.09
4	16.29	8.17	infinity	70.71	13.31	21.35	282.83	15.50	17.41
5.6	11.64	6.81	infinity	50.51	12.38	24.29	202.02	15.17	17.85
8	8.15	5.44	infinity	35.35	11.20	30.59	141.42	14.70	18.55
11	5.92	4.35	infinity	25.71	10.01	45.28	102.85	14.14	19.51
16	4.07	3.26	infinity	17.68	8.51	227.03	70.71	13.31	21.35
22	2.96	2.51	infinity	12.86	7.21	infinity	51.42	12.43	24.08
32	2.04	1.81	infinity	8.84	5.74	infinity	35.35	11.20	30.59

10. View Your Camera and Computer as Part of One System

Once images are in the digital domain there is an infinite field of possibility open to you that can move your photography to new levels. It is time to stop thinking of your camera gear and computer gear as separate things.

Digital photography is as massive a paradigm shift in photography as the invention of photography was in the first place. The paradigm shift is one in the thinking of the photographer, and many of us haven't yet caught up with this. Let me explain.

Let us create a hypothetical 'normal' photographer and a 'new paradigm' photographer for comparison.

The normal photographer shoots pretty much the same way they did with film, though they may shoot more. They have their camera gear and they have their computer gear. The computer gear replaces their old darkroom equipment and the trips to drop off and pickup film and prints that they were not equipped to handle in their own darkroom. Their thinking is inherently two-stage in nature. They go out and shoot with their gear, then later they get into their images on the computer. When they shoot they take some heed of what they may do on the computer, just as in their darkroom days they exposed so they could get a decent print without too much prestidigitation in the darkroom. A hangover from this thinking is an effort to handle as much with the camera as possible. This may include overly tight cropping of the image and a failure to shoot enough variety.

The new paradigm photographer has an inherently one-stage thinking. Everything is their photography and everything is their camera gear, even the computer. They think in terms of what is the best way, within their present means, to address a particular issue. They understand fully the effect of every decision on their workflow and structure things to get the maximum quality they can out of what they have, and have the most fun doing it. So they may have a workflow that uses the best camera and lenses they can afford and use appropriate software to reduce image noise, correct lens aberrations and achieve image modifications that allow them to do the photography they want to do in a way that suits them.

On the discussion lists too often you see photographers who are struggling with the camera gear they have and limiting what they shoot because of it. Yet computational photography, as I call it, opens up so many possibilities. Rather than not doing night photography because they have a fairly noisy camera and cannot afford an update, a cheap software purchase may do the trick. Likewise a cheap lens with aberrations that make architectural photography difficult can be addressed with software. Panorama stitching does not need a special camera. Likewise using HDR techniques can extend a low dynamic range camera. Software can extend depth of field in macro work and even allow you to choose the focal point and depth of field after the shoot. And the list goes on.

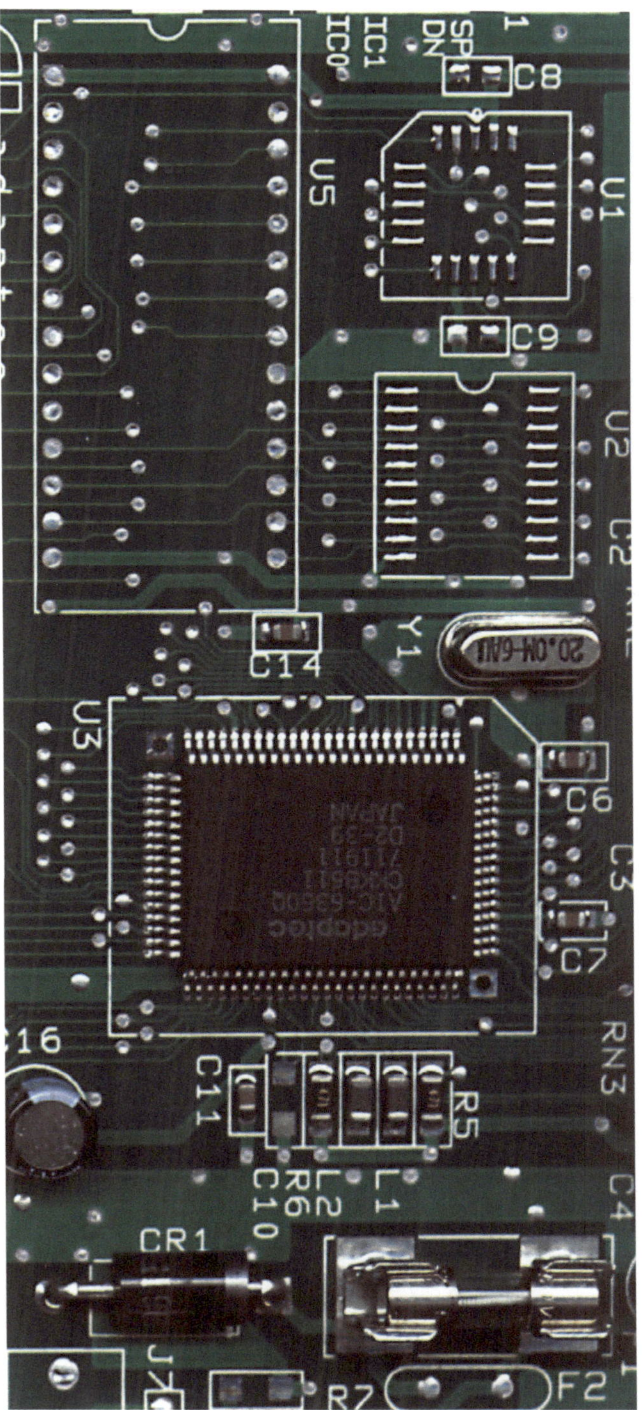

Beyond technological solutions there are also solutions of perception. Not every image has to be sharp and perfect. Blur can be highly effective, a soft image can add atmosphere and burned out highlights and blocked shadows can be used in creative ways.

I sometimes think we like to be limited so we have something to complain about or have an excuse for not testing our creativity. Perhaps it is an avoidance mechanism so we do not have to risk failure. Whatever it is, it is worth blocking it away and taking the risk of changing your thinking. You just might like it.

11. Watch Out for Your Accessories and Gear

Mostly our camera equipment, including accessories, work for us, but sometimes they get in the way. The solution can be a bit of do-it-yourself.

Over recent months I have been experimenting with long exposure photography. To do this in normal daytime lighting requires the use of a very heavy neutral density filter or something like an infrared filter. These filters cut out so much light, sometimes eight to nine stops worth, that your full sun exposure stretches into minutes.

One of the filter systems I have been using is that by the French company Cokin. This system uses square resin filters and a filter holder that you fit to your lens. This is a great system and works extremely well in normal situations with normal filters. However, what I found in actual use with these very dark (effectively opaque to the eye) filters is that the filter holder allowed light to leak in behind the filter and fog the exposure. With such extreme filters there was nothing that you could do to cut it completely. I tried draping a cloth over the filter holder but this only helped a little. This is not an issue with the screw in filters because they have a tight fit to the lens.

The solution was a bit of do-it-yourself. The standard Cokin filter holder has three slots to take multiple filters. But even with a filter in the slot closest to the lens there is still a gap that lens can leak through. So what I decided to do is to glue some black leather scraps around the filter holder so that with a filter inserted the leather sits up against the filter but still allows the filter to be slid in or out without scratching.

With these modifications in place most of the flare was gone. One more thing had to be done. I needed to use the eyepiece cover incorporated into the camera strap of my Canon 400D. Without it in place it was clear that some light was leaking around the mirror when it was up. With the cover in place (oh how I dream for a camera with a built-in blind) there was no more leakage and the images were clear and sharp.

Don't be scared to modify your gear if you need to. The results can be great.

The above story also illustrates that your normal camera gear does not always work as expected. The eyepiece blinds are supposed to be used simply to stop light entering the pentaprism and skewing the exposure, since on many cameras the light metering sensor is located in the pentaprism of an SLR. However, what I have

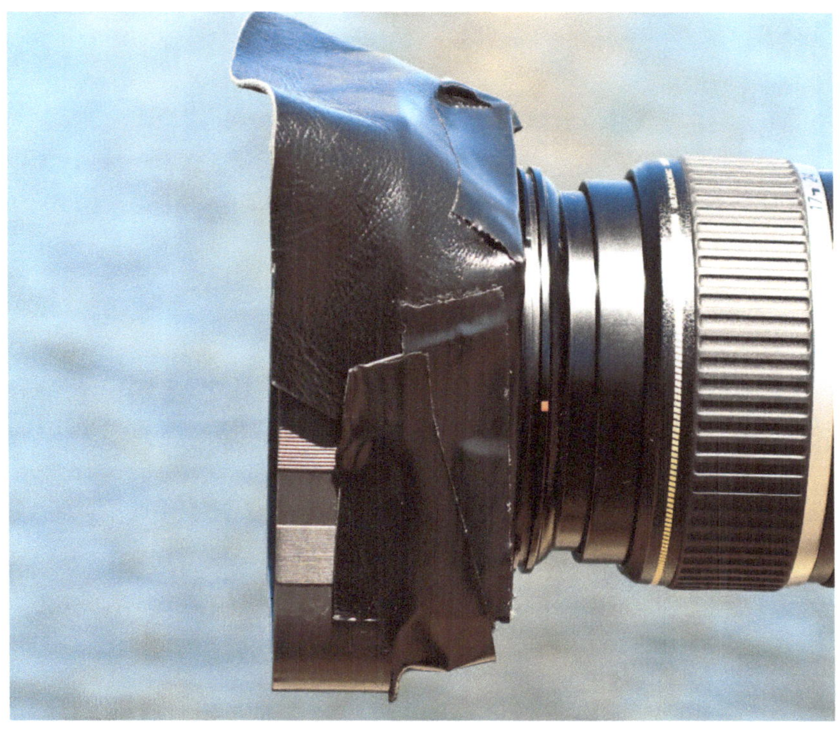

found with a number of SLRs is that with the mirror up during a shot, what should be a tight fit between the mirror and the pentaprism is not so tight and so light can leak around the raised mirror and fog the image sensor.

I've also found a similar issue to the Cokin case with a tool I use for panorama photography called the GigaPan Epic. This is a little motorised robot that sits on your tripod and has your camera attached. You set the start and end shots and it happily moves and shoots for you to allow you to capture a very high resolution panorama with less effort on your part, which is certainly a benefit when capturing a hundred or more images for one panorama. While designed for small and light compact cameras it will actually fit a small dSLR if you fiddle with it a bit. But because of the way the device is built you can't keep the camera perfectly level even when you level the base of the unit properly. This is because it has quite a bit of mechanical slop on its rotation axes. This seems not to be an issues when you use GigaPan's own panorama stitching software but is a pain when you use some other software that works better with RAW images. I know one person who has disassembed his GigaPan and rebuilt it with proper bearings and metal rather than the plastic gears it comes with.

Modifying your own gear is a long tradition in photography.

12. Use What You Have

In a consumer society it often becomes a programmed response that we need a new camera, lens or the latest software to life our work. But have we really obtained all we can from what we have?

It is very easy to fall into the trap of thinking that we can just do something when we have that certain lens, or whatever, and that we can't do anything until we have it. This is a common condition and whilst obviously reasonable at some level, is often a manifestation of our consumer society and/or an avoidance mechanism to avoid actually putting ourselves to the test. Coupled with the above is the fact that we often lust after a new piece of gear when we have only used 10% or so of the capability of the gear we already have that we intend to replace.

It is worth trying to overcome any tendencies to these above traits that you may have. In reality all they do is hold you back and stop you from achieving. No matter how great the circumstances, there is always something that is less than perfect. You may have a really good close focusing zoom but not that dedicated, single focal length macro lens you lust for. Yet that close focusing zoom lens could still produce stunning macro images if you worked at it. Perhaps you might need to invest $30 is a really good closeup filter to aid its close focusing, but perhaps not. Do you really need that top power studio flash set or could a couple of secondhand Sunpak flash guns and some cabling do the job for now? Or even a reflector made from white card or aluminium foil and your single flash? Or is that software upgrade really necessary?

There is another, hidden side to upgrading our software and gear: the time it costs you. How much time do you spend researching the purpose, daydreaming about it and then learning how to use it? Particularly with software upgrades but also with some gear there can be a huge learning curve involved in coming to grips with it so you get the best use from your money. You might be better off putting all this time into your photography or art. Remember too that there can be ripple effects. Upgrade that software and suddenly you need more memory, an operating system upgrade and maybe even a new computer to handle it, all with their attendant costs and time cost.

Most photographic and art gear and software can be used in many more ways than any one of us do. Most have under utilized potential just sitting there. Different types of shots, extended uses, creative uses and more. When was the last time you turned that lens off autofocus and shot everything out of focus to see how it looks? How long have those extension tubes sat in the cupboard unused? Have you explored the full potential of your bounce capable flashgun? Have you used its wireless capability and got it off the camera and in a different relationship to the subject, such as behind?

Of course there can also be a bit of the collector mentality to overcome too. Do you really need that battery grip for your camera or is it just to complete the look? Must you have every prime lens in Canon's current catalogue? And so it goes.

Discipline is the key to overcoming these traits, which keep you stuck and not performing and in saving all the time you will waste in indulging them. Put that time to better use and make more images.

Activity

Spend some time and make a complete list of all the photographic and computer gear, plus software, that you have.

In a cold and calculating way go through this list and make an estimate of what percentage of its capability you have exploited.

Pick the item that you have least exploited and set yourself a program to fully use it over a reasonable time frame.

When you have done this, move on to the next least utilized.

Don't buy a replacement item until you are comfortable saying that you have pretty much exploited all the capability of what you are replacing.

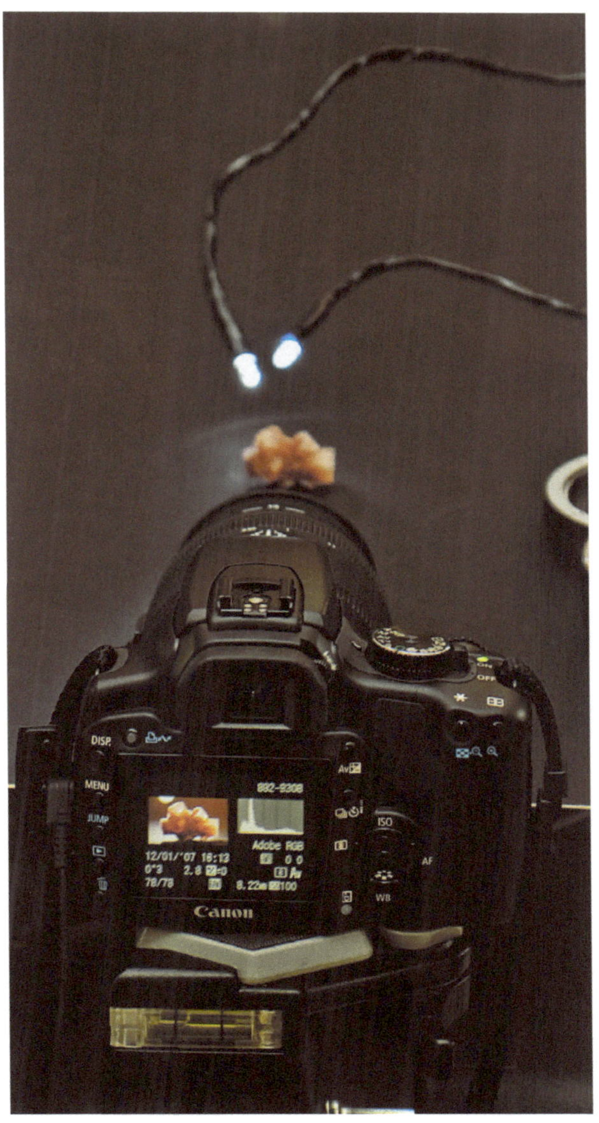

While I'd love to go out and buy a fibre optic lighting system for lighting the small rock and crystal specimens I love to shoot, I really could not justify the cost. So a couple of hours, two white LED lights, two battery holders and switches, some wire and a box gave me a perfectly workable small light for selective macro lighting for a total cost of around $10. Pretty well anyone could knock one of these together. All you need is a soldering iron and some solder, though I suspect you could probably do it with push on connectors if you looked around a good electronic supply store. Problem solved at virtually zero cost. Extension tubes can also be a cheap alternative to a special macro lens, as can closeup filters. After all, it is what people used to use before macro lenses were developed and there is no shortage of great but old macro photography.

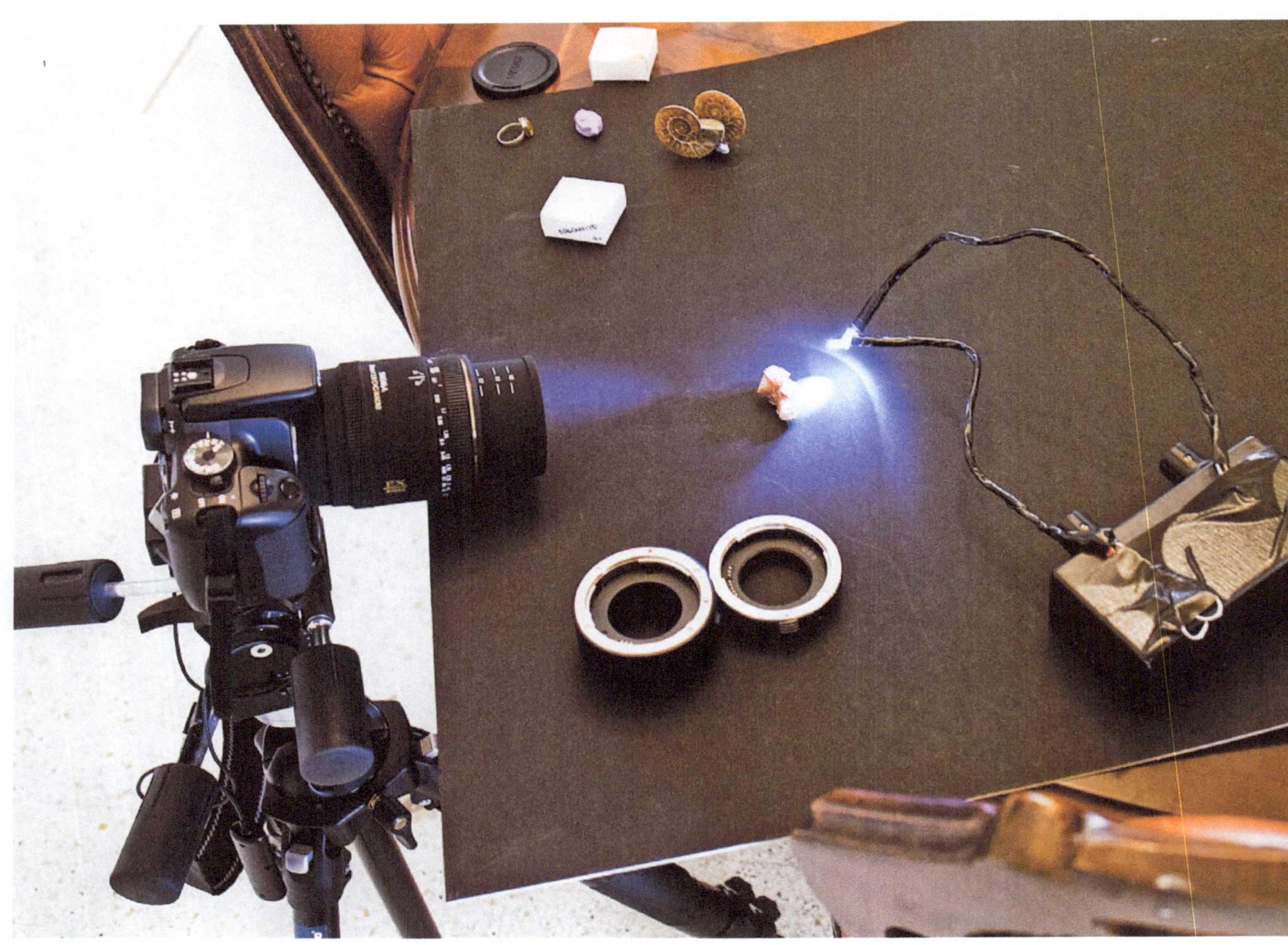

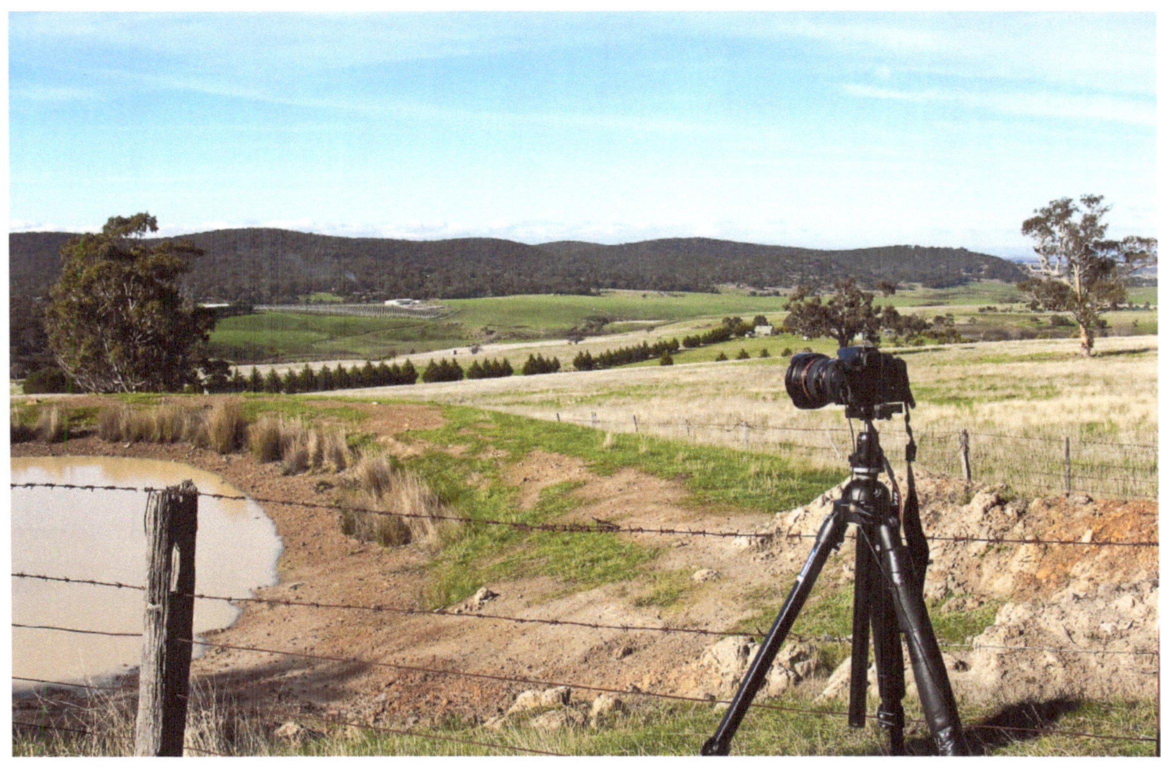

You don't have to have the latest carbon fibre tripod and magnesium head to take great shots. An older, solid tripod works fine. This is often the case with a lot of equipment we lust after.

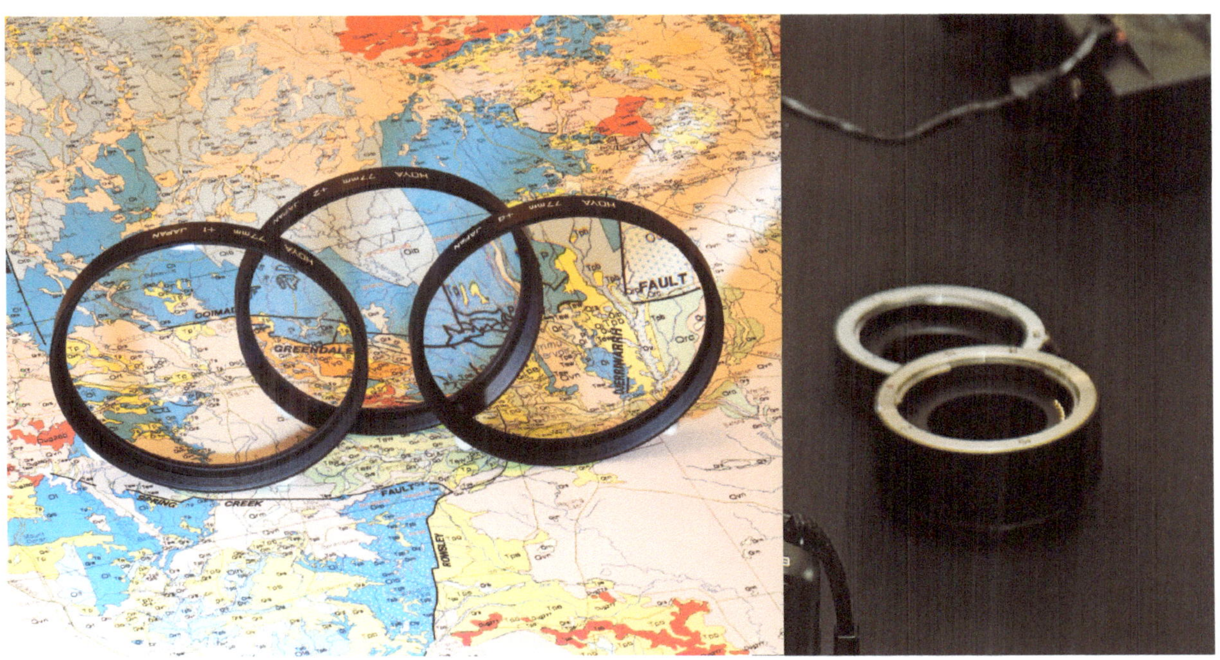

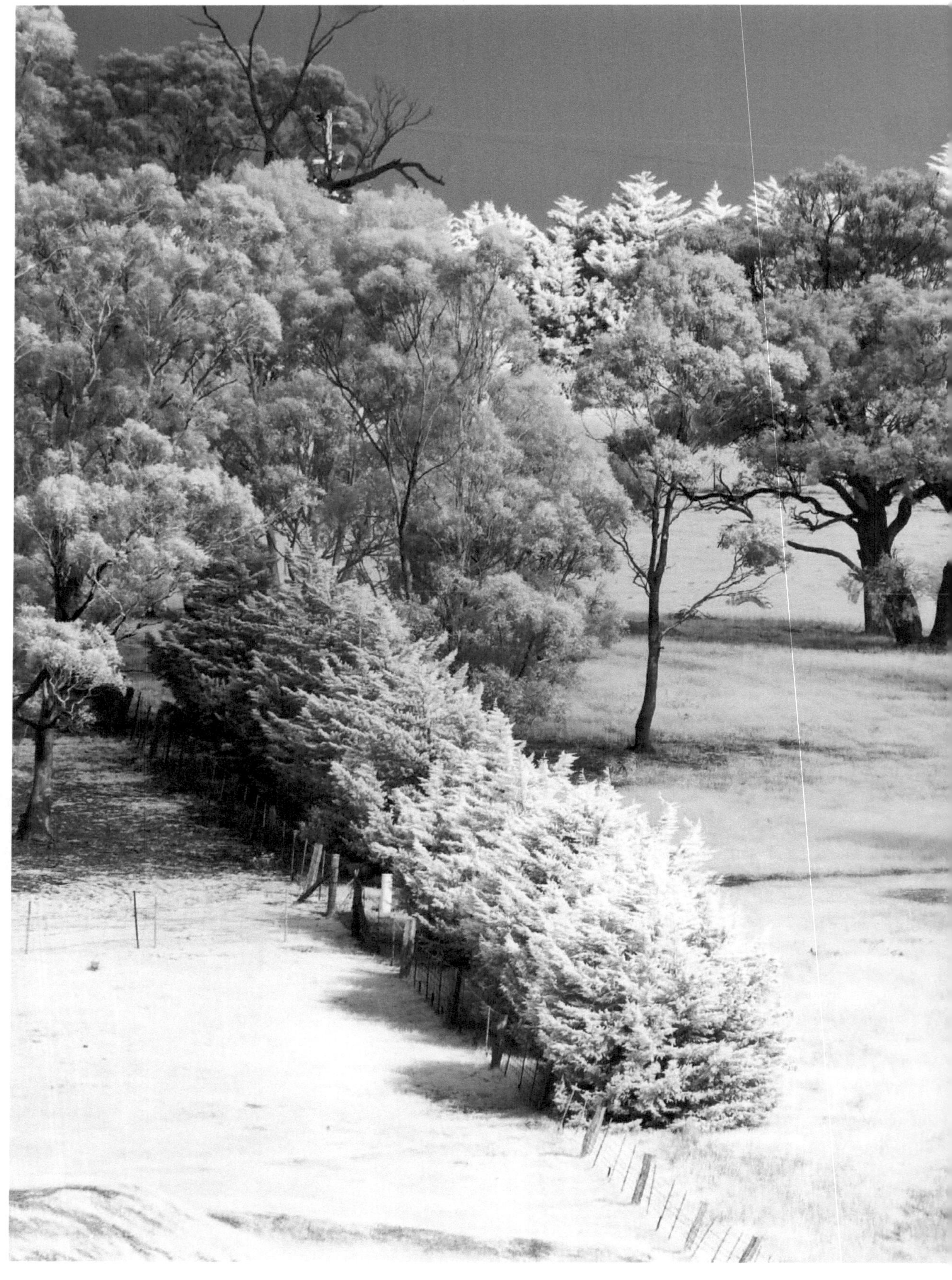

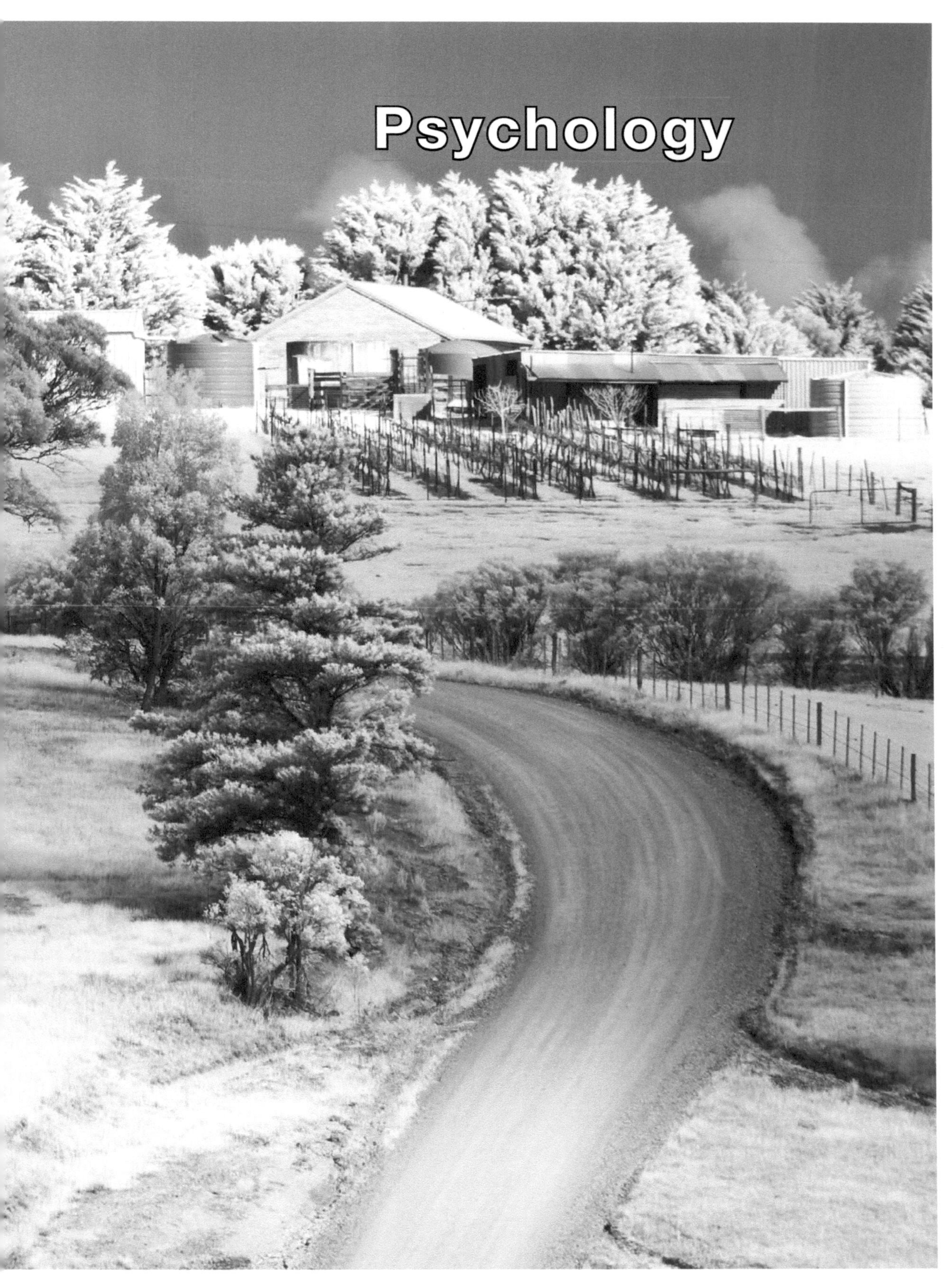
Psychology

13. Balance Intuition and Intellect

It is ok to be an intellectual about your photography. It is not wrong to think, plan and be methodical. Some of us are natural planners, list makers and thinkers. Others of us are not. But a bit of this is good for everyone. If this is not natural to you, cultivate it. Make lists before you go out on a shoot of what you want to capture. Take notes, keep a photographic diary, make use of the data your camera records with a RAW file, draw diagrams of what you want to do before working in Photoshop, etc.

It is also ok to be driven by instinct and intuition with regard to your photography. Whatever works for you is good. Some of us are naturally intuitive, others less so but can develop it.

Intuition is a vague term but it can include knowing something without being conscious of how, gut feelings about what to do and even that state of doing things 'automatically' without being consciously aware of what you are doing. Many call this 'being in the groove'. Probably many of us have had the experience of losing time when we have been out doing photography, or indeed doing any other activity we were involved in. In such a time we do have an awareness of doing things, it is just that we seem to be in a flow and not trying, just doing. What in fact is happening is that through being totally focused on an activity we enter an altered state of consciousness. Meditation leads to an altered state of consciousness too, and not all forms of meditation require sitting cross-legged on the floor staring into space. There are also active meditations, and that is, I think, what is going on when one slips 'into the groove'.

Learn one of the many different forms of meditation (there literally is one to suit everyone). Practice it before going out to do photography and again when you are out on location.

Mixing intelligence and intuition is fantastic. Some situations require one, some the other, whilst still others require a combination. Many of us naturally favour one over the other. If this is the case, try to develop the less natural one. Then you can consciously choose which will serve you better in a given situation rather than just being limited to what you habitually do.

Those rational types should learn some meditation and listen to their inner voice more. Intuitive types would benefit from consciously trying to plan their work and making lists and notes.

None of this comes easily and, in fact,

the quality of your work can deteriorate at first. However, if you stick with it, you will come out of the tunnel and your work will start to improve. I have seen this happen with many people, including myself, and so can only encourage you to push forward.

Activity

Before going out on a shoot make a list of what you would like to capture.

If you are into making image montages or composite images, try sketching a plan of what you want to create before you start. Also make a list of the component images you need.

If you are a rational, thought dominated photographer you would benefit from listening to your intuition more. This requires trust.

So next time you are doing some photography and a little voice in your head tells you to try something that seems dumb, do it. It sounds stupid, but trusting the intuition makes it stronger and makes the impressions clearer over time. Like everything, it requires practice.

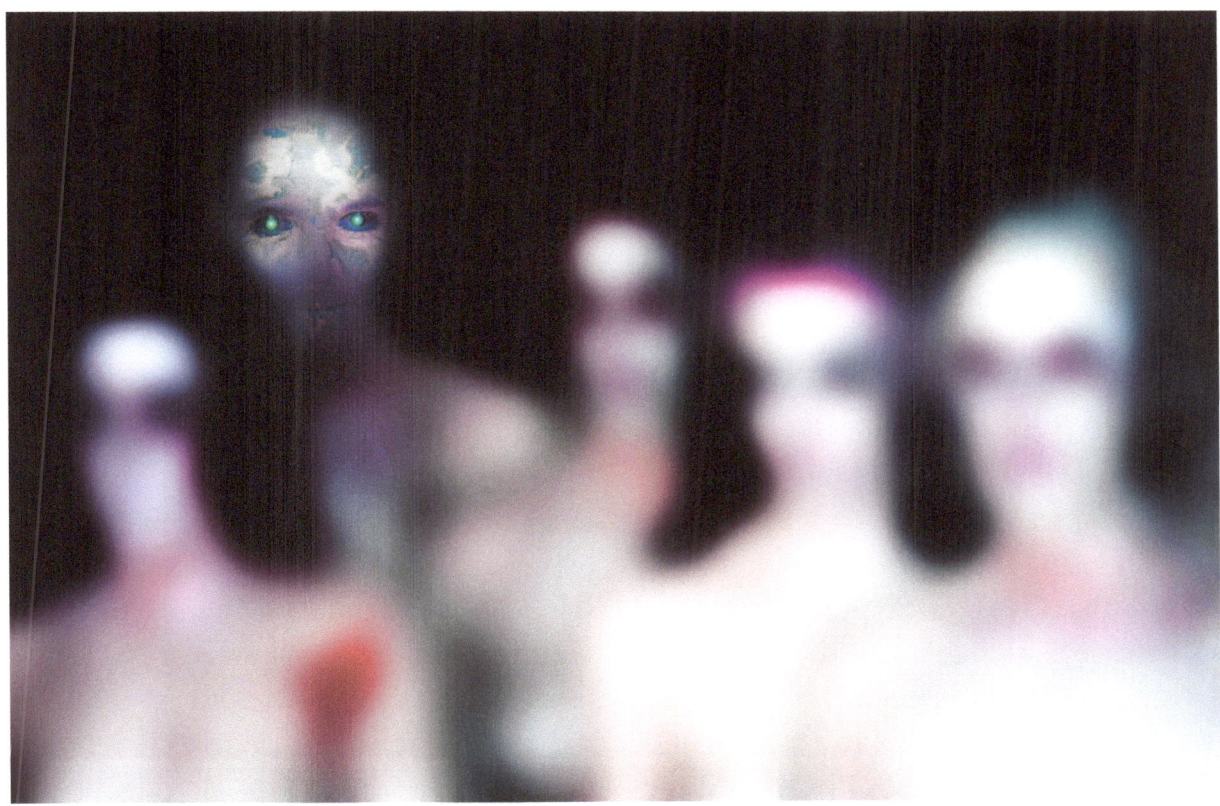

14. Restrict Yourself

Sometimes we are so overwhelmed by choice that we actually do nothing. There is a fix to this.

Choice is a wonderful thing, it is the freedom we crave and so many in the world do not have. Yet choice can be a double-edged sword, especially when it comes to creativity.

Whether we are a photographer or a digital artist, most of us are presented with so much choice. We have a range of lenses to use, and even a substantial choice of focal lengths with just one zoom lens, exposure options, processing techniques, subject matter and much more. This can be great. But if you are like me, there will be times when you are overwhelmed by this choice. Where do I go, what camera and lenses do I take, what tool will I use in Photoshop or Painter?

A way out of this dilemma is restriction. I don't mean putting the handcuffs on, though if that makes you more creative, go for it. What I mean is to deliberately make the choice not to use all the options available to you. So pick one camera and one lens and go shoot the whole day with just that. Set one shutter speed and use that, no matter what the lighting. Or pick one process in your software and use

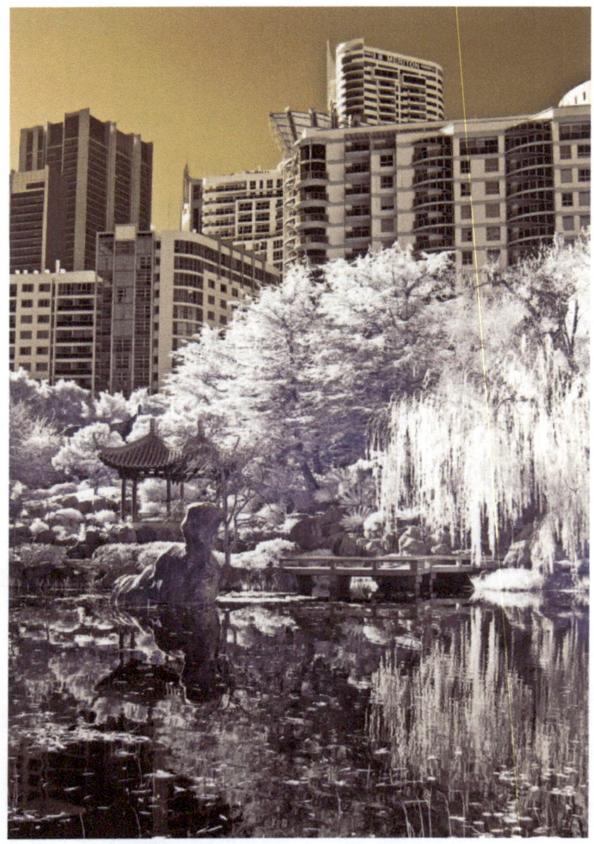

that only for some time.

Restriction shifts your thinking into problem solving mode, forcing you to try things you might never have chosen to do before. It forces you to accept compromises you might not like, or to find a way around them. In fact the very restriction liberates your creativity. I will often put a short-range zoom or single focal length lens on one camera and go out shooting for the day. Or I'll apply one Photoshop technique to all the images I process in a day or week, to see where it takes me.

See for yourself if restriction sets you free.

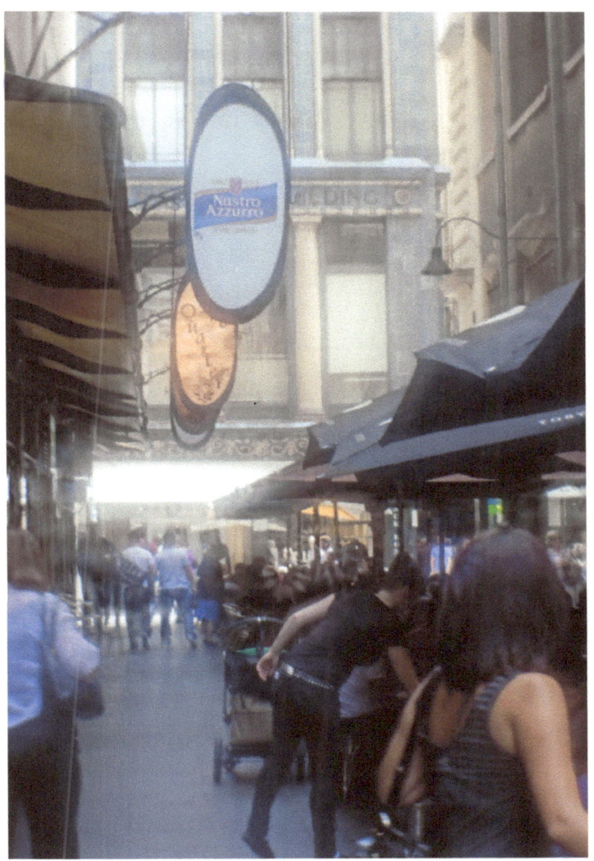

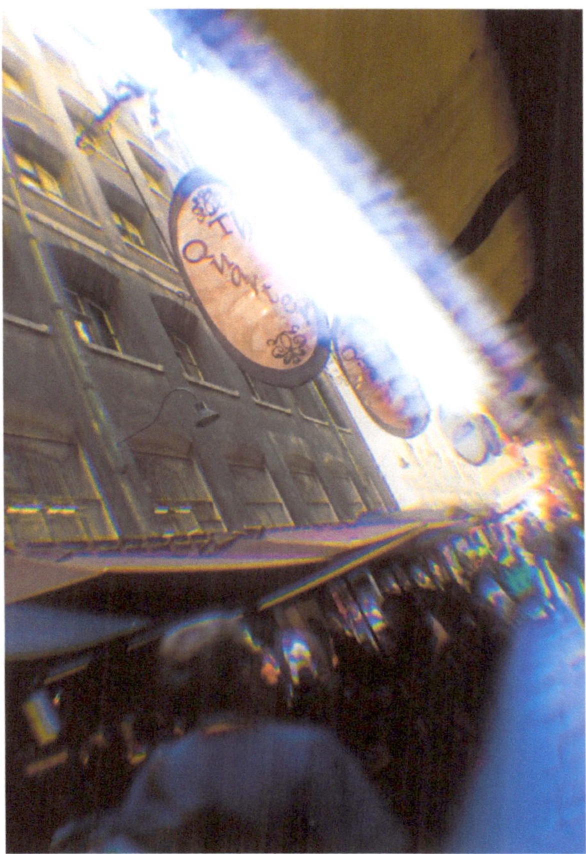

Activity

Look at the way you shoot and the gear you have and makeup a list of things that could constrain you. Then set an assignment around each constraint and shoot it.

Be disciplined about these constraints and don't cheat. After all, you will know if you cheated.

When you have exhausted equipment-based constrains, come up with others based on time, subject matter, shooting angle and whatever else you can come up with. You will be the better for it.

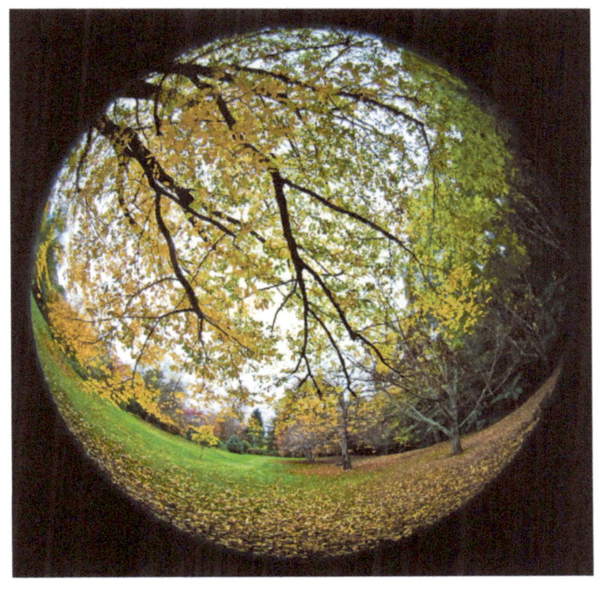

15. Stay Outside of Your Comfort Zone

The concept of a comfort zone is a useful one. Your comfort zone encompasses everything you already know, can do readily, people and places you know, and such. When we are within our comfort zone we are, as it goes, comfortable. It is a nice place to be, except when you are trying to develop.

Outside of your comfort zone is everything you do not feel comfortable doing, techniques you do not happily use, aesthetics you do not like, as well everything you do not already know, understand and have integrated into yourself.

If you are interested in growth and development, whether artistically, photographically, in business or in your personal life, you need to step outside of your comfort zone. By stepping outside our comfort zone we expose ourselves to new things, new ideas and new experiences and eventually we make them our own. This expands our comfort zone, which is what growth is about. You have pushed your own boundaries, expanding them in the process.

Now there is an interesting thing about comfort zones. Step too far outside of it and you risk the 'Oh my God, I can't deal with this' response. How far varies from person to person and time and situation and so you must know yourself. The OMG reaction sets you back, people retreat back into their comfort zone and sometimes don't step out again for some time.

So what you want to do is get yourself out of your comfort zone as far as you can without provoking the OMG response. After you've been out there for a while you will find your zone has expanded and you can push further.

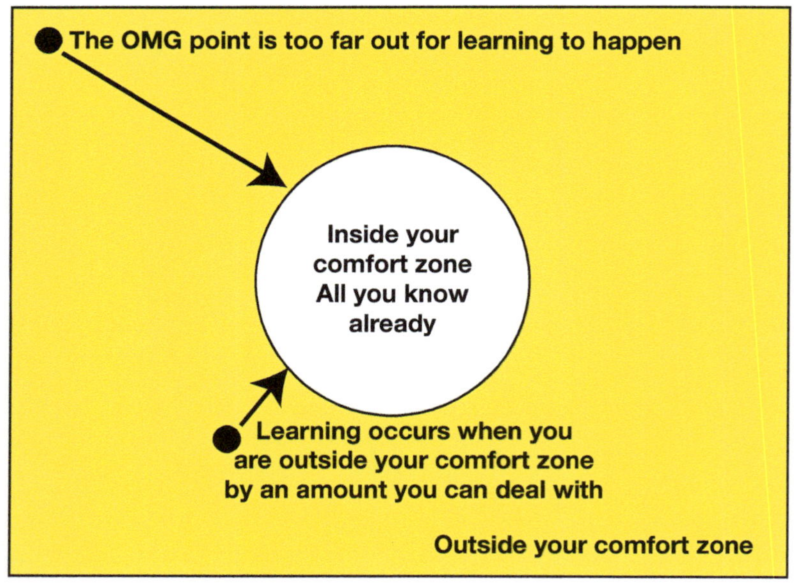

Photographically and artistically, our comfort zone includes the tools we regularly use, the techniques we use, the subject matter we like to shoot and the places we shoot. Pushing our envelope can be trying a new lens or filter, a new processing technique, using different software, shooting in a new way, tackling new subject matter (always been scared of shooting people, for example), trying some new ideas on composition or image design, etc.

Note that just because you bring an artistic style or technique within your comfort zone this doesn't mean that you will necessarily like it or want to use it in your own work. What it means is that the blanket fear and hate of it will tone down and you'll see it as a valid approach, just perhaps not for you, at least at the present. Always leave open the possibility of change.

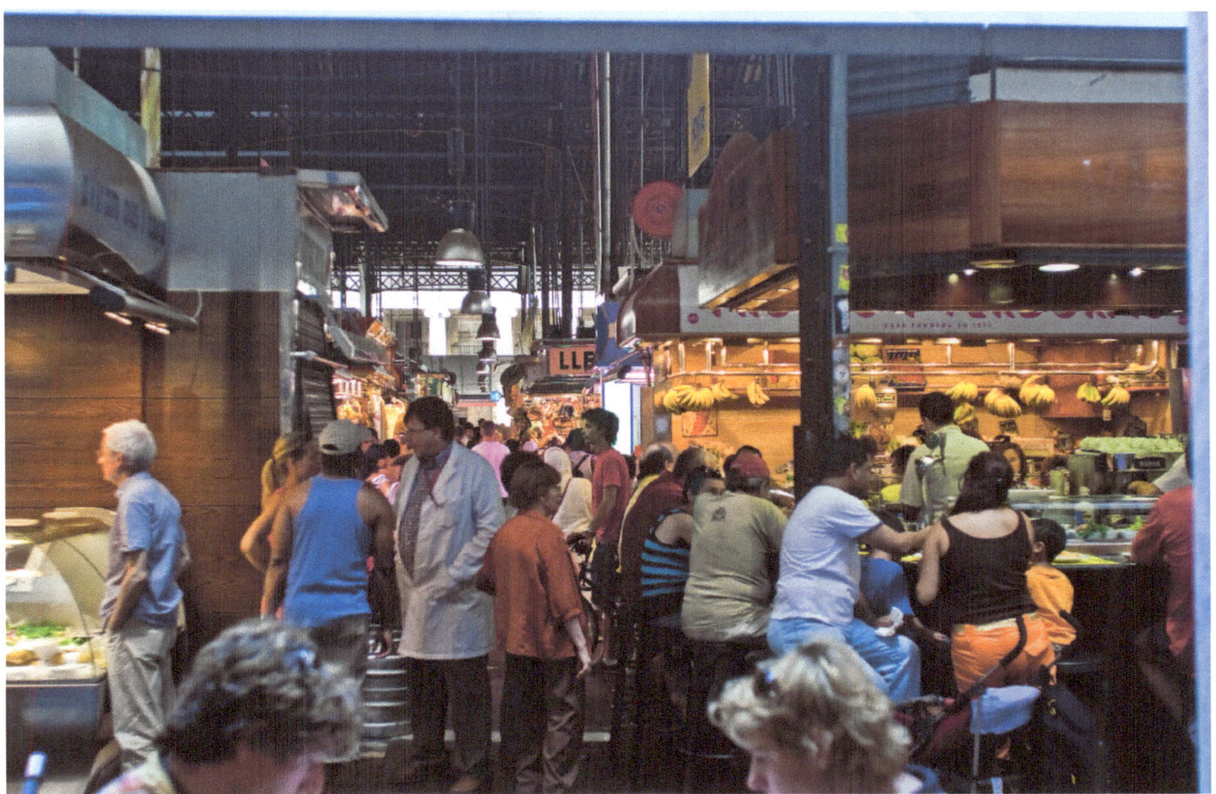

Many of us find shooting people quite confronting, and thus well out of their comfort zone. If this is the case for you, then the careful construction of slightly uncomfortable situations can stretch your comfort zone gradually. This is what training does for you, an expanded comfort zone.

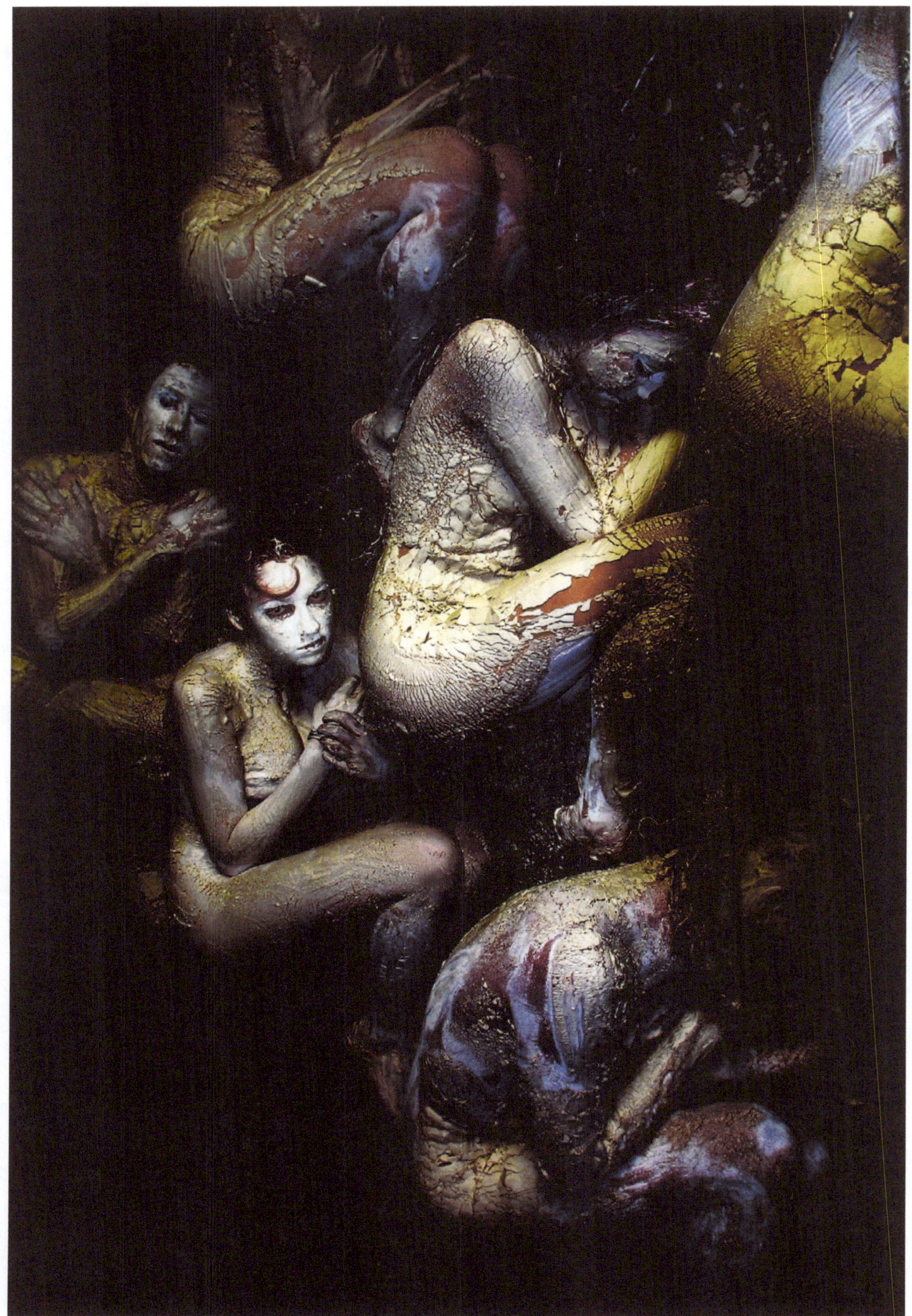

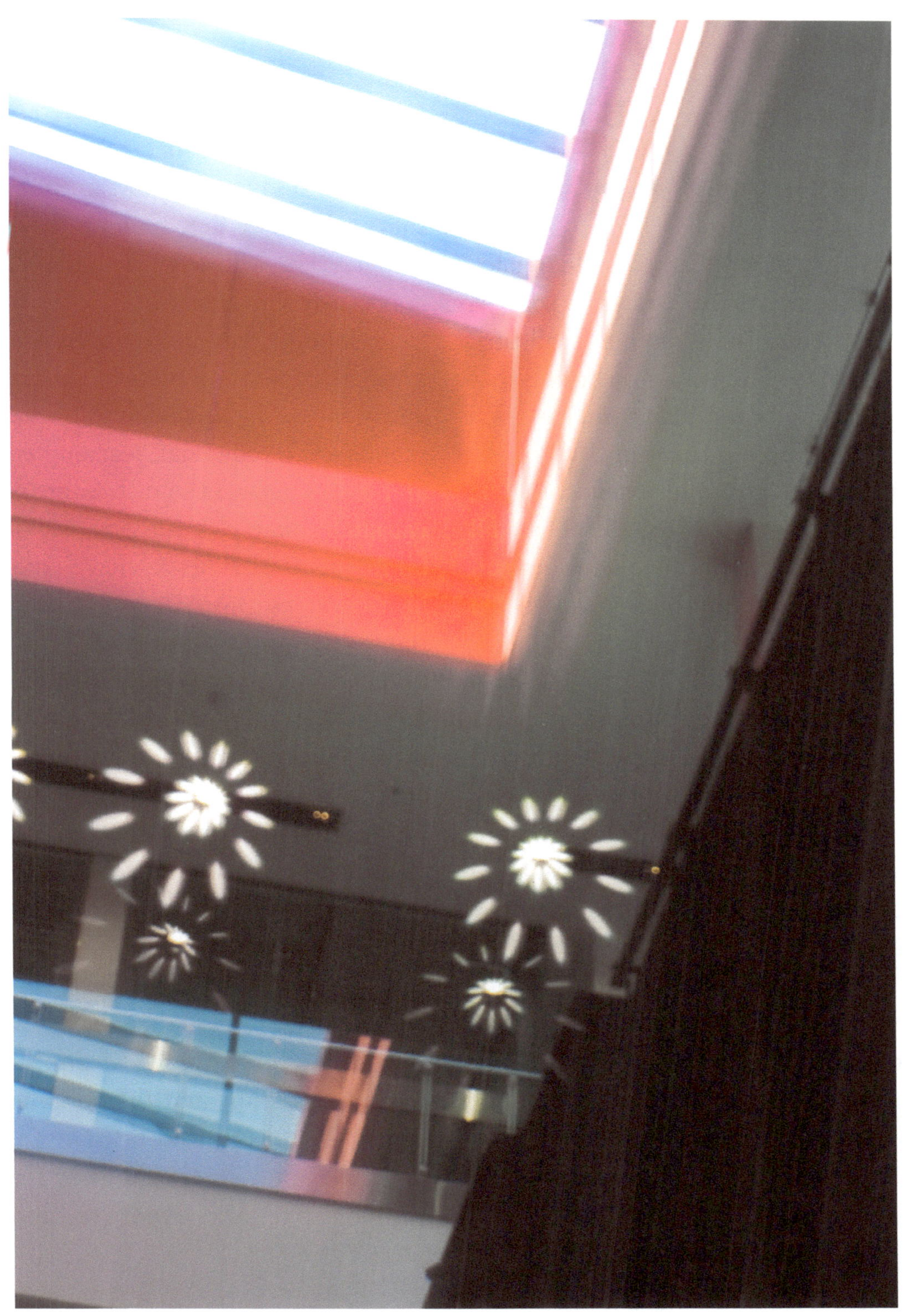

16. Push Yourself That Little Bit More

You may be tired and decide to pack it in for the day. And of course as soon as you pack up and leave the light will turn wonderful. Do you give up on trying that night photography technique you have told yourself you are keen to try just because it is a bit cold or your favourite show will be starting on TV? Or you may have put all your stuff away ready to try a new location and an opportunity presents itself. Do you get it all out again or do you go home or move on?

Pushing your photography requires pushing yourself. I don't know about you, but lugging that big, heavy but oh so nice tripod around is hard work. Same with taking some of that extra gear. So do you leave it in the car or at home or do you make the effort?

Pushing your photography is a lot more than just pushing your technique. In fact, I would argue that really it is only the pushing of your thinking that advances your photography. Techniques are only the vehicle by which you demonstrate this change in thinking.

Arnold Schwarzenegger said that it is that last extra repetition of an exercise, after you wanted to stop that builds the muscle. When your dad told you that life was hard he may not have meant exactly that, but rather that sometimes you have to persevere even when you have little to apparently show for it.

Taking great photographs or making great art is not easy. In fact, it is a complex and demanding task. Some of those demands are intellectual, learning exposure and optics and all the rest. Some is physical, such as carrying the gear, walking that bit further for that great view or crouching in a cramped position to get exactly the right point of view. But some is also emotionally and spiritually demanding: how do you keep going when it is just not coming together and the shots are lousy or how do you summon the motivation to drag yourself out of a nice, warm bed so you can shoot before dawn?

Activity

To borrow a phrase from the movie 'We Were Soldiers', there is always one more thing you can do. So apply this to your photography and to your whole life, in fact. There is always one more angle you can shoot, one more change in the lighting you can try or one more technique you haven't given a go.

Push yourself. Try getting up and out

with your camera an hour earlier or stay out an hour later.

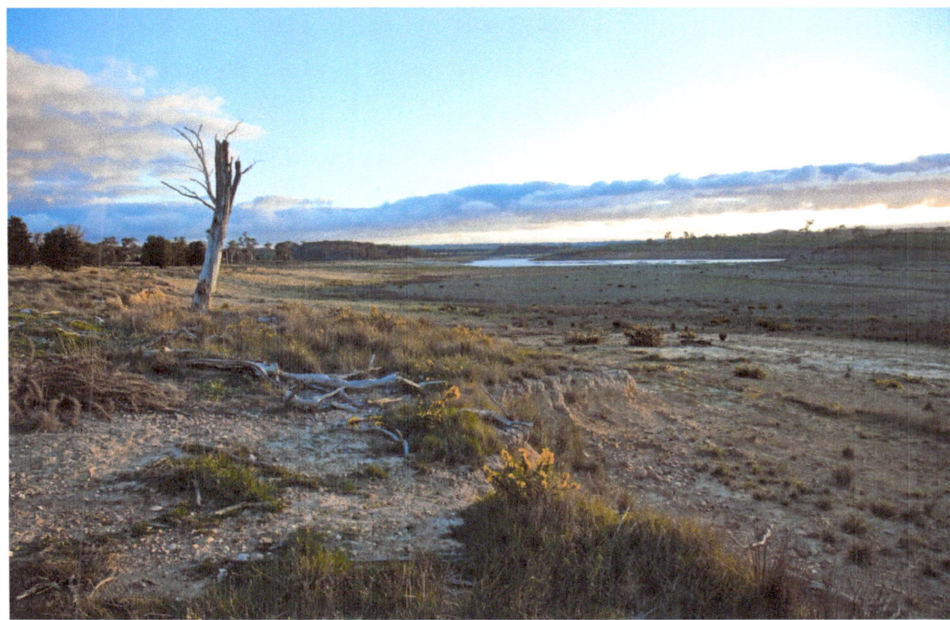

Staying out later, walking further from the car or being out in wet weather gear and with an umbrella is often the way to not only shake up your photography but also capture great images. The image below was taken moments after a storm had rolled over San Francisco Bay.

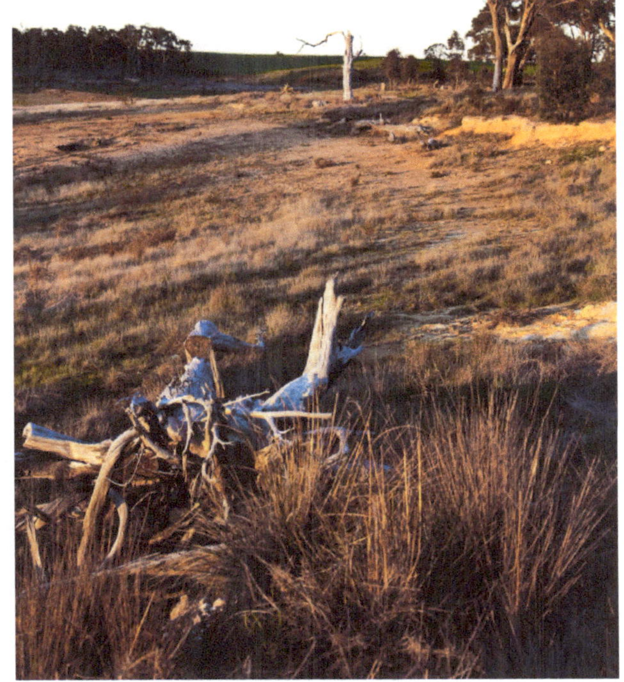

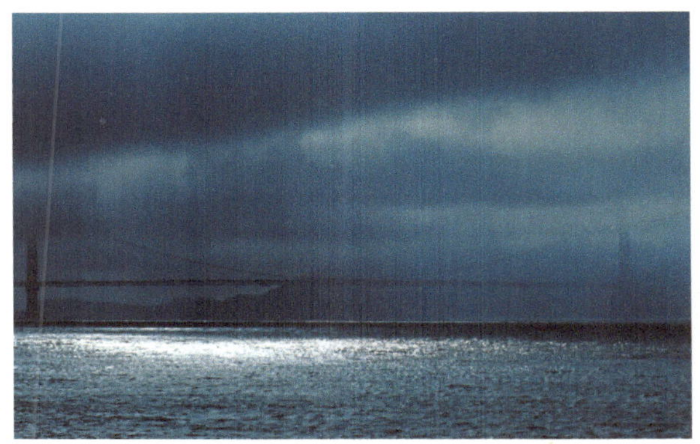

17. Reconsideration Is Good

For many of us there is such a rush to new creation of images that we do not reconsider our old ones.

Especially for those shooting digital, but even for film users, there is a perpetual focus on our latest images. We may do a lot of work on an image but then put it away as we move on to the latest work. We may also shoot so much that an individual image gets dismissed in comparison to more obviously strong images, and left untouched.

The history of photography has shown some photographers who, rather than doing this, develop a lifelong relationship with an image. They come back to it time and time again, re-evaluating, re-considering and re-working an image. Over time, such an image relationship builds an interesting document in its own right, your changing view of photography, of life and of this particular image.

We all grow and change as an image maker. Our technical skills hopefully grow, whether in the darkroom or on the computer, as well as at the camera. Our sense of aesthetics change as we look at more work, expand our sense of what is possible and grow to accept new visual possibilities.

All the above means that re-evaluating previous work is a great idea. The best image you will ever take may be sitting in your archives. It pays, every so often, to re-evaluate old work, to take the time and effort to go look though your previous work, both in its raw state (film or RAW file) and in its interpretation (prints or Photoshop file) and see just where you can take some of these images today. If nothing else the process will show you just how far you have come and even whether you have moved away from a very promising approach.

Re-consideration and perhaps re-work of an image can be very enlightening.

Just as revisiting your previous work to see if it can be improved is good, so is revisiting favourite subject matter or places.

With the wealth of subject matter and locations that most of us have access to, there is a huge urge to not revisit something or someplace we have already worked but to constantly try for something new.

Throughout the history of art, many artists have revisited the same subject matter over and over again. It might be a favourite place, subject or topic. Recurrent topics can be the self-portrait, a favourite landscape location, the same type of flower or whatever. Why would they do this?

When you revisit something or somewhere you are familiar with you are freed from the novelty and thus able to perceive through to a deeper level, explore different techniques and of course see completely differently as we have, hopefully, grown as an artist or person. Of course when it comes to locations, you are also exploring it over time and thus can explore how the time of day, season or development changes the location. Our equipment may also change over time, or our technique of using it. As photographers we may have new lenses or accessories, even new cameras, that open up new picture taking possibilities. As artists we may also have developed techniques, new software (or new versions) and new art making tools, from a graphics tablet to new papers or materials for working over a print.

Personally, I am doing a lot of landscape photography at present. I've fallen in love with a particular broad location, about an hour from home, and I am now exploring it and reshooting it as often as I can, with all the gear I have and with whatever gear is coming in for testing, at differing times of day and as the seasons shift. I am loving it. My photography of the place is getting better (in my view) and I am learning more about the place.

Give it a go. Indeed it may be a lifelong study as even while you work other subjects and places you keep revisiting the familiar, find new things or just new things to say. Give it a try.

Remember that your aesthetic tastes, skills and perception will change over time, as will your thoughts on a topic and thus what you want to say and how you want to say it. If they are not changing then perhaps you have become stagnant.

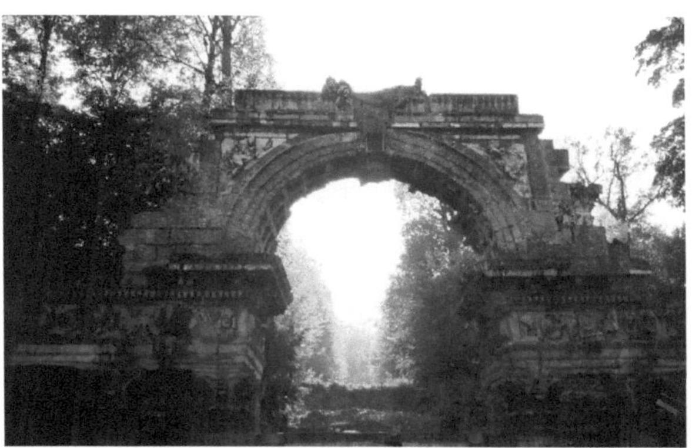

I am currently going back over many of my old images shot on black and white film and reworking them digitally to fit my current thinking.

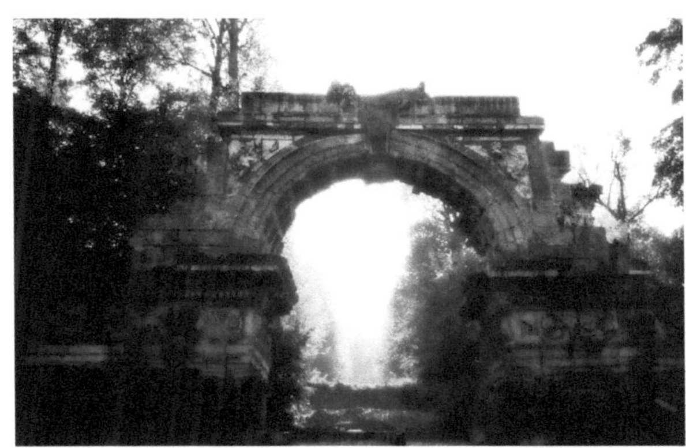

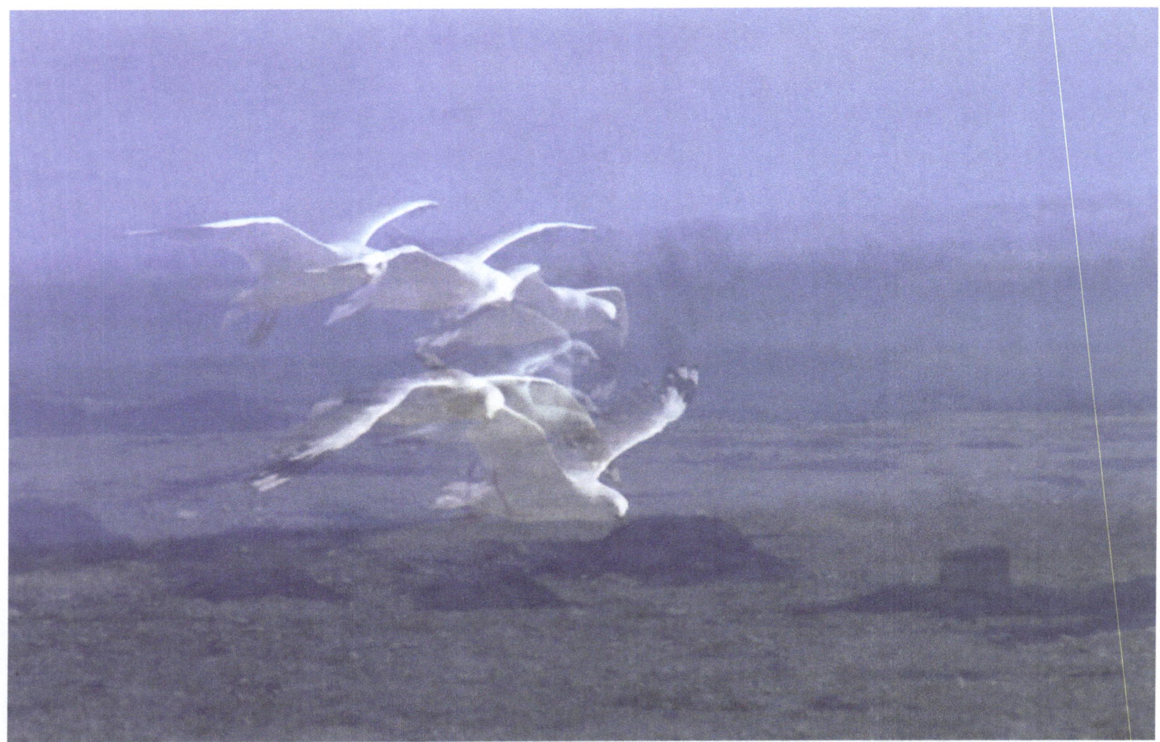

The above image and the one at top right were shot many years and it seems many lives ago on high ISO slide film on the same day. Both came out of being on an uninteresting beach that forced me to try something new. Remembering my camera, a Canon T-90, had multiple exposure. They are thus grainy but have remained some of my favourite images. They were originally exhibited as large Cibachrome prints. Both have been revisited recently and processed to reduce grain, tweak colour. I don't believe I have finished this process and will revisit them again. I will also try shooting similar again, digitally, for lower noise and perhaps a different effect.

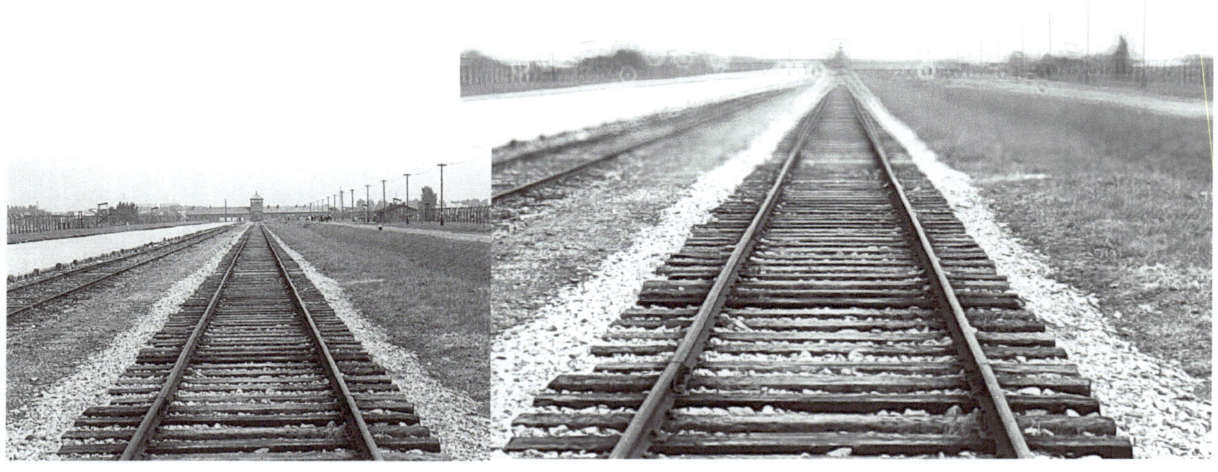

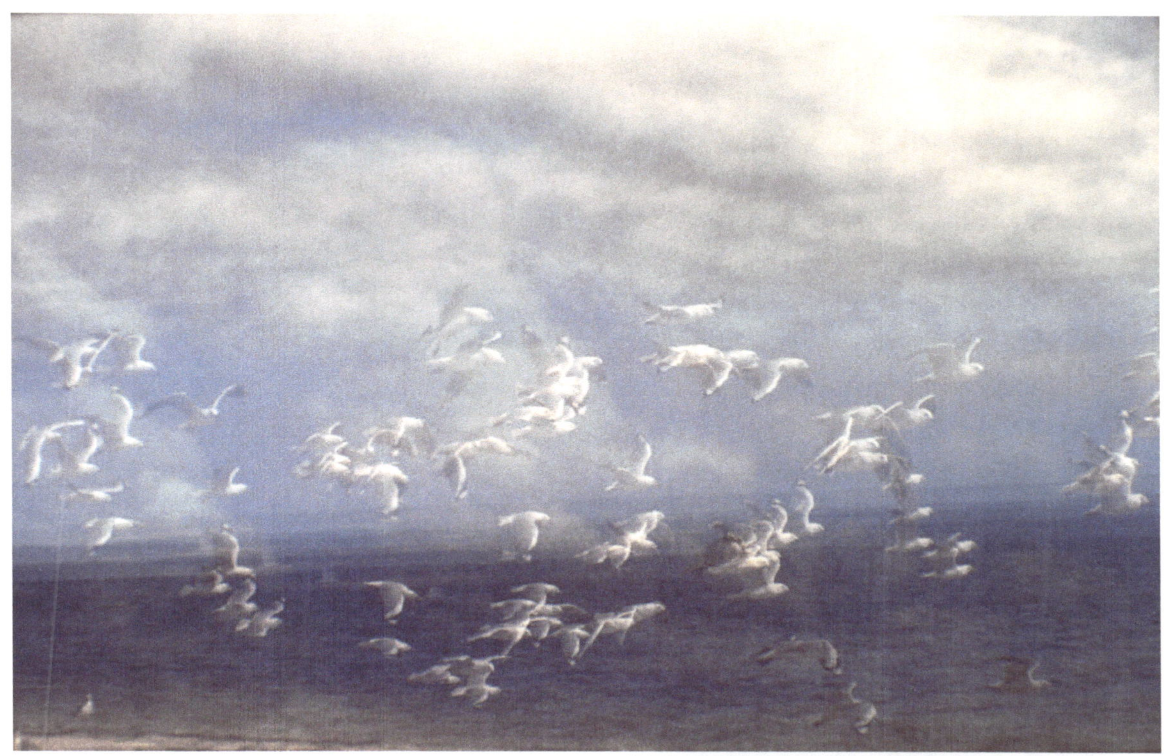

These Auschwitz images bottom left and this page show the images as I originally printed them and recent reworks. Time will undoubtedly cause me to revisit and rework these images in many ways.

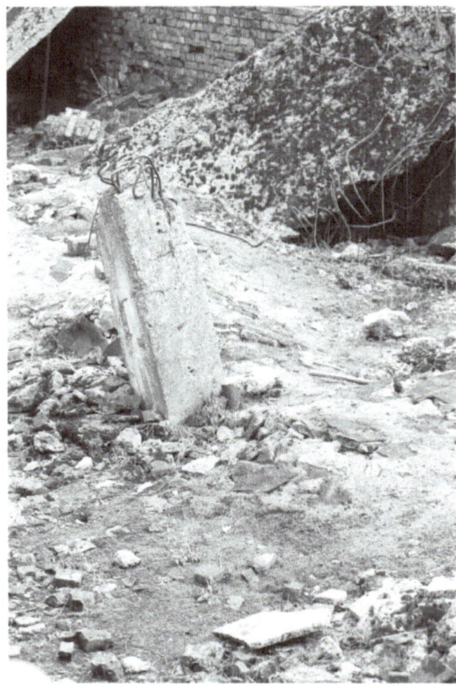

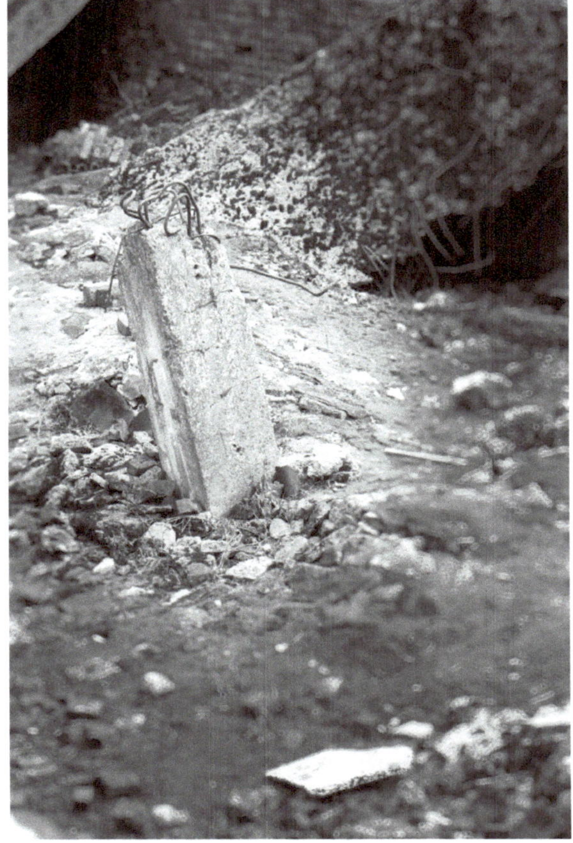

18. Plan, Then Shoot

Shooting spontaneously is great, and can produce stunning shots. But with most of us time limited, a bit of preparation ahead of time can maximize your chances.

Many people have the impression that photography needs to be spontaneous to be creative. This is true for some people and for some of the time. But like all human activities, sometimes a bit of preparation can increase the likelihood of creativity triumphing over mediocrity. Call it creative foreplay rather than planning, if it makes you feel better and tricks you into doing it. Also some personality types would benefit from developing their planning, rational sides.

Studio photographers plan ahead all the time. They may need to book a makeup artist, get in props, hire equipment, construct sets and more. All of us also plan ahead in some ways, such as packing our camera bag and making sure the batteries are all charged up.

I am mostly a landscape photographer. Planning a shoot can be little more than checking the weather forecast and consulting a map to know how to get there. But it can be much more.

Let us just consider landscape photography for now as an example. Before a landscape shoot, we could do the following:

- Check the weather, plus high and low tide times if in a coastal area;
- Determine sunrise and sunset times, plus moon rise and set and phase. You can also determine the azimuth points around the horizon of the rise and set points;
- Google for shots of the same location;
- Go look for books at the library;
- Use Google Earth to examine the ground;
- Consult a topographical map to look for potential vistas, shooting locations, approach routes, etc;
- Even learn to read a geological map so you can get an idea of soil or rock types;
- Write up a list of the shots you want to take.

The above list is, of course, only representative and similar lists could be prepared for other types of photography. A bit of preparation helps to maximize your chances of success. For example if you know that the moon will rise at 3pm in the afternoon and that there is a particular location with an appropriate vista then you can arrange to be there a bit before three. Without knowing it you will not be sad for what you missed but you just might have completely missed what might have been a stunning shot.

Don't get me wrong, I do not plan all the time. Sometimes I just have to get out and so I grab a selection of gear and just drive. But sometimes planning lets you get far more out of whatever time you have available for shooting.

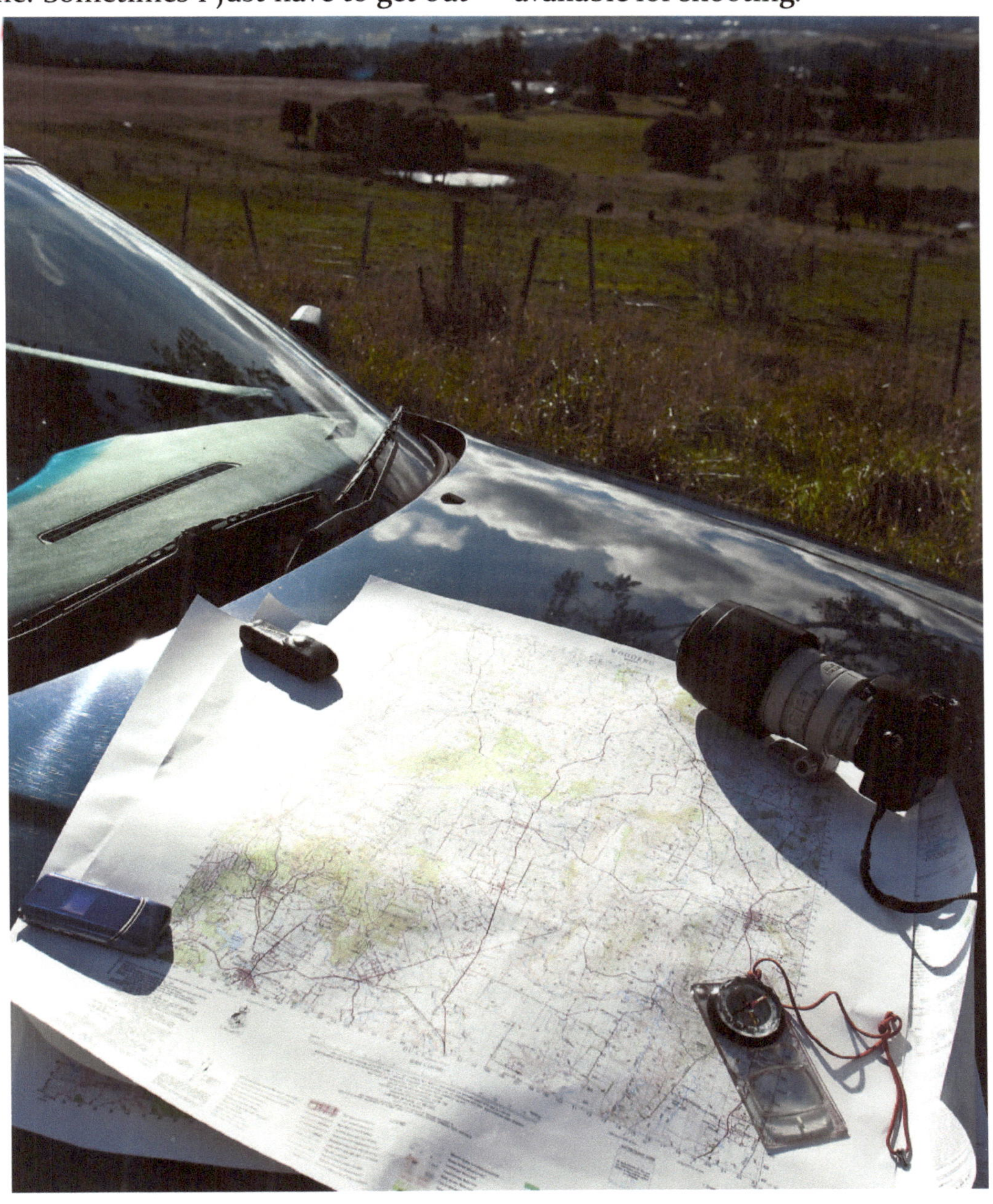

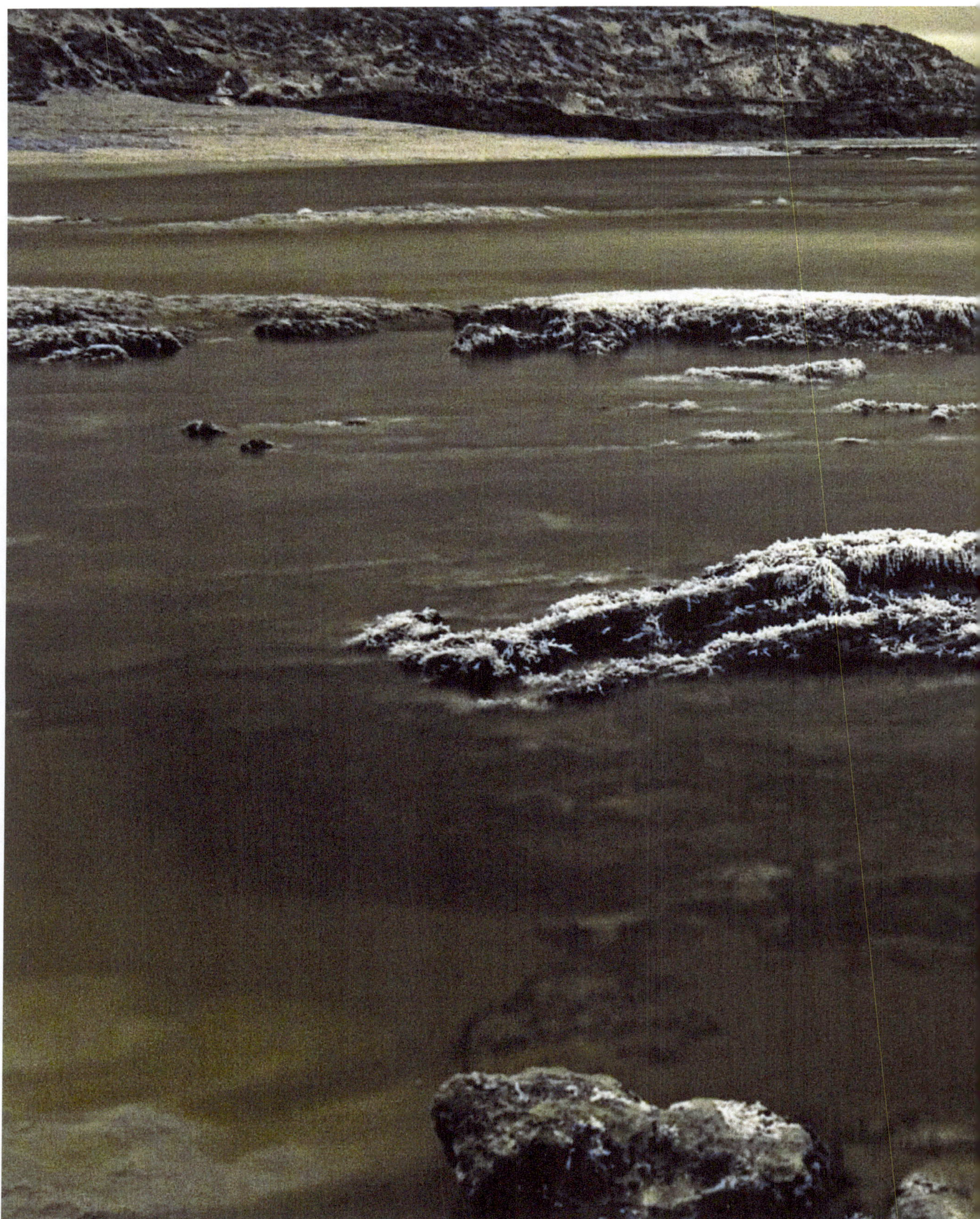

Rules

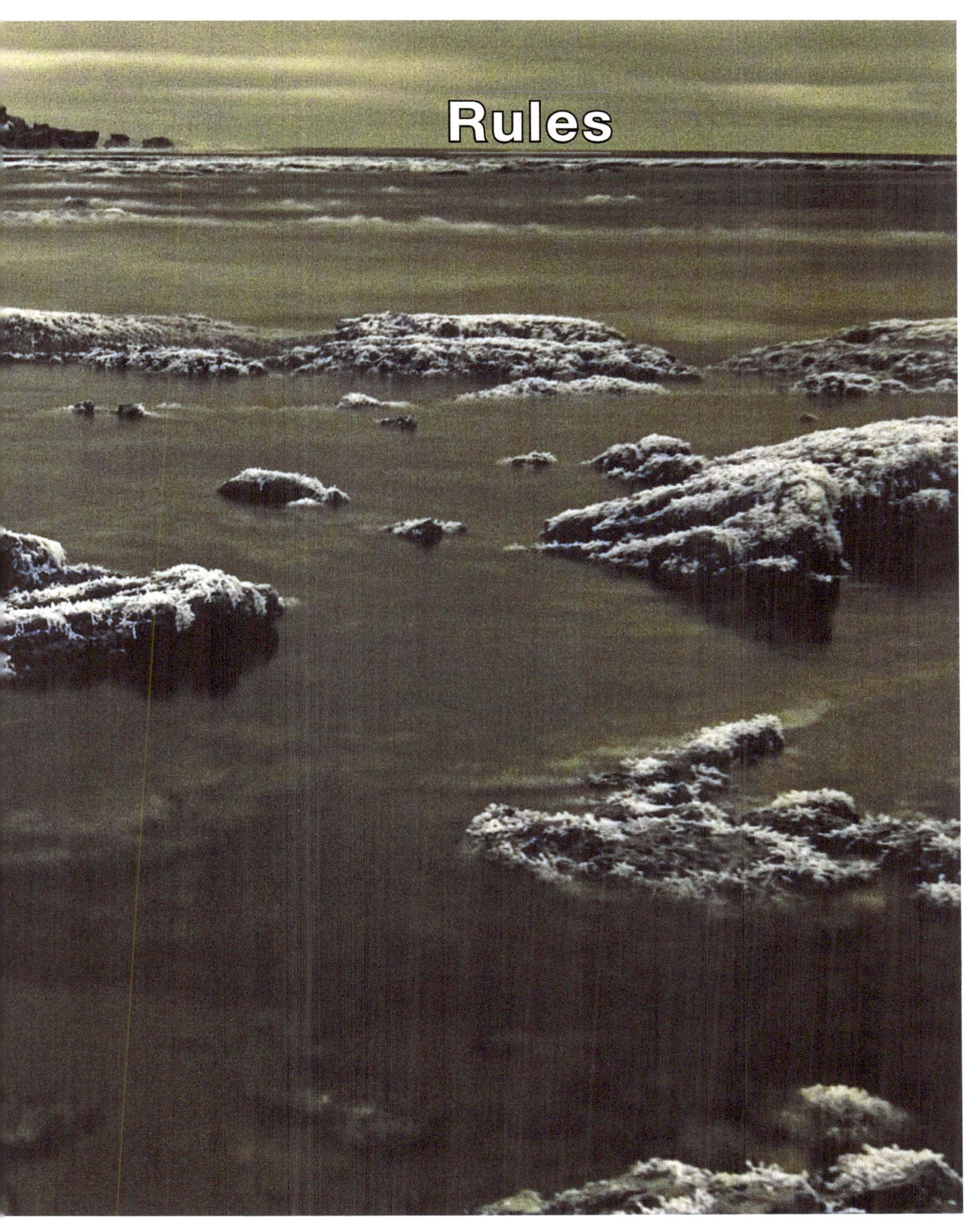

19. Understand the Rules

Photography, like everything else, has some guiding principles in many areas. This can be the rule of putting the sun over your shoulder, rule of thirds in composition or the one about the slowest shutter speed you can handhold is 1/focal length. There are many of these rules that it pays to learn. Why? Because they represent real knowledge and can save you in a tight moment. These rules represent hard won knowledge by photographers (and artists) who have come before us. Learn from the experience of others.

More important than just learning the rules is understanding them. What is it that the rules are really telling you?

The rule of thirds is really an approximation of the older and deeper Golden Section or Golden Mean principles that go back at least as far as the ancient Greeks and probably further to 1st Dynasty Ancient Egypt.

The Golden Section says that there is an ideal proportion that offers perfect aesthetics. This ration is known as phi (Φ) and has the value of 1.61803.

Likewise the idea that you can only handhold a camera and get sharp images if the shutter speed is at least 1/focal length is a gross approximation. What it says is that if shooting with a 50mm lens you should shoot at 1/50 second or faster. But inherent in this are many assumptions: how big you will blow up the image, how sharp is sharp enough, how steady your hand is and even that your sensor is a full frame 35mm sized one. Understanding all this gives you the basis to determine your own personal rule, that takes into account your gear, steadiness, general blowup size and desire for sharpness in your images.

Activity

Learn and understand the rules of composition, colour theory and design principles.

Test them out to see if they make a difference. Take shots that follow them and break them and see which works better.

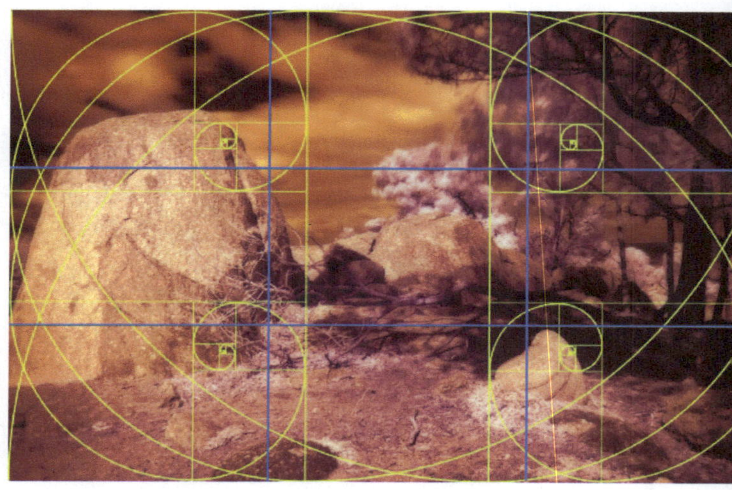

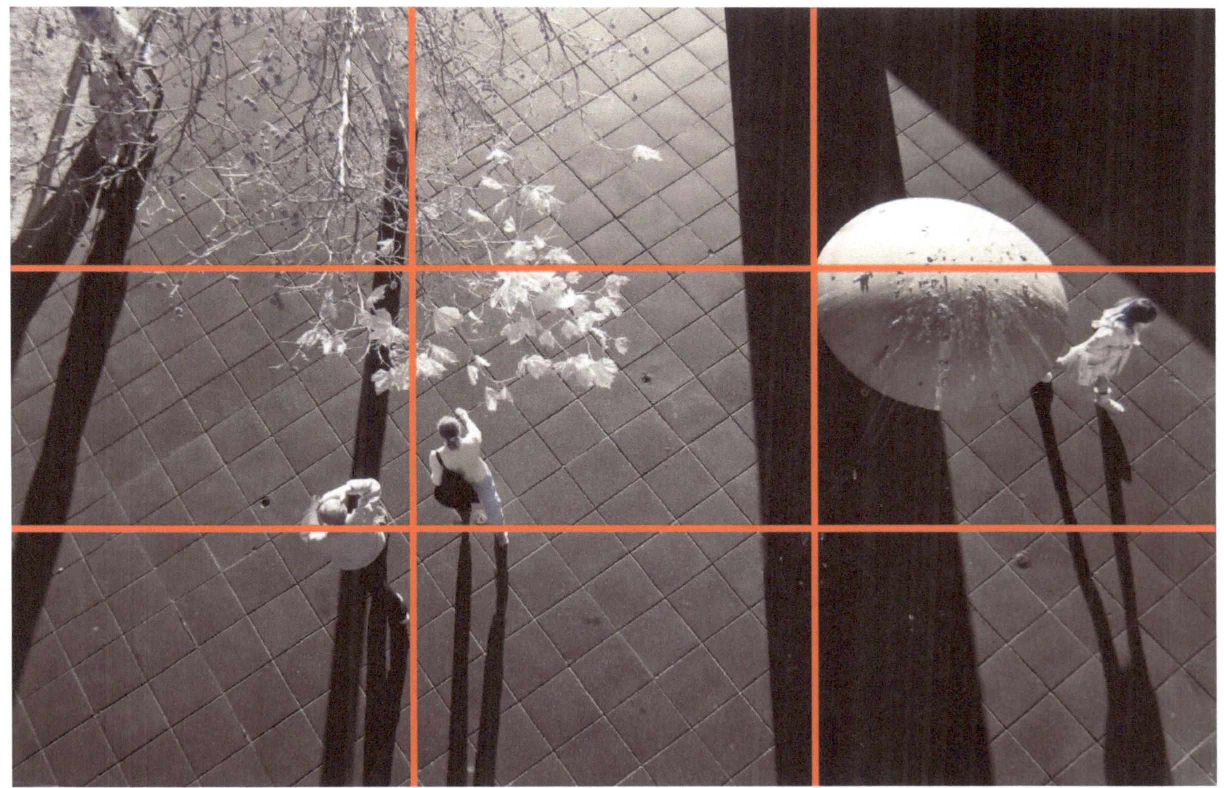

The rule of thirds (above) is only an approximation of the much harder to apply Golden Mean ideas (see below).

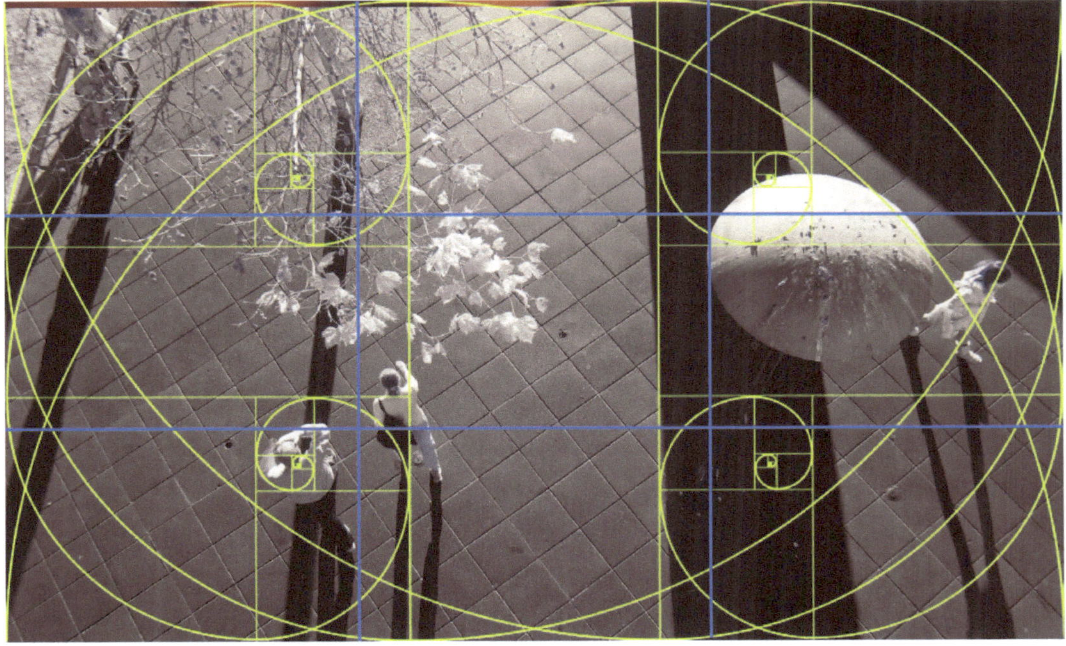

20. Break the Rules

Photography, along with other art forms, has so-called rules: rules of composition, colour theory, and so on. Rather than being called rules, they really should be called principles.

Part of our growth as an artist is to know these principles. Study of composition: ideas of rhythm, mass, line, form, contrast, repetition and position is a core part of our education. Likewise colour theory and ideas of symbolism in colour are important. We all know of the rule of thirds, but there is benefit in knowing how this is merely a simplification of ideas of sacred geometry and the golden section. All these and more should be part of your study, not just in the beginning of your creative path, but throughout it as we all forget and we will also get more out of the study at various times as our thinking and visual vocabulary become more developed.

But none of these principles are, in fact, rules. There are famous photographs that break one or more of them. Main subject in the centre, odd colour choice, imprecise rhythm, all these and more have been used to create stunning images. Does this mean the rules are wrong? No. It means that, occasionally, breaking them makes for a stronger image. The trick is knowing when to break them.

The beginning photographer and artist violate them constantly, because they do not know better. The developing artist follows them slavishly, hoping they will make their work better, which it usually does. The master knows when the subject or their interpretation of it requires something different. Then the violation in itself becomes a tool. But you have to know the principles to know when you really must break them.

Practice is the key. Examine great images, yours or others, check the composition, analyse how it is constructed and how things are places, the colour choices, etc. Practice and analysis is the key.

Activity

When your intuition or intellect is telling you this is one shot where you should break the rule, do so. Just shoot one that does obey the rules as well, if for no other reason than so you can reassure yourself later.

Practice a deliberate policy of rule breaking. Set yourself assignments that break one rule or another for a while and examine the results. This is a VERY important exercise for you to do. It will help you understand when the rules apply and when it is the right thing to break them.

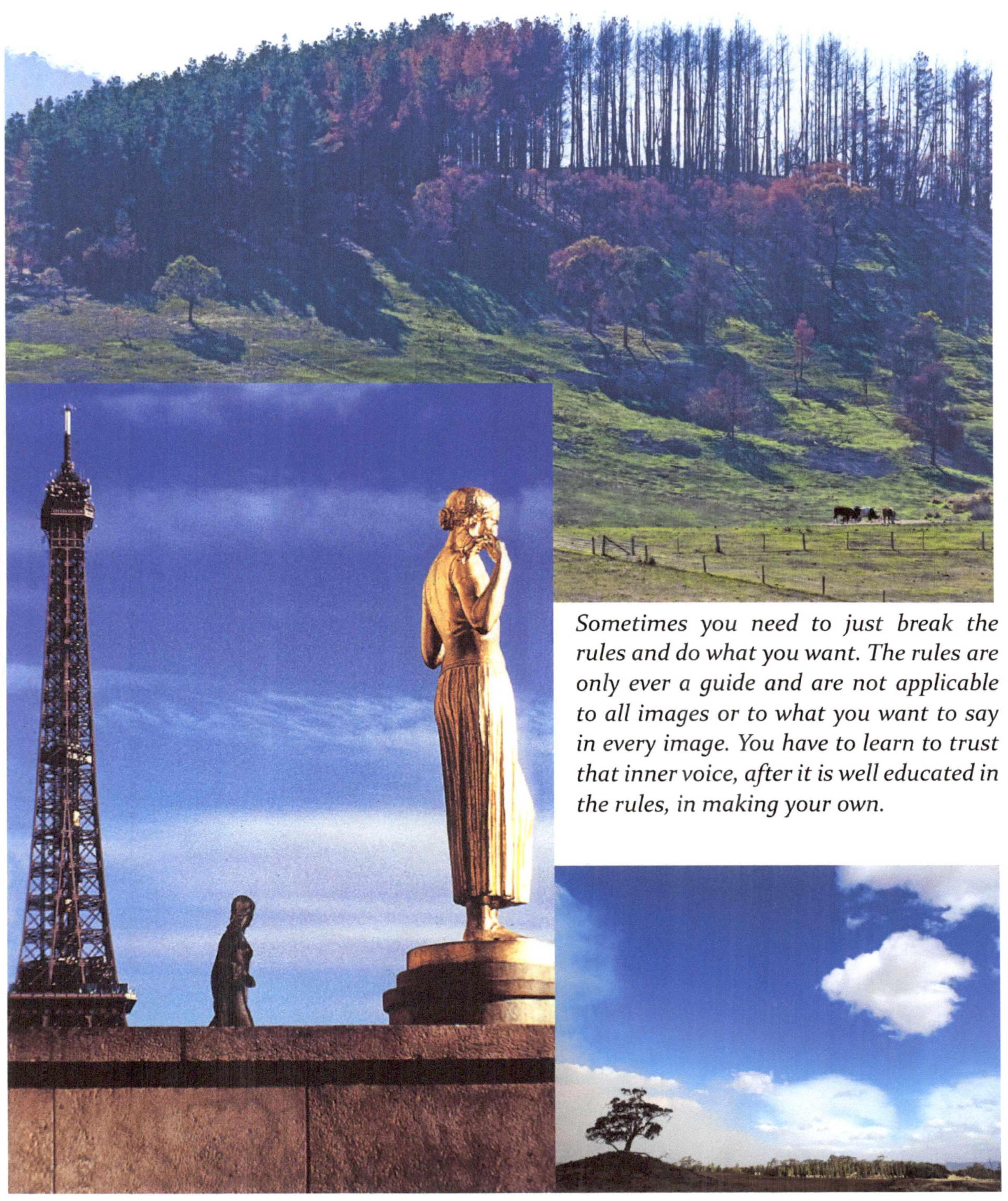

Sometimes you need to just break the rules and do what you want. The rules are only ever a guide and are not applicable to all images or to what you want to say in every image. You have to learn to trust that inner voice, after it is well educated in the rules, in making your own.

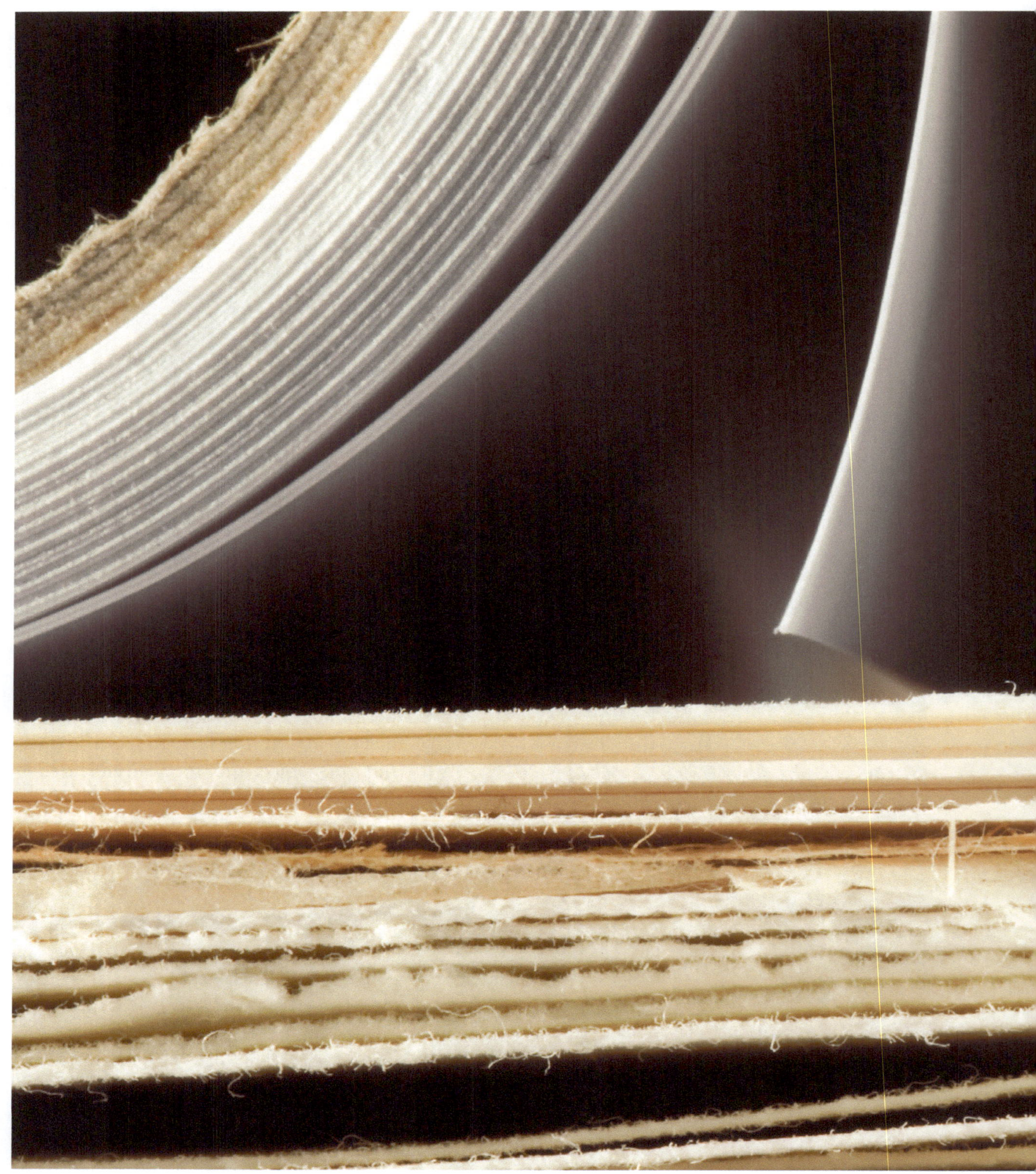

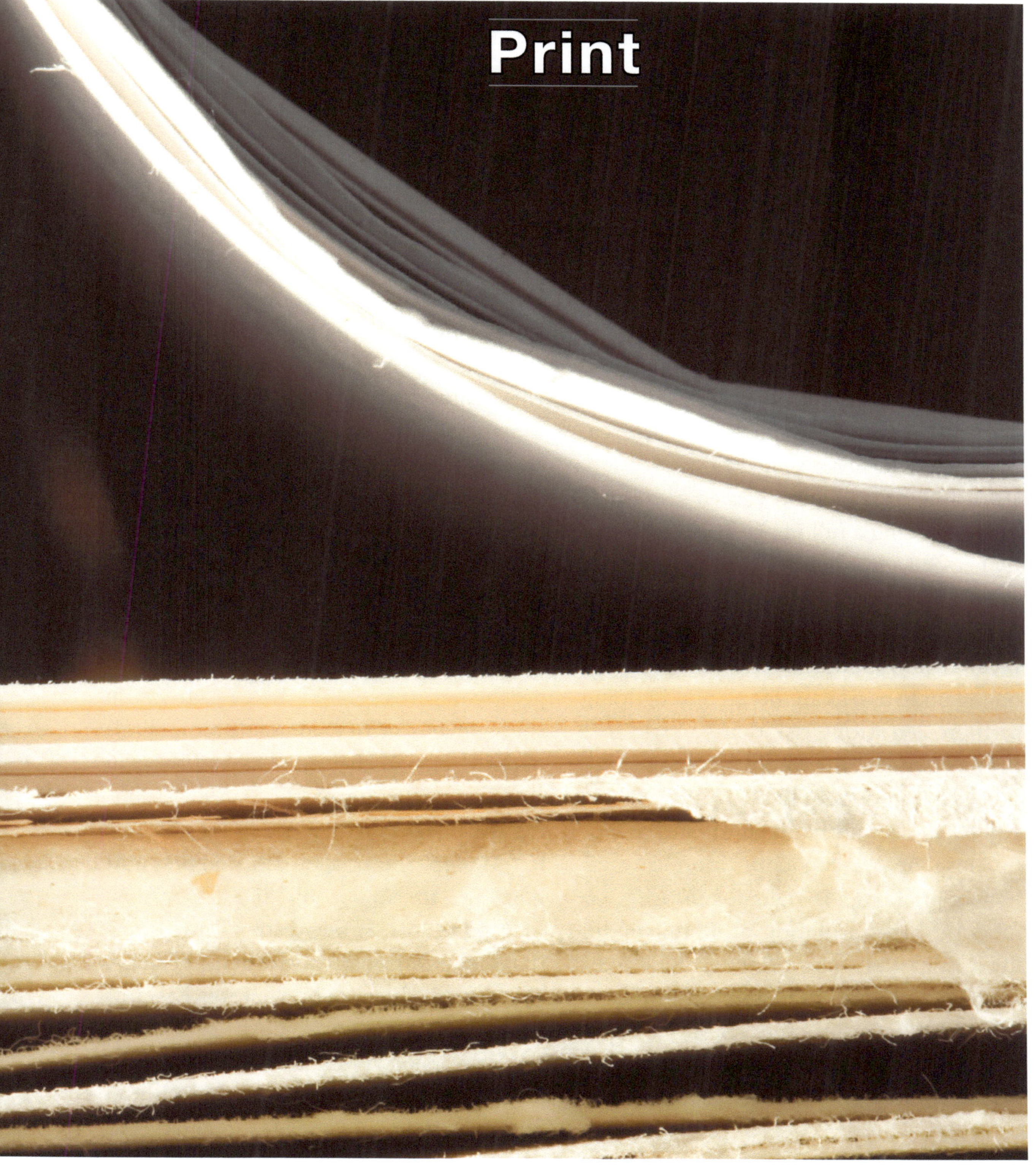
Print

21. Print More

Especially since the arrival of digital, many of us do not print images as much as we used to. Images look different in print than they do on the screen. You can gain a different perspective.

The key to the value of prints lies in the resolution. With any camera above around 2MP, if you view the full image on screen you will not be seeing the actual pixels, but rather a scaled down version. With higher resolution cameras you may only be seeing a full image at 16 to 20% of real size, or even less. It is not possible to judge anything like detail, sharpness or focus from such a reduced size image. This means that you must zoom in to 100% and out again to assess an image, and in doing so there is a strong risk that you will lose perspective over the whole image.

An appropriate sized print can show you all the detail that is in the image. For up close viewing a 300dpi (more correctly 300ppi) image is right for printing on modern, high resolution printers (360dpi for Epson) that have print resolutions of 2000dpi and above. The table below gives the minimum print sizes for various digital camera resolutions. If you print at least this size you will see all the detail in the picture.

5616x3744 21MP Canon 1Ds MIII 19" x 12.5"
4672x3104 14.6MP Pentax K20D 15.5" x 10"
4368x2912 12MP Canon 5D 14.5" x 9.5"
3888x2592 10MP Canon 400D 13" x 8.5"
3456x2304 8MP Canon 350D 11.5" x 7.5"
3008x2000 6MP Nikon D40 10" x 6.5"

Note that these are not the maximum sizes of prints you can produce with these cameras, since you can usually increase these camera images by at least 2x in each dimension with no real loss in image quality and at larger print sizes you can drop significantly below 300dpi and get a good result. Larger sized images are commonly viewed at much larger distances than the short ones used to get the 300dpi requirement.

In the old days in the darkroom I'd get my negatives, take a loupe to them on the light box or to a contact proof, eliminate the obvious flawed ones and then do small prints, for me usually 8x10's, to examine the images further, get an idea of how to 'develop' the image with dodging and burning, etc. Now with a digital workflow we tend to look at low-resolution versions that our viewing software, whether Bridge, Aperture, Lightroom or whatever has prepared. You can judge composition from the low-res version. But you can't judge composition in relation to sharpness from the down sampled version you see on screen,

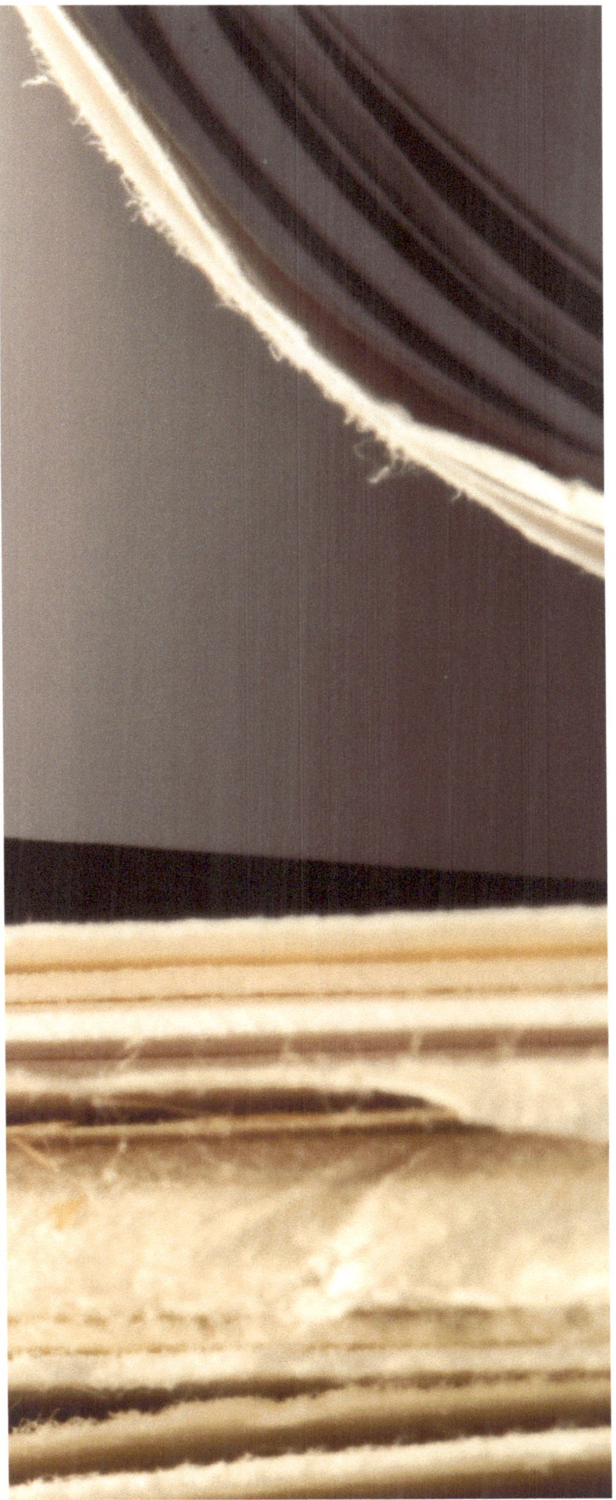

and so things like considering sharpness contrasts across the image (sharp areas vs. blurred areas), for example, aren't possible and you need to zoom in. But when you do this you lose the overall perspective.

So doing a suitably sized print allows you to judge and compare all aspects simultaneously and thus keep the whole image in mind at all times. I find that a far superior way to judge an image and plan what to do with it. This is a great aid for you in understanding your images and in advancing your art.

Activity

If you have a reasonably high-resolution camera you have probably not been printing your images large enough. So take an image that can show great detail and print it at both your normal print size and at the size recommended in the above table. Compare them and see how much you have been missing in your images.

Artists who work on paper develop a love affair with papers, and it benefits a photographer to do exactly the same. Go visit art supply stores and examine the papers, not just digital or photo papers, since a digital coating can be readily applied to most papers.

22. Print In More Sizes

It is easy to become stuck on one or two sizes of print. Break out of the rut and try something different. Photographs and art work can look very different depending on the size.

There is no right size to print every image at. We tend to fall into habits with regard to everything, including our printing. Sure, we can work out what size print a given camera can produce at 300dpi. But this is really only the starting point. A print resolution of 300dpi (or 360dpi for Epson) works well when you are up close and personal to the print. But with larger prints we don't hold them in our hands up close, we look at them hanging on the wall, typically, and also from some distance so we can take in the whole image in one go. You can lower the resolution you print at and thus print the image larger. Think of this as the packing density, how close the camera pixels are packed together on the page.

The other thing that affects what resolution you need to print at is the type of paper. High gloss, photo papers demand the highest resolution to produce a print that will look great up close. Matt papers can sometimes take a lower resolution and still look fantastic. Non-digital art papers, especially the heavily textured watercolour papers, can look great at even lower resolutions. For example, I have printed an image at as low as 25dpi (image resolution, not printer dot resolution) on a non-digital watercolour paper and the result has looked great. I have even used very low actual printer resolutions, such as 300dpi. This has partly been a result of the texture of the paper making the lower resolution image look more detailed and also because when you print on non-digital papers, the ink bleeds into the paper, spreading the dots out till they blend together, creating the illusion of a higher resolution than actually used. Particularly suitable to this approach are the non-digital watercolour textured papers and the Japanese, Korean and Nepalese handmade papers, often called Washi, and especially those with inclusions, such as bark or flowers.

Some images work well when small and intimate. Many don't. My observation is that probably a majority of people print their images smaller than is ideal for the image. This is perfectly natural because of issues of having suitable equipment and the cost of the gear and the consumables as you go up in size, but is still something to be worked on. You could argue that images have a natural size at which they work best that is determined by a combination of factors. The amount of detail in the piece and how important it is plays a part. As does the style of the work: is it intimate or bold and brassy? The desired impact on the viewer and what it is you are trying to say play a major part. When discussions of what size should work be printed at comes up, I am always reminded of a time soon after returning from a trip to Poland where a lot of shooting at Auschwitz had been done. I had been printing my images fairly large, approximately 24" x 36". There was an exhibition at a local photography gallery by a photographer who had also shot Auschwitz. His work was printed very small, in fact no larger than 8" x 10" and mostly noticeably smaller. With such small work the automatic response was to move in close. You were then confronted with the subject matter that had not been obvious from a distance. This drawing you in worked well with these very detailed, medium and large format images. My approach had been to play with the graphic elements, the shapes and textures, and I found this worked better for me large. Who was right? Frankly I don't know and I suspect we both were because although our subject was the same, our photography was very different. I preferred my approach though I could see what the other photographer had done.

So how do you change your printing size or even judge what size works best? There are several approaches. The easiest is to make sure you can move well back from your computer screen so you can vary the viewing distance. Fill the screen with the image and then vary your viewing distance from close to far away and see how the image responds. Zoom right into the image and judge how dependent it is for success on the detail it contains. For those who can, a data projector is a wonderful tool. It lets you explore the really large sizes before you have to print. Just remember the projected image will be much lower resolution than your print will be. Think about the psychology of your image and how you want to use it. Should the viewer have an intimate and thus close engagement with the image or will a huge, in your face sort of impact work better? You will generally find the same size will work well for most, if not all, images within a body of work. This certainly makes for a more cohesive look in an exhibition, though some variety can also work in your favour when it comes to selling work, since not everyone has the same size spaces to hang work in at home or the office. It depends on what suits the work.

Overcoming equipment and cost issues can be a creative exercise in itself. What about tiling your prints together to make a larger one, taping them together

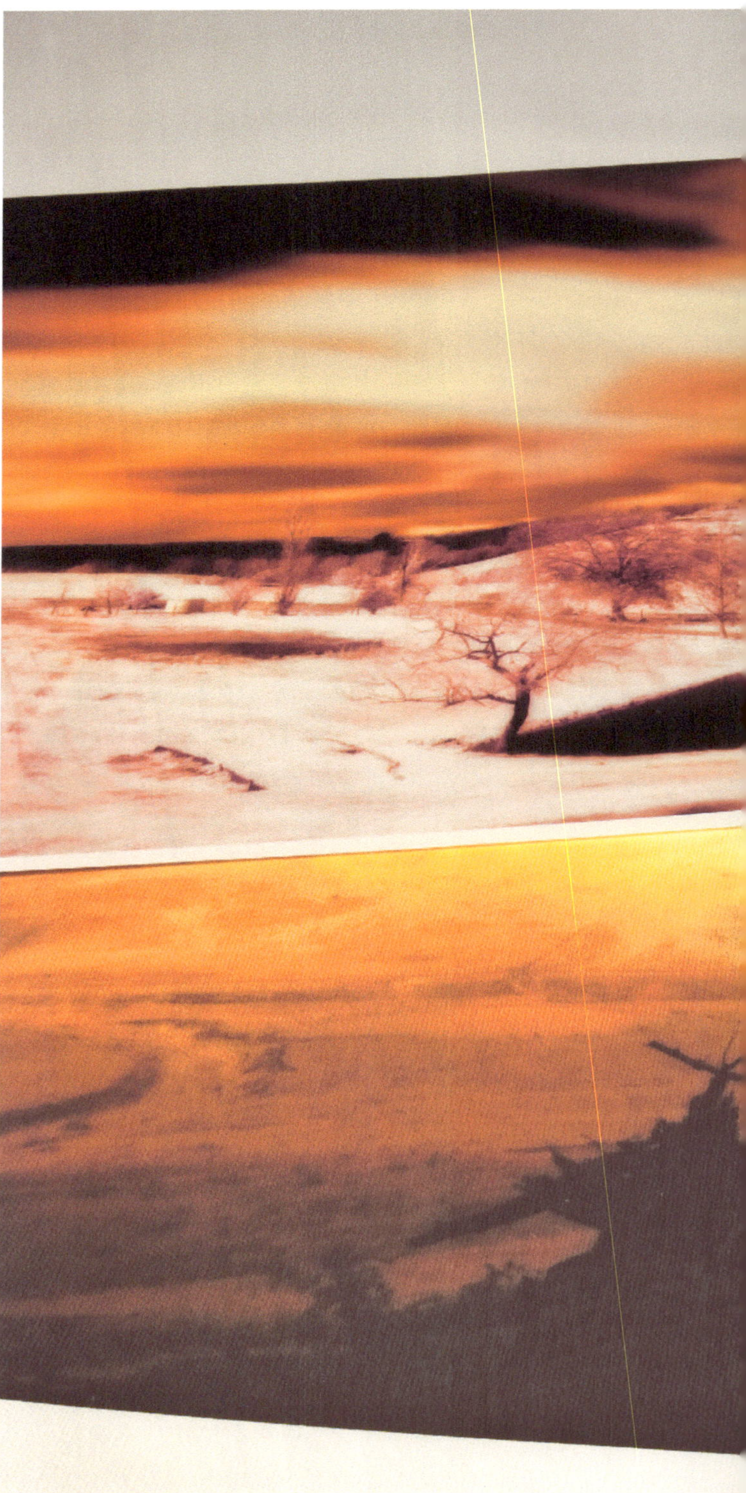

even or mounting them as separate pieces that hung together form a whole? Look at the work by the Starn brothers to see how effecting taping images together can be. Do a trade with a friend who has a larger printer so you do something for them that they need in exchange for some larger prints. If you want to, there are ways around most limitations.

Activity

Explore your available print options. An A4 or Letter printer cannot print any wider than the carriage, but most can print longer to print panoramas. This is the same with the larger A3 and A3+ (13" x 19") printers. Many people can manage larger printers, but many can't. Look into your options. Do you know someone with a larger printer who you could pay material costs to? Is there a nearby college with a larger printer than you can come to an arrangement with? Or is there a local print shop or sign store that can print your work at reasonable cost?

Experiment with printing sections of your images on the largest paper or film you can and then tape them together to see if you like this approach. It does take some getting used to and you can be as rough and ready as you like, since the hand done look can be very effective.

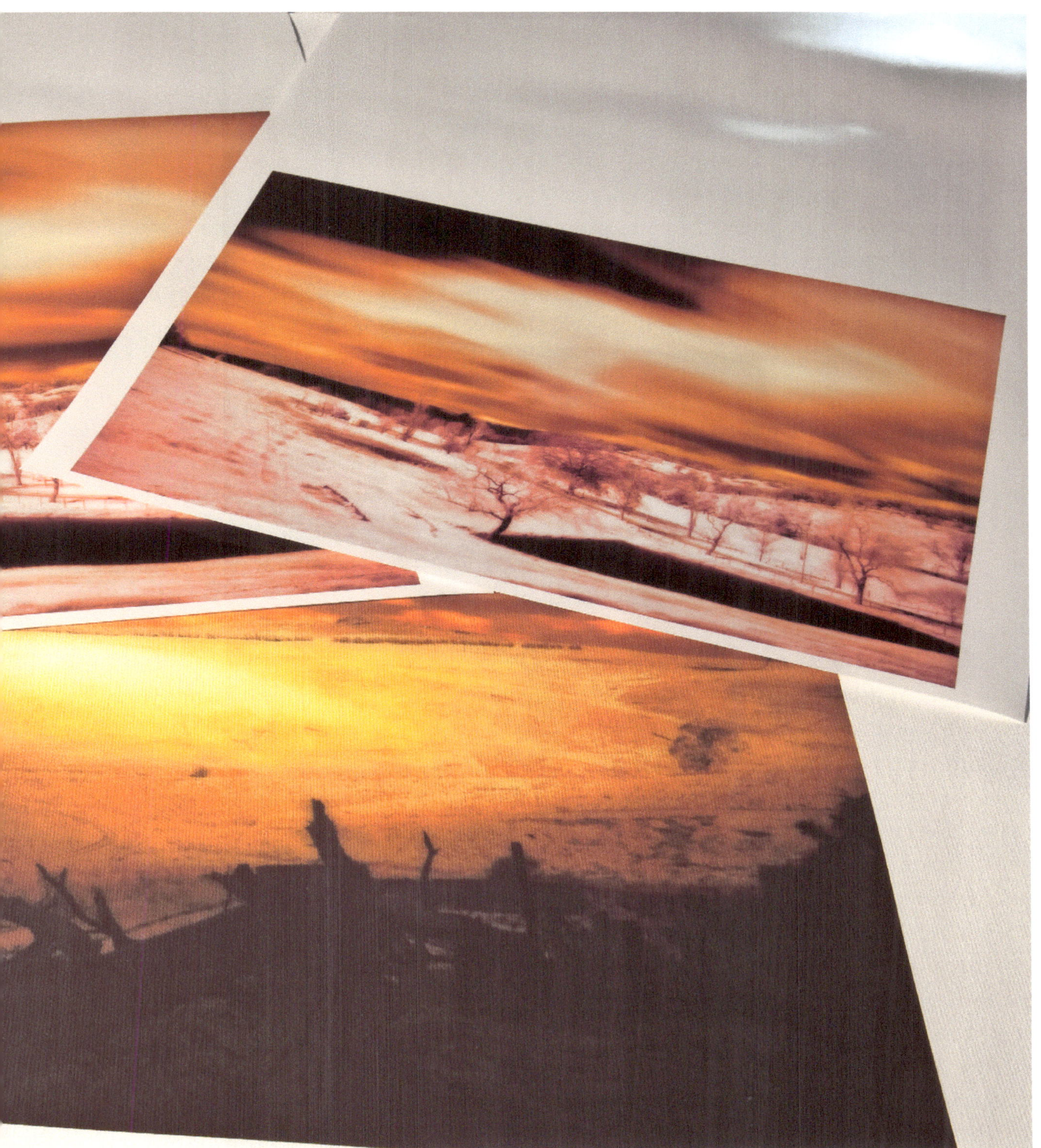

23. Vary Your Paper

It doesn't always work to print on gloss paper. Try matt, semi-gloss or rough. Sure, gloss can bring out the highest sharpness and colour saturation, but is this always the best thing for all images? Variety is the spice of life.

Variety is one of the huge benefits of the digital shift. You can still print on photographic paper, if you want, by having the work printed on the Fuji Frontier, Durst Lambda or similar. However, you also have access to the full range of artist papers as well as the digital papers. In fact, depending on your printer, you are not just limited to papers of the conventional type but can use aluminium sheet, plastic or all sorts of thing if it is prepared properly with a precoat like InkAid or Golden's Digital Grounds to accept ink. All that you need is a receptive layer that will allow the ink to 'take' to the surface. Most papers are absorbent and so the ink can soak in. Nonporous surfaces, like metals, will not allow the ink to soak in and so it has nothing to adhere to, as ink does not have the ingredients to allow it to adhere to a hostile surface. The coating products overcome this by covering the surface with a layer that can accept the ink and hold it.

I said in the above paragraph 'depending on your printer', and this is true. The printer that you have, and its ink technology, can limit your choice. Many printers, for example, cannot accept very thick paper. Also printers that use dye inks, rather than pigment, can make some experimenting difficult. However, most printers can accommodate far more experimentation than most users ask of them.

Activity

Check the limitations of your actual printer with regard to paperweight and thickness.

Start with the manufacturer's papers and see just how the paper changes the way an image looks. Perhaps pick a few images of yours that are quite different and try these so that you can compare.

Try some non-digital papers, particularly art papers, for a different look. With non-digital papers your colors and contrast are likely to be more subdued, unless you coat them, but some images respond well to this.

Try some alternate digital papers to see if you prefer the results.

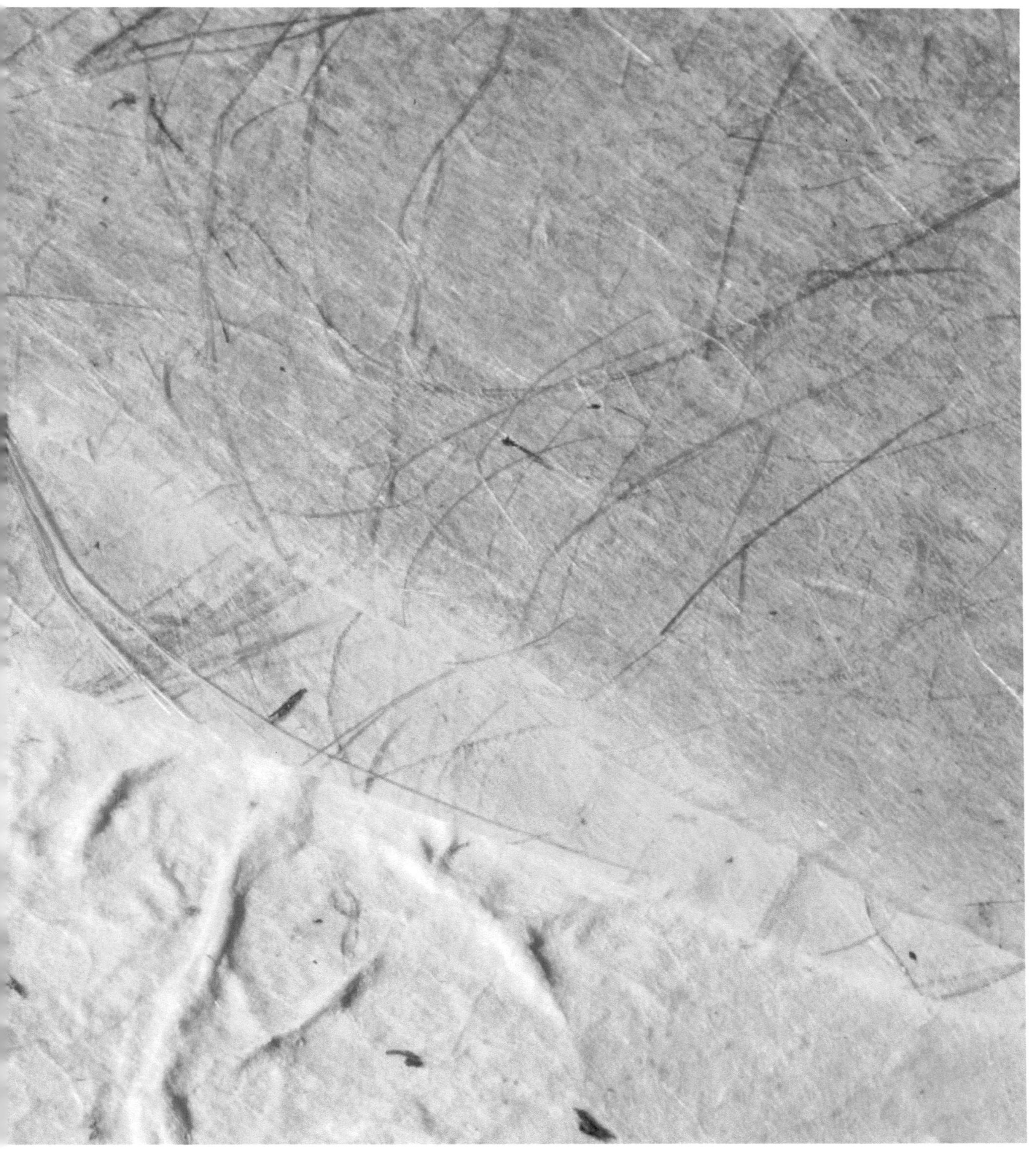

24. See Your Prints

I am a big believer in spending time with my images so I can form a proper opinion of them. So get your latest images up on the wall and live with them for some time.

Getting your images on paper and up where you can see them gives you a chance to see if you become bored with your image too quickly, whether a glaring fault becomes obvious once the initial enthusiasm passes or whether you have an award winner on your hands. You can't do this by looking at your images for 10 minutes and then putting them away. Remember, someone who buys your image will have it on the wall for years. Also looking at your images only on a computer screen is a very poor substitute for a print, since the screen cannot show you the whole image and most of the detail that the image contains. A screen is just not high resolution enough.

Use any technique that suits you (and your household) to display the prints. Use magnets and display them on the fridge. Tape them to the bathroom mirror. Use bulldog clips to attach them to another framed work hanging on the wall. If you have a dedicated office or studio space, or a very image friendly spouse, you can use a metal whiteboard or even mount a sheet of steel to the wall (it has to be steel or magnets will not hold on it) and use this as a quick mount gallery. If you go the sheet sheet route, it need only be thick enough for stability when mounted and can have paint put over it to blend with the decor as the magnets will still hold on it. If you only want to hold the images by the top edge you only need a strip of steel rather than a whole sheet. Whatever it takes.

Activity

Find various places in your house where you can display prints.

Look for a variety of experience, from the location where you will look in passing to somewhere where you can contemplate the image for some time, as some images work best in high traffic areas and others require a more quiet setting.

Prints have so much more resolution than screen images, so their is really no substitute for nice, large prints. An A3+ sized printer is a huge advantage for a photographer to have. Not only are the ink cartridges generally larger and so the running cost may be lower, but you get to do the odd larger print yourself. I use a cheap semi-gloss paper for these 'proof on concept' prints, which can then go on file and then lovely paper for those that warrant a final print.

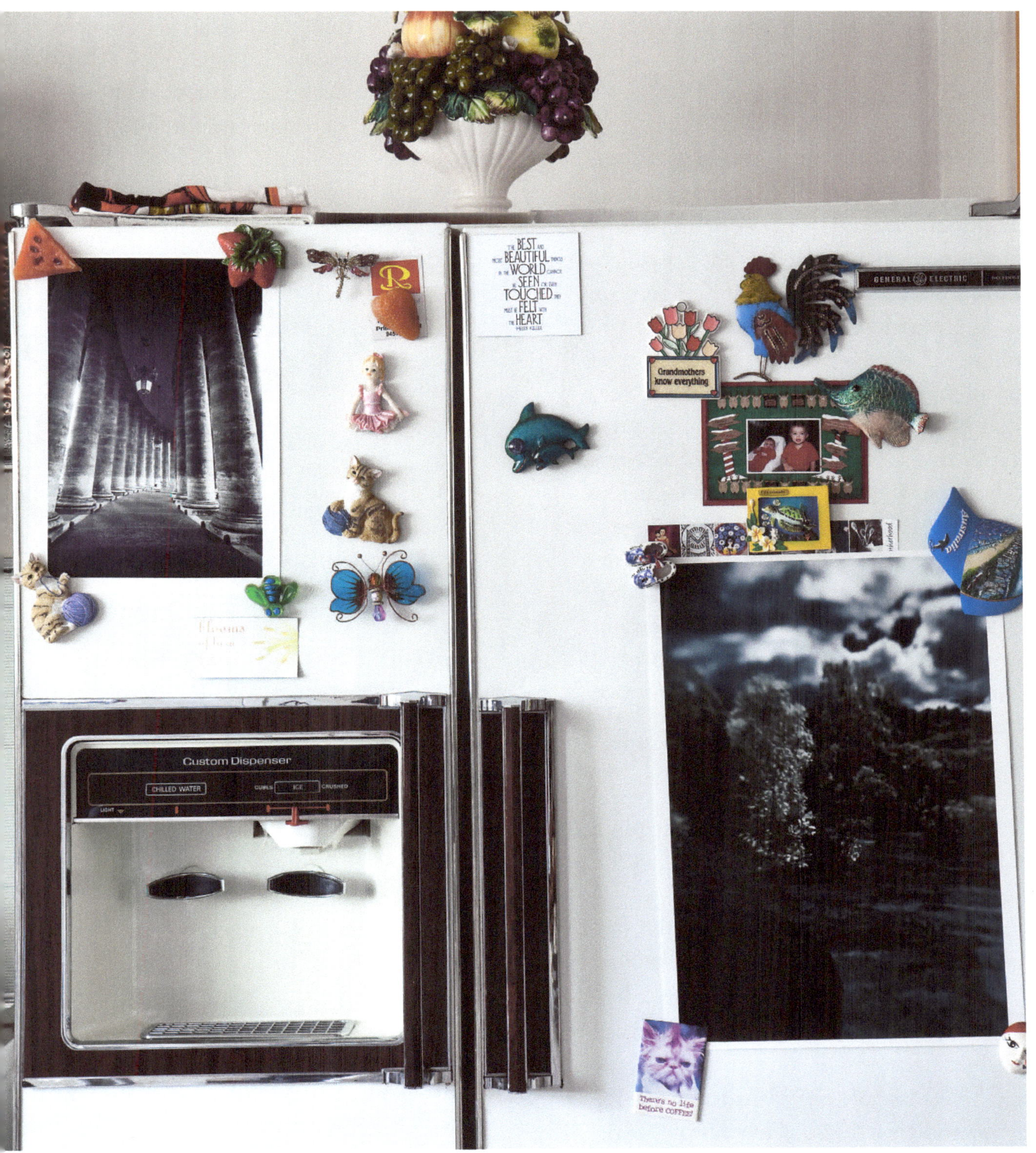
GENERAL ELECTRIC
Grandmothers know everything
Custom Dispenser
CHILLED WATER
ICE
CRUSHED
There's no life before COFFEE!

25. Finish

Finish what you start. Take the images that you capture to a conclusion and save them away. If you never finish anything you will never have good work to show, work to submit to that competition you discover just before deadline and you will never experience the satisfaction of completion. Aside from that, it is a very good habit to get into. In the modern day of multiple sources of distraction, it seems to be a growing issue of people failing to complete what they start. I know I have been prone to this, partly because I am interested in so many things and partly because the completion process is often not very exciting. For our own sake we need to overcome the distractions and our own weaknesses and learn to complete.

Activity

Make it a point of personal discipline to finish a piece before moving on to the next.

Build a diary of your completed images.

File your finished prints away carefully so they will be well preserved and accessible.

Make use of your historical work for review and growth. Look at your old work, see where you can do better, in fact even revisit and rework old images if they cry out for it.

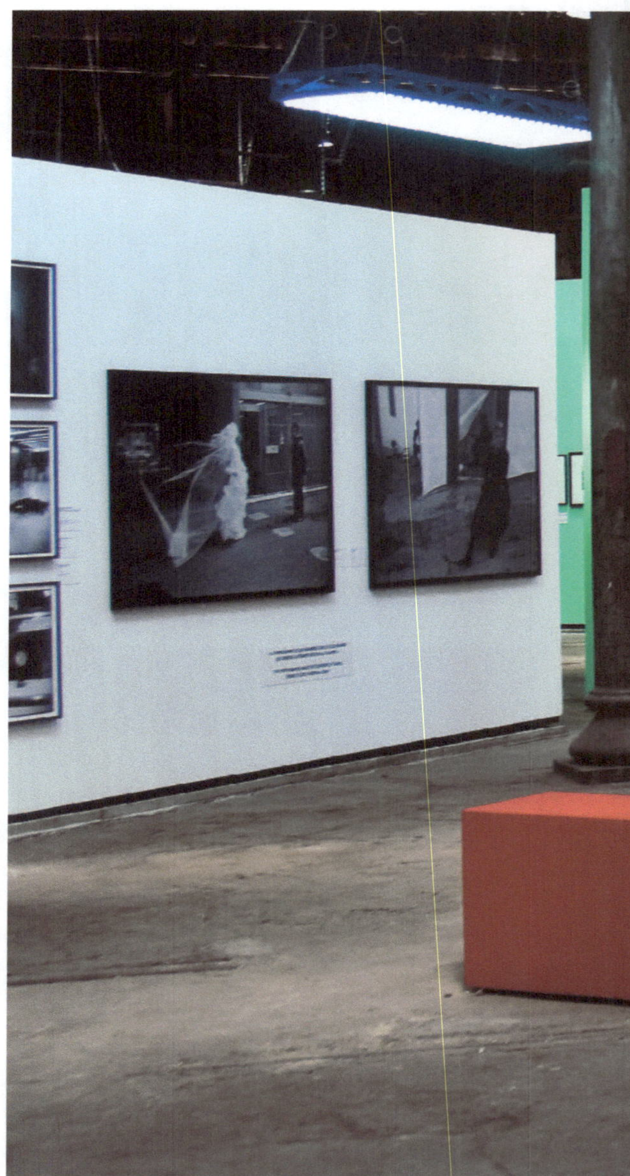

Make it a point to finish each image as if you were going to put it in an exhibition. This discipline will have you to approach your images in a more professional and serious manner and is actually more time efficient than putting it off. When you are in the flow of working with an image you will get a better result in less time if you just complete it.

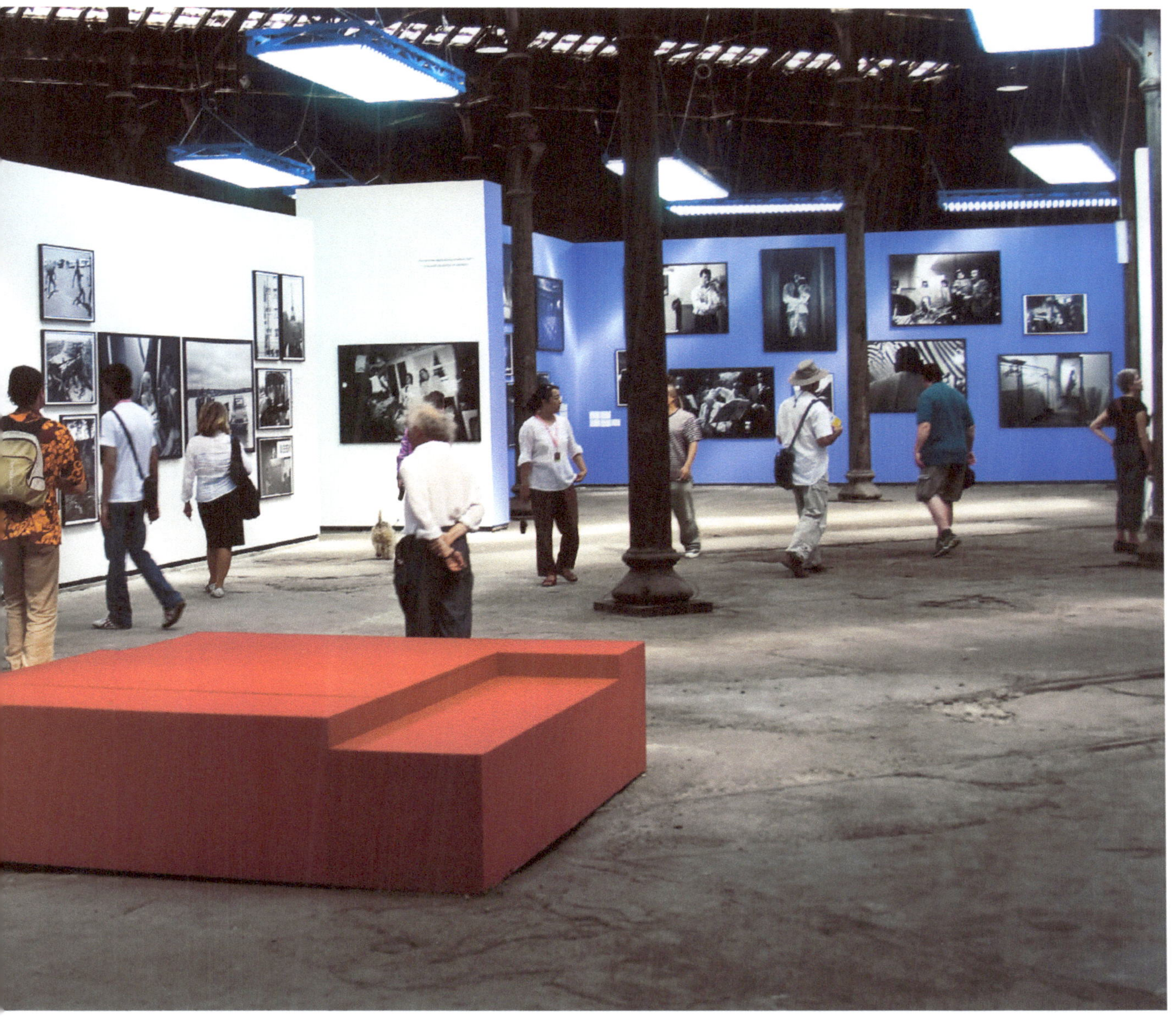

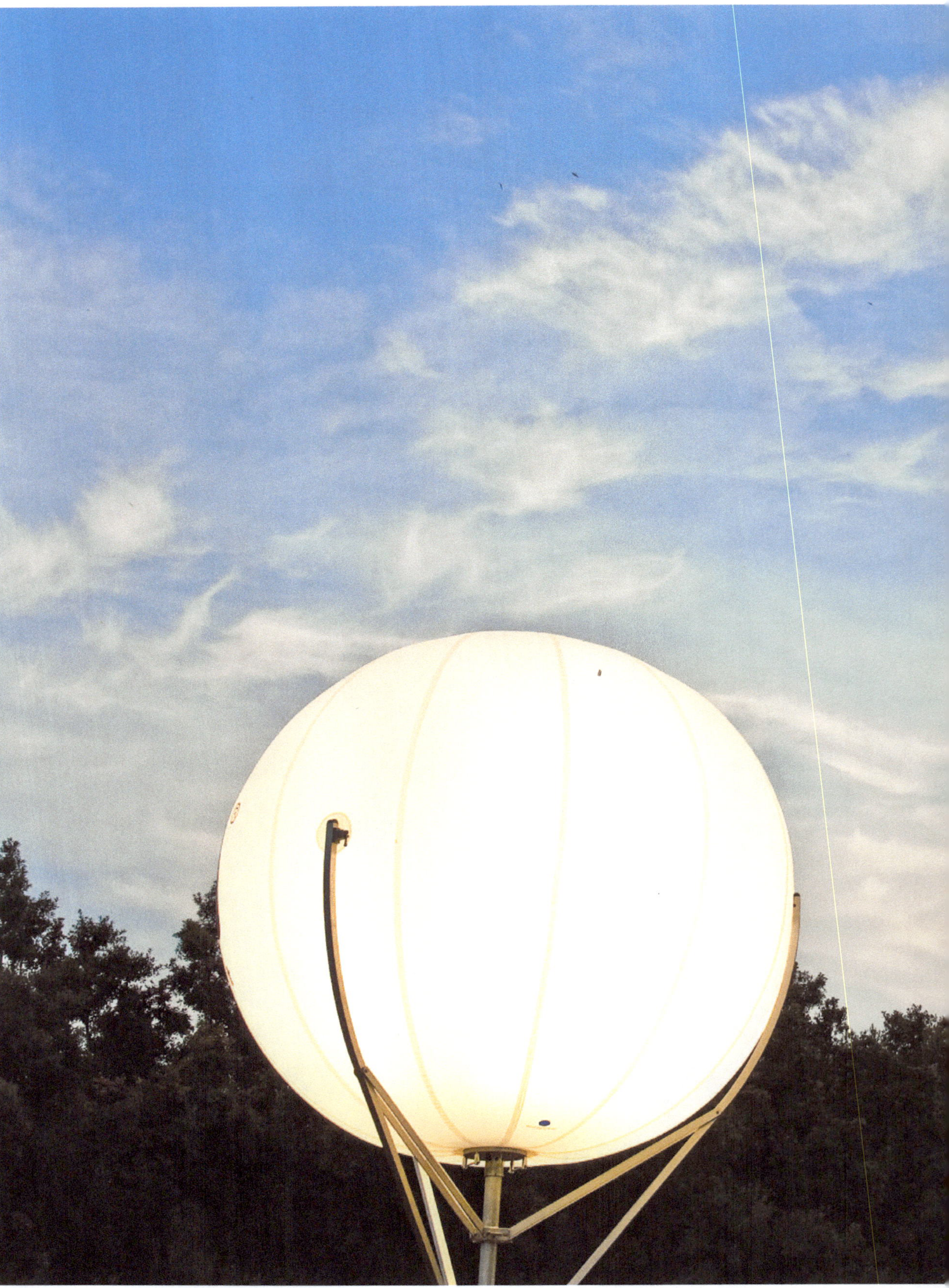

Learn

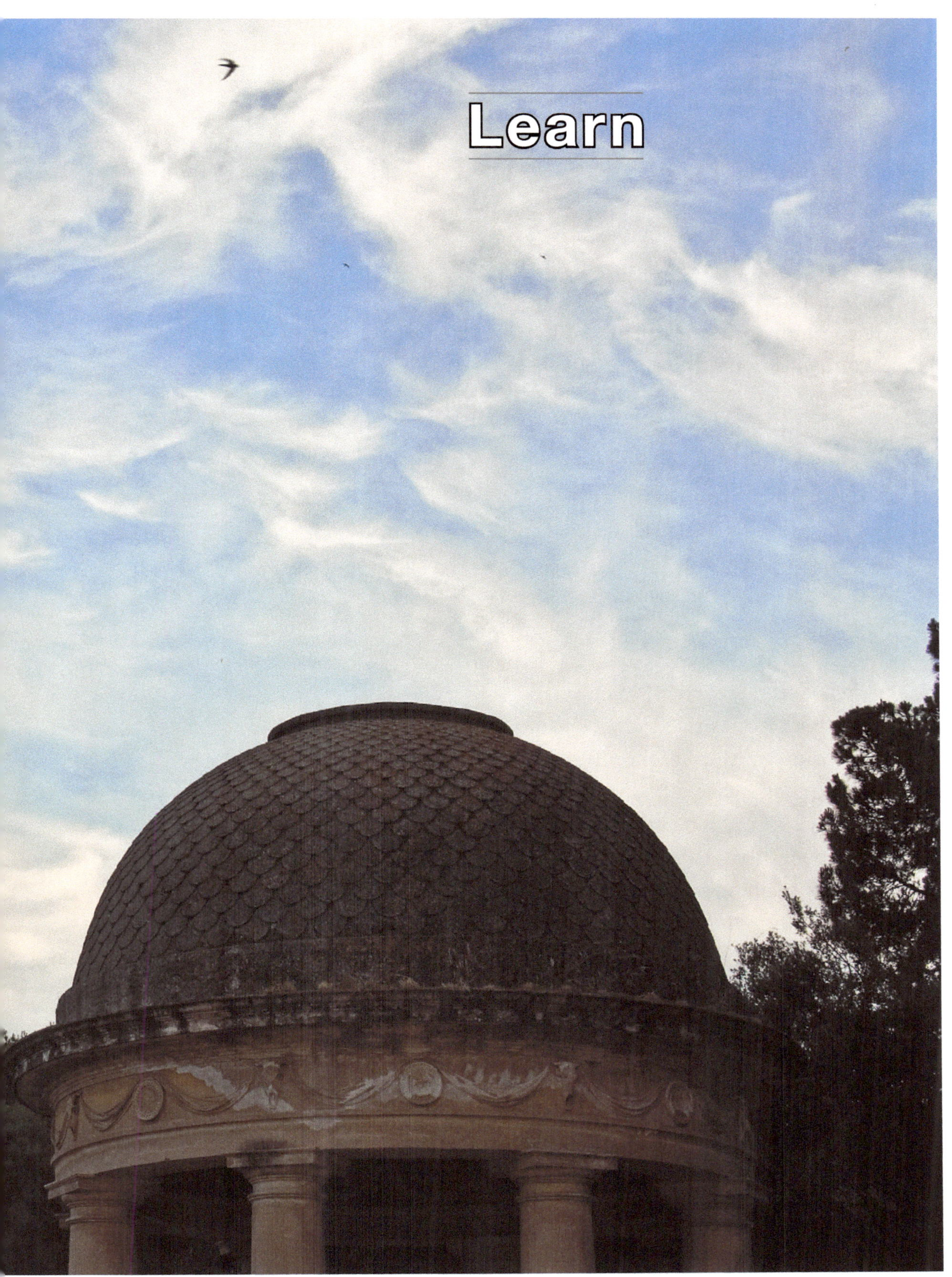

26. Learn the Lingo

Photography is a dialogue between yourself and the viewer. Like all dialogues, it requires a common language. In the visual arts the common language includes the rules of composition, colour theory, aesthetics and symbols. Yes, at one level all art and photography is about symbols. Some are culturally based, others seem to be universal. A symbol is a shorthand way to bring up, in the viewer's mind, all that they know and associate with it. So if you include a cross in an image it brings up whatever the viewer knows about Christianity and the Church. Now you can't control exactly what comes to mind in the viewer. Someone with a positive view of Christianity will bring up one set of concepts, whilst someone who had a bad time associated with Christianity may bring up another. But the benefit is that you will, with one simple image element, bring up a whole series of ideas and emotions.

Like all languages, a rich vocabulary allows for a richer conversation. So learn all you can about symbols. There are great books on symbols, read them. Look at symbolic art and read books on it. There are great art documentaries available on DVD that will walk you through great paintings and even photography and explain what is going on. Don't forget DVDs over books: they can be great for us visual thinkers. Just because you are a photographer, rather than a painter, does not mean that you cannot apply the same lessons and method.

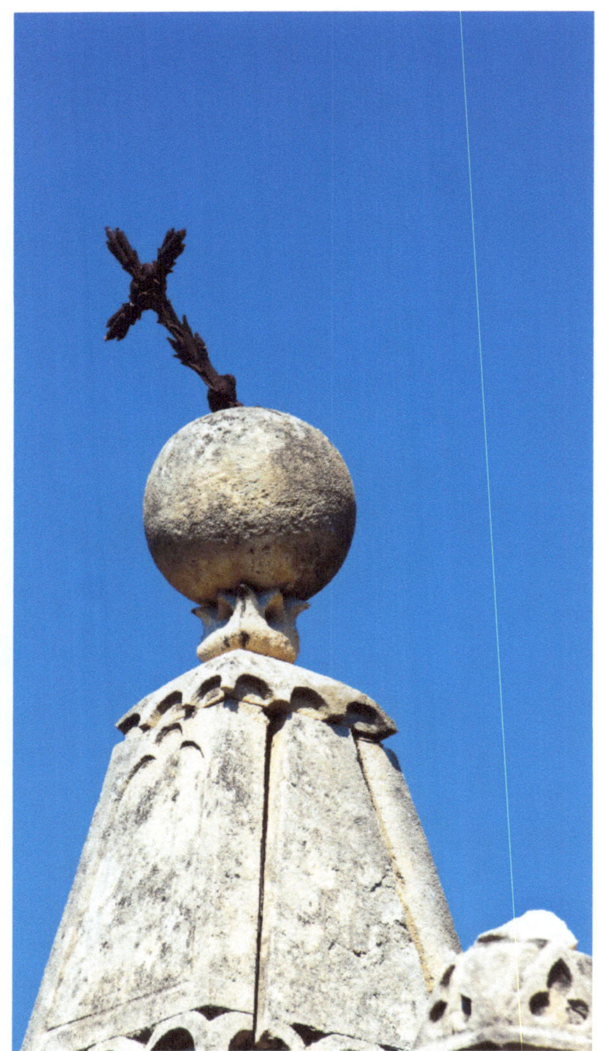

Activity

Read, read, and read. Get yourself some books on symbols and read them.

Buy the better ones and keep them for reference.

Set yourself assignments to explore symbols in your photography.

Set out to construct an image with specific symbolic content. Make a list of the symbols and then go out and shoot appropriate material to combine or construct a set to photograph that contains the symbols you want. You may or may not like this way of doing photography, but it will teach you to better consider the content of your images.

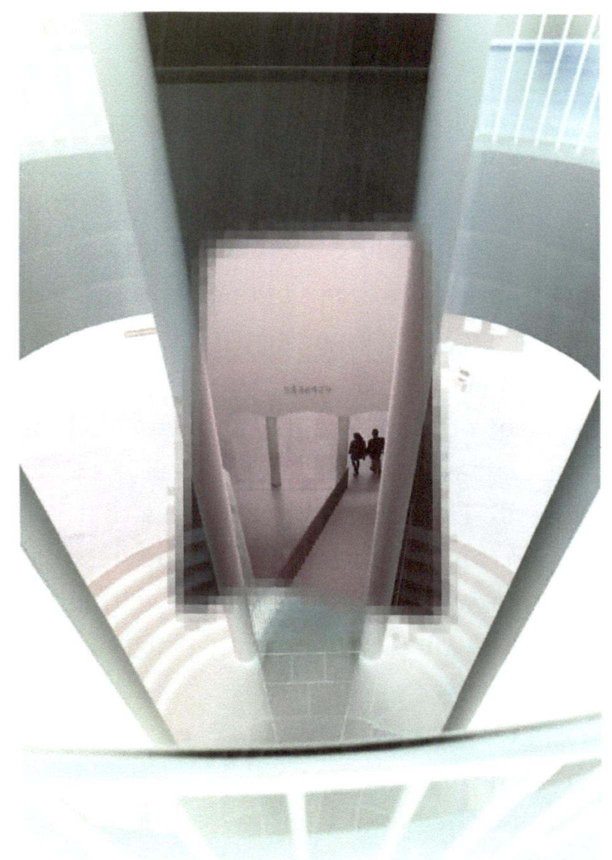

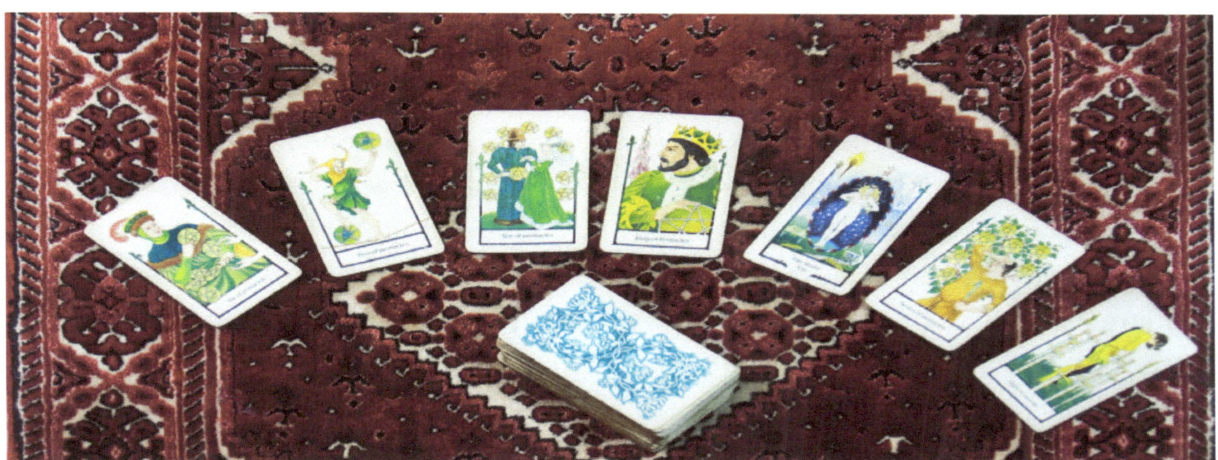

Tarot is another system, like photography and visual arts in general, where symbolism is the vocabulary you have to work with. There are books that will explain the symbols used by the artists who create the cards, offering insight into how it all comes togather.

27. Look At Photography

Now there is a valid argument for not allowing yourself to be unduly influenced by others. However, this needs to be balanced with the huge benefits that can flow from making yourself familiar with the work of other photographers and making a critical assessment of what you can learn from it. There are so many ways that you can do this: on the Internet, through books and magazines, camera clubs, visiting exhibitions and folio viewing programs, to name a few.

One thing I cannot over emphasize is the value in looking at real, high-resolution prints rather than the low-resolution versions placed on websites. When we were judging entrants for the International Digital Art Award, which I was involved with for many years, we had a number of surprises between judging the low-resolution emailed entries and the high-resolution prints. Some works looked much better in print form and had been ranked lower than we would have from seeing the prints or the high-resolution files. In other cases the works actually looked much better at low resolution and we were disappointed looking at the final prints. Since we are still at the point where the major way of viewing and displaying photography is the physical print, this is the best way to judge and learn from photographs.

To a lesser extent, the previous comments about the difference between Internet resolution images and print images also applies to reproductions in books and magazines. If you have ever had the opportunity to compare a real print to the same image in a magazine you will know what I mean.

What all the above means is that you should take every opportunity to see real prints, whether digital or analogue prints. There are a multitude of places you can do this, including museums.

Activity

Determine the galleries in your area that exhibit photography, go visit and get on their mailing list for invites to openings. Keep an eye out for new ones.

Go to the openings. The advantage of openings over just going to the gallery at another time is that there are bound to be other photographers there that you can easily start a conversation with. 'What do you think of the work' is often a good icebreaker.

Look At Art

Other forms of art are very valid as a source of inspiration, education and ideas.

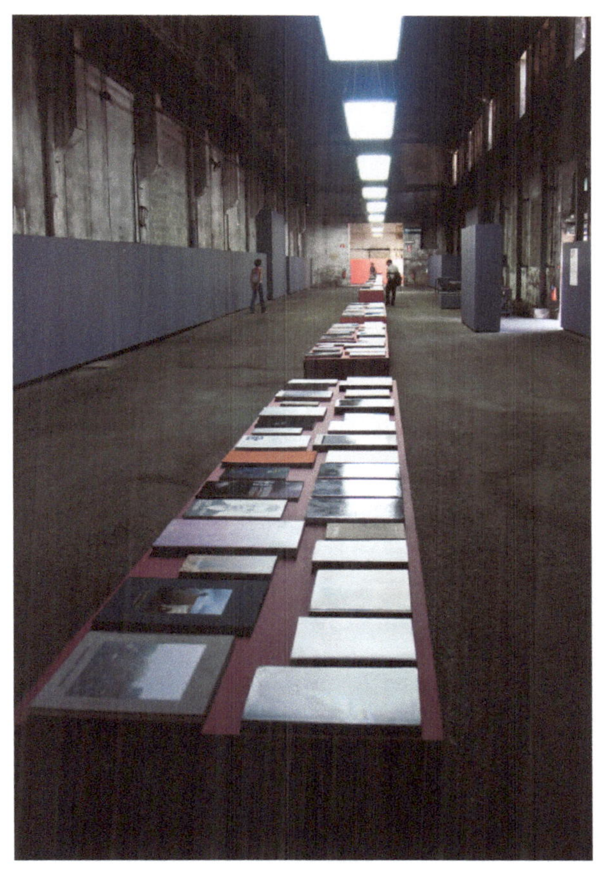

All forms of visual art effectively use the same principles of colour theory, composition, symbolism and use of design principles as photography. Plus of course the themes and subjects are universal, just the medium differs.

All the visual arts have a common language. That language uses the principles of design, composition and colour theory as the grammar or structure of the language and symbolism as the vocabulary. Since their use are often more explicit in the other visual arts than they are in much photography, it can sometimes be easier to learn this language and way of thinking by looking at other art than photography. Also, more so than photography, there is a rich body of writing that analyses and deconstructs paintings, drawings, etc.

Activity

Look into learning about art theory and art history. Take courses, watch videos and read books. Many adult education centres and community colleges run introductory courses that can get you started.

Start to think about and actively construct your photography using what you are learning about art. As you learn a concept try to create a photographic work that demonstrates what you have been learning.

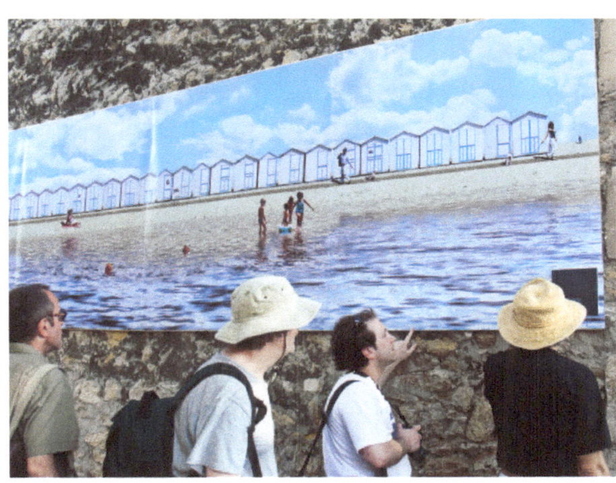

28. Read the Manuals

Your camera(s), lenses, flash units and accessories all come with manuals of various sizes. Read them. As I like to say to my wife, they hide useful information in books, and this also applies to manuals. I make it a habit to read each manual fully when I buy new equipment and I am always amazed at the information I can get from them, the hidden features I didn't know about, etc. If you need motivation to help with this, get yourself a nice glass of scotch, cup of tea or coffee or box of chocolates, put your feet up and read the manual.

If you are following the previous item about keeping a creative journal, you can summarize key points from the manual in there, such as features you want to try or key settings you want to remember. I know some people will find this advice hard and a violation of childhood learning, but I like to write in, highlight and annotate manuals and books. Most of the books in the libraries of the great thinkers, like Newton and Einstein were heavily annotated in the margins, indeed that is partly what margins are for, so I figure if it was good enough for Newton it is good enough for me. I call this active reading and have found over years of teaching that it makes the reading process much more effective for many people. This is especially effective for those of you who may suffer from dyslexia, as my wife and daughter do.

Activity

Make it a matter of personal discipline to read all the manuals for your photographic and computer gear, as well as the software.

Make sure that as you discover new aspects of a piece of equipment that you go and actually try them. Make notes if appropriate.

Backs and bottoms of equipment can be great places to tape a cheat sheet. So the head of your accessory flash gun, underneath of your handheld light meter (they still have a place in a digital world) and even the base plate of the camera is a great place for a reminder note of modes, etc.

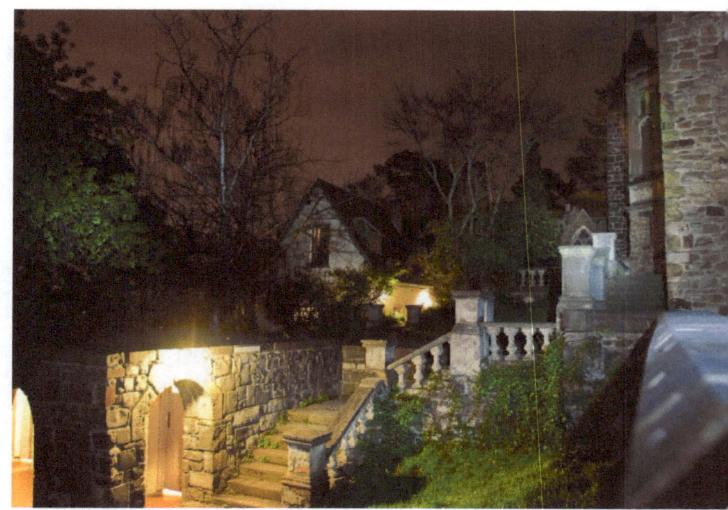

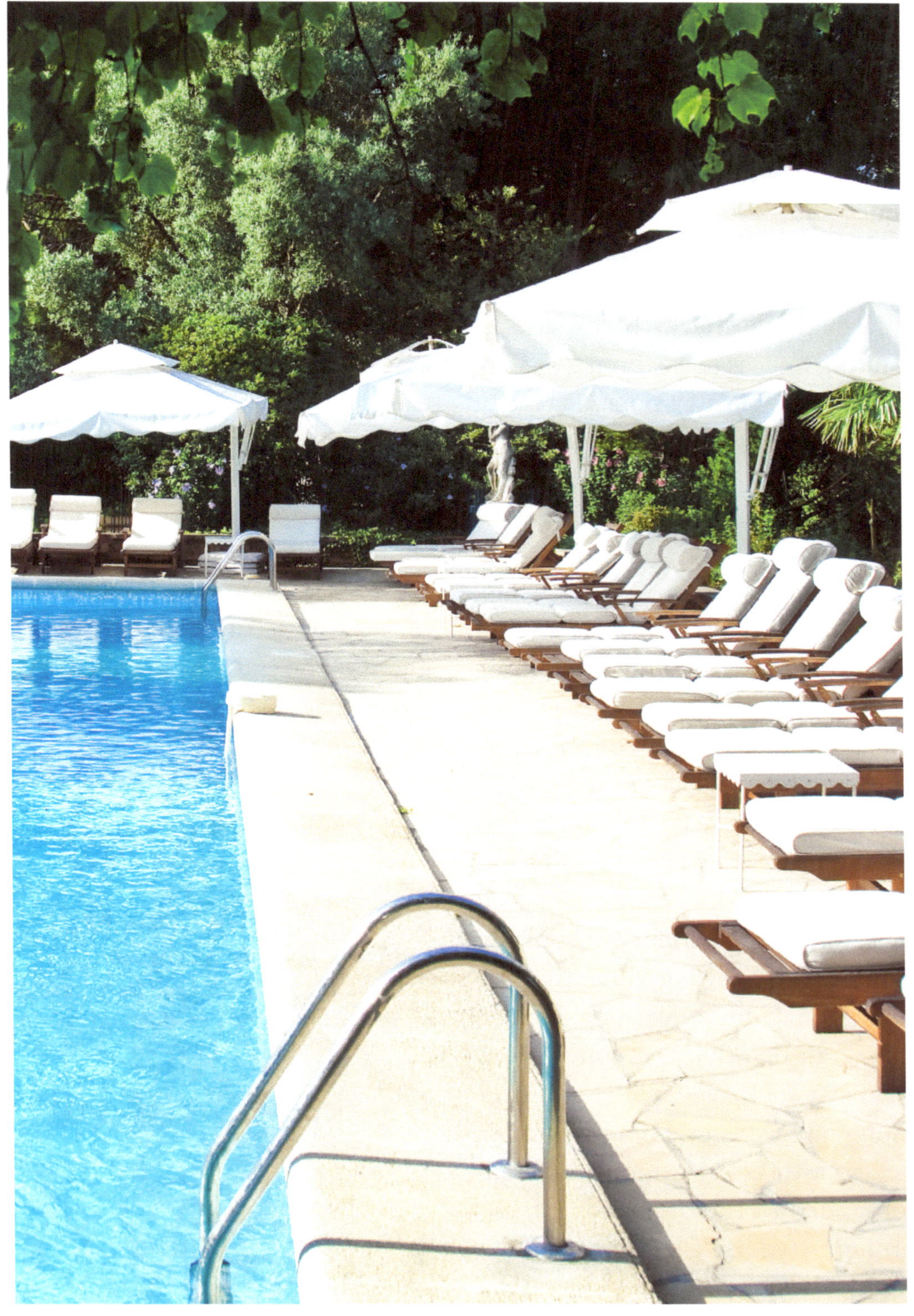

29. Experiment Widely

Try all those weird and wonderful techniques you have read about, seen or thought up for yourself. You may never use them again, but you never know, you just might. Even if you don't, the experience and resulting images may stimulate you in another direction. So next time you read or see or hear of some weird technique, go try it immediately.

Before you can get the most out of your learning you need to follow the effective learning steps: learn about, think and contextualise, discuss, practice and analyse. After we learn about something new, say a technique or approach, we need to think about it in our own context so we can determine how we can use the knowledge. We then often need to discuss this to assist the process and then it is essential to put it into action. Lastly you need to look at your own experience in applying the knowledge. Following this sequence gives you the maximum learning and the best chance to determine if you wish to integrate what you have learned into your own photography or not. Some aspects of this process are easier in group learning situations, such as the discussion. If you are learning by yourself it helps to find a community, perhaps online, where you can perform this discussion.

Activity

Keep a creative journal. This can be a physical diary, an electronic one or even an online one, using a blogging tool like Wordpress. Be sure to add material to it constantly.

This journal becomes your way to document what you learn, the experiments you try and analyze the results that you obtain. It becomes effectively a dialogue with yourself.

At set intervals, say once a month, review your journal to see if you have followed up on the things you have put in it. If not, schedule some time to do so as soon as practical.

The image opposite top came out of a thought of could I photograph a flower that was lit from inside. A whole in cardboard let me pump the light in.
Bottom right is an experimental shot with the Soft Focus optic from Lensbaby.
Below is the Gigapan Epic that I use for panorama photography. I modified it to fit my dSLR.

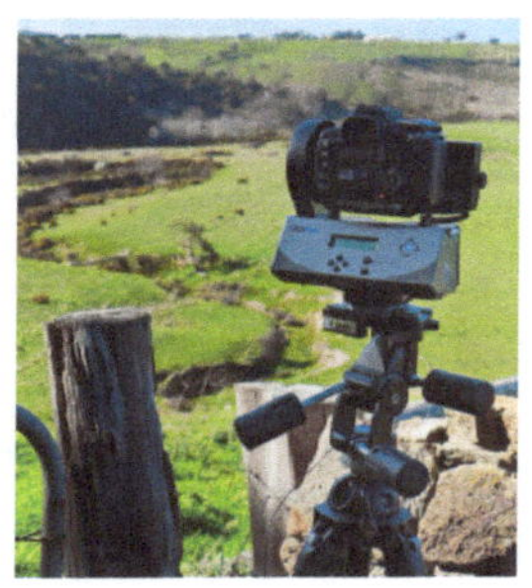

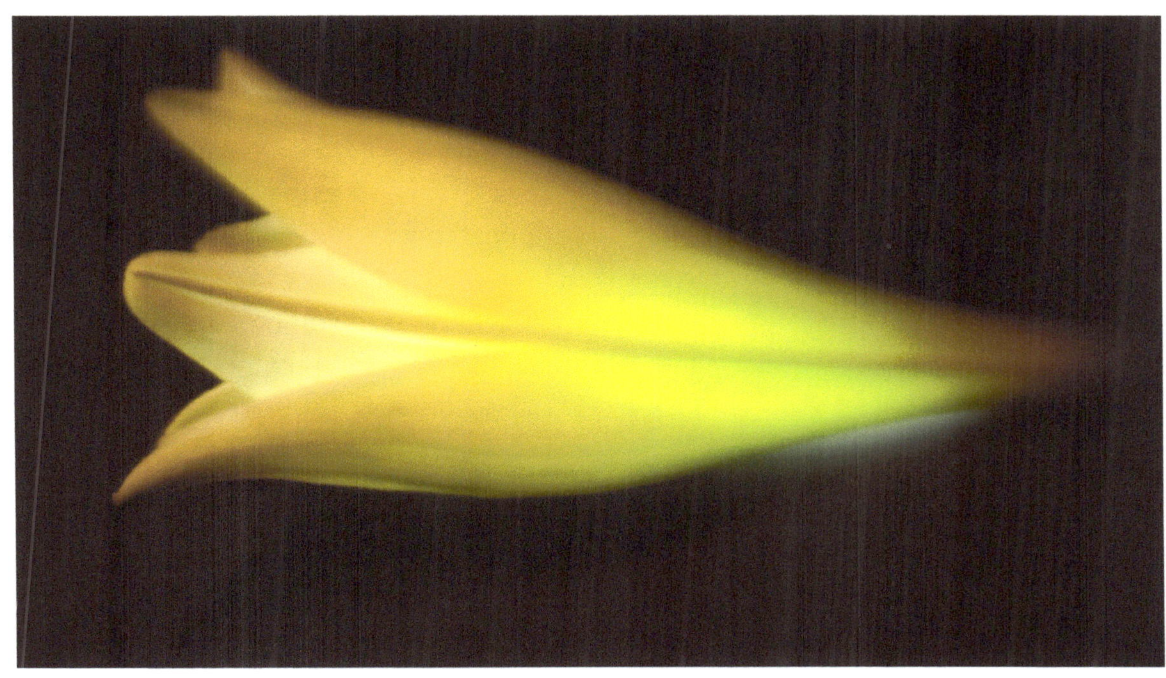

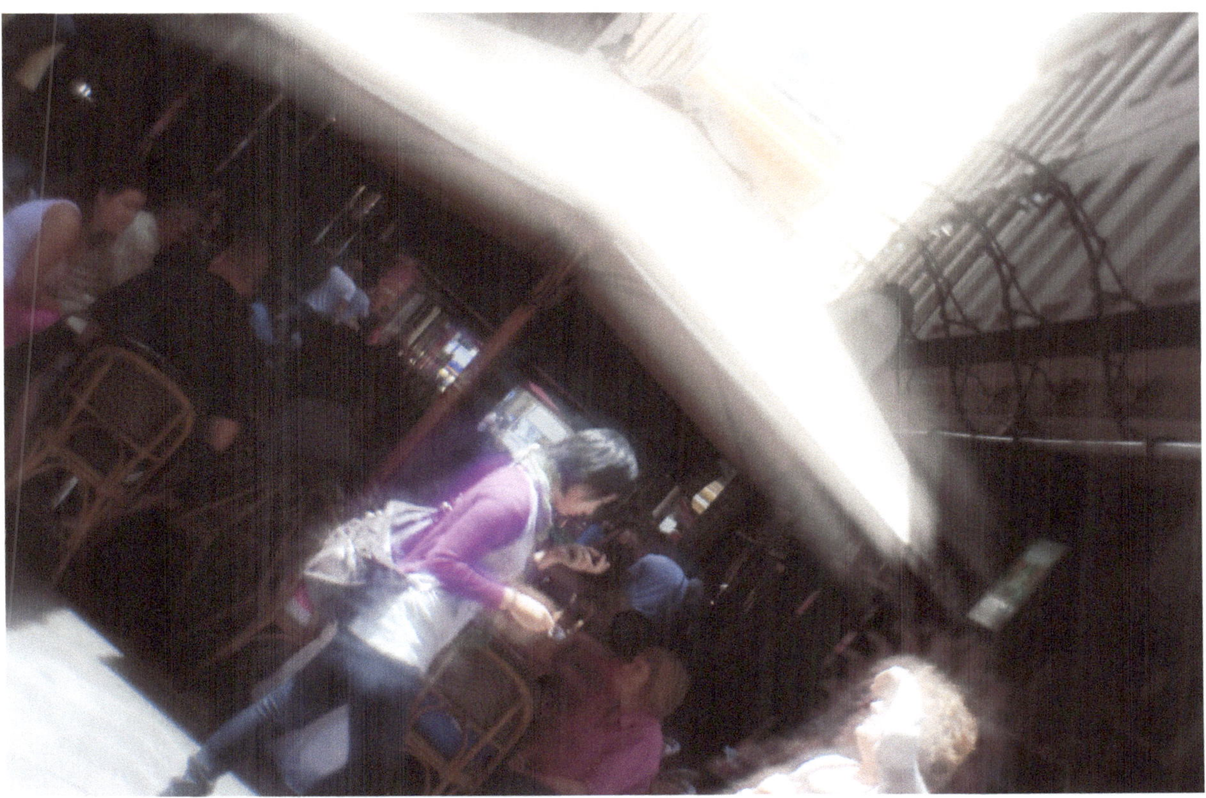

30. Apply and Practice What You Learn

There is no point reading a magazine article, book, getting a great answer on a forum or spending money on a workshop if you do not apply what you learn. Classic learning patterns show that effective learning happens when you hear, see, say, put into action, evaluate and conceptualize (check this). You see people failing to do this all the time. They rave about a great how-to article in a magazine and six-months later still have not tried what was in the article. Or they do a workshop and then don't practice what they have learned. Don't be one of these people.

The thing is, what you learn you may not decide has a place in your photographic practice. That is fine. But if you don't really try it how can you be sure and you also reduce the amount of benefit you get from the process. It is often surprising just how frequently learning about something in one area opens up something in another. So, for example, a workshop on macro photography with the inherent shallow depth of field from close focusing could lead to an interest in shallow depth of field in portraiture.

Activity

Make it a matter of personal discipline to put into practice the things that you learn. Do not take on a new piece of learning until you have done this.

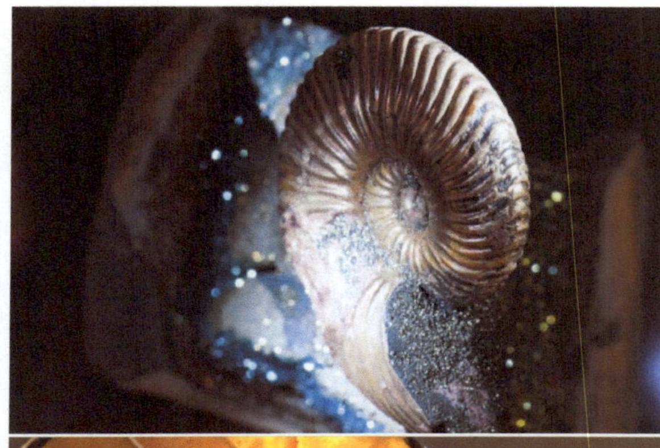

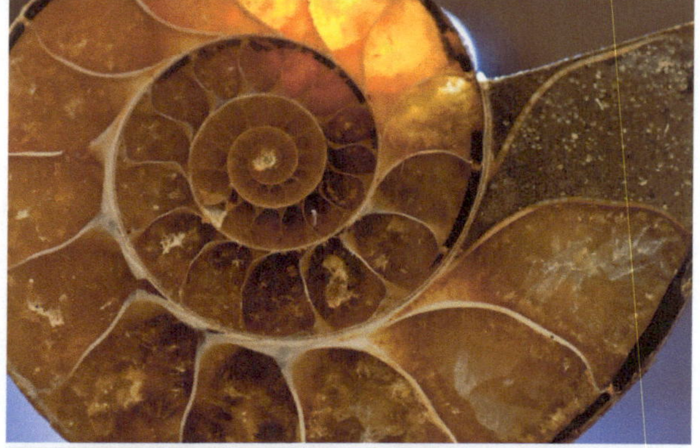

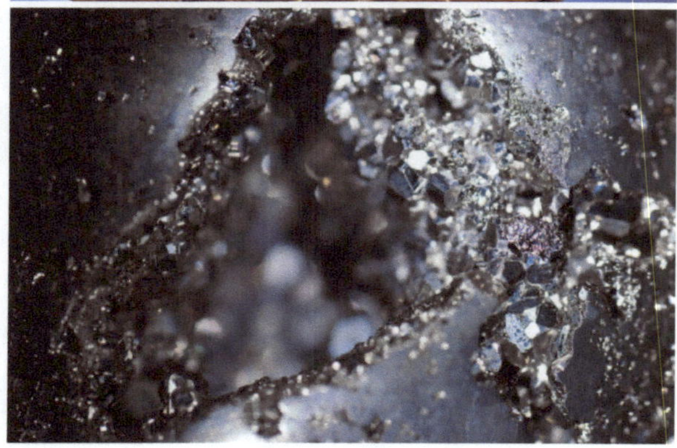

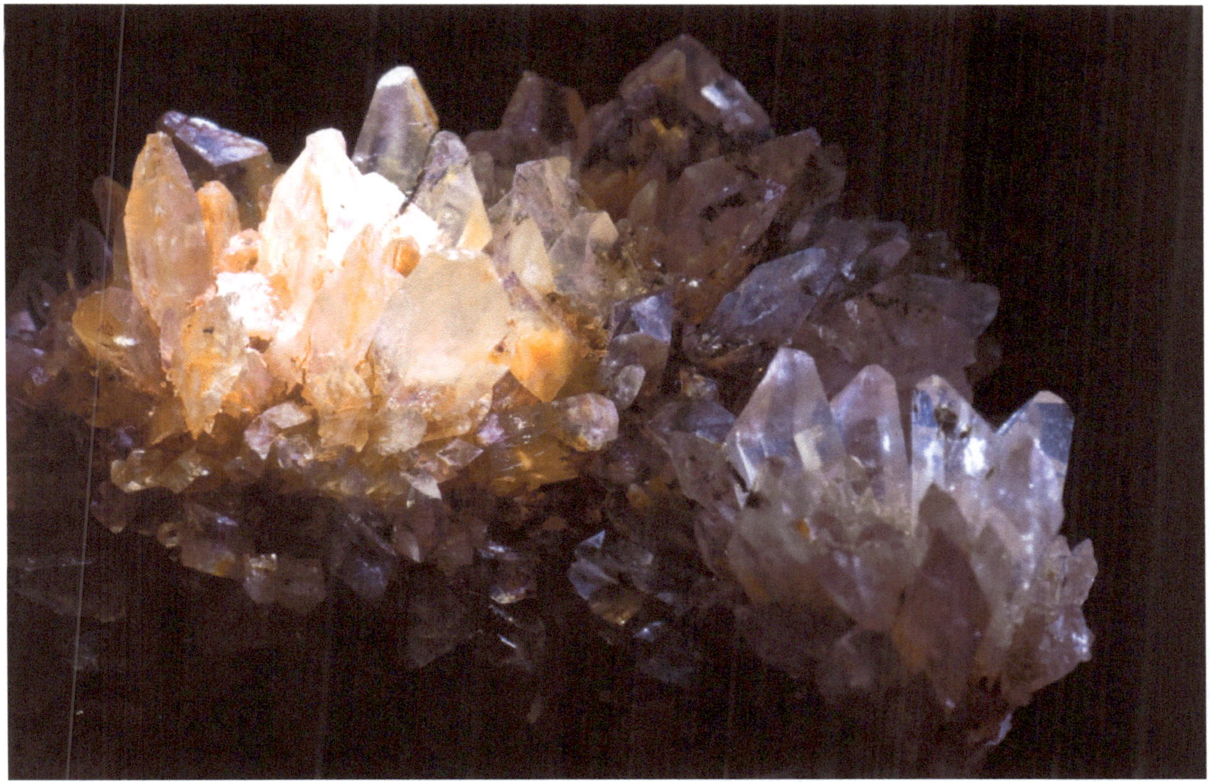

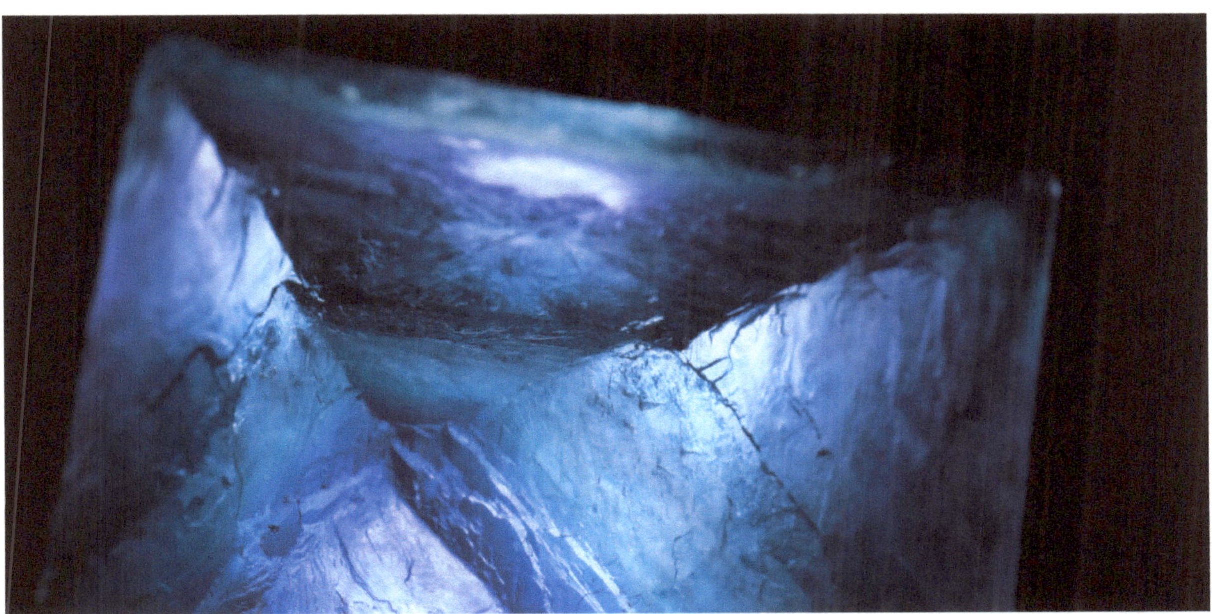

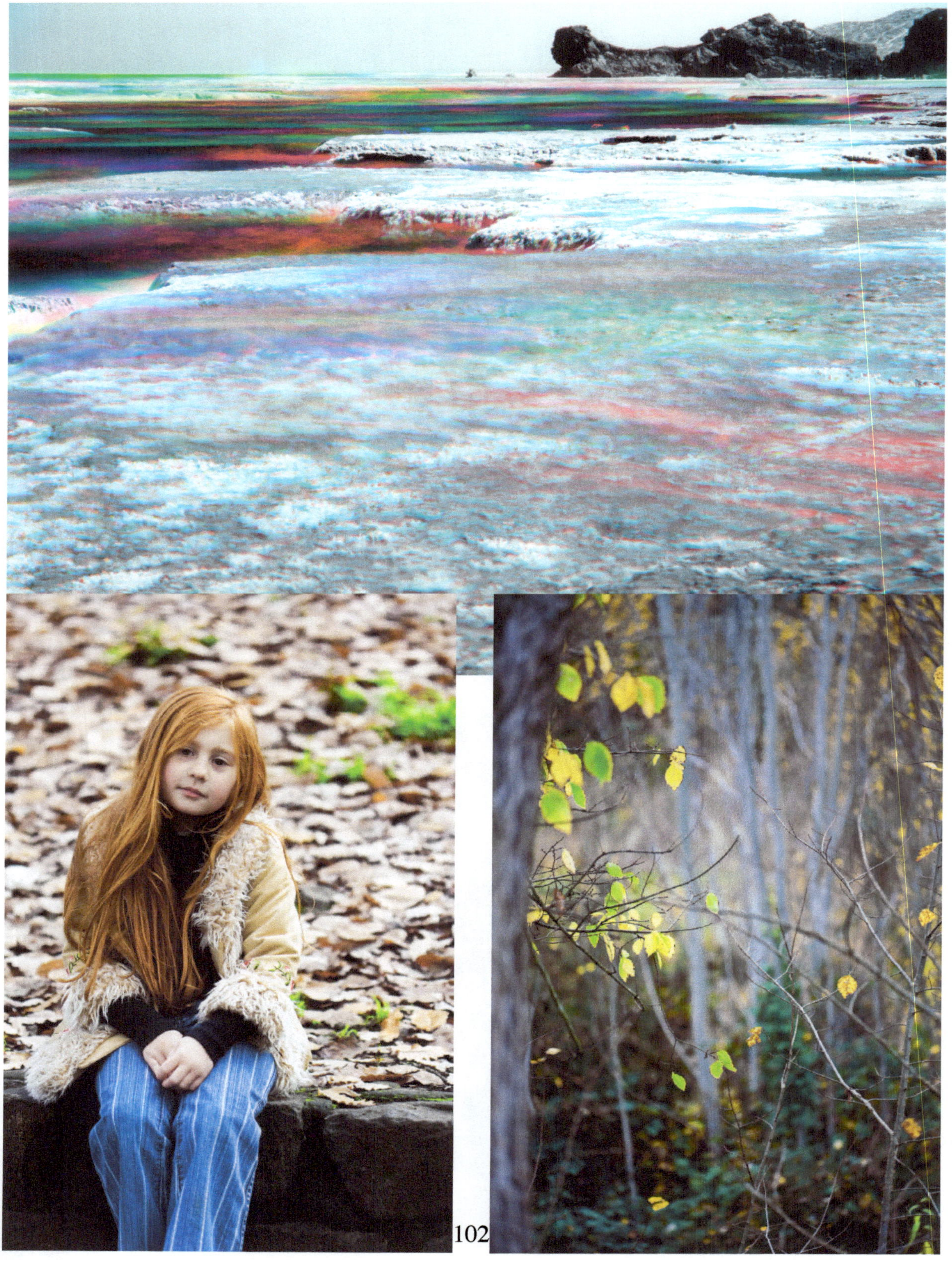

The images on the top left and below use the tricolour photography technique. I learned this many years ago from a magazine article and involved taking three exposures onto the same piece of film, with each exposure taken through a different coloured filter: red, green and blue. I dusted this off recently for digital photography by taking three successive shots and then taking the red channel from one, the green from another and the blue from the third and combining them together in Photoshop.

Practicing what you learn can be applied to any area of photography. On the previous spread we have some macro shots. Macro is an area that needs lot of practice to not only master the techniques but also to start producing strong images. It is also a perfect way to practice your lighting without a model getting frustrated as you keep changing things.

For people photography you also need to practice. I have shot my daughter over the years as a convenient and a happy to be photographed subject.

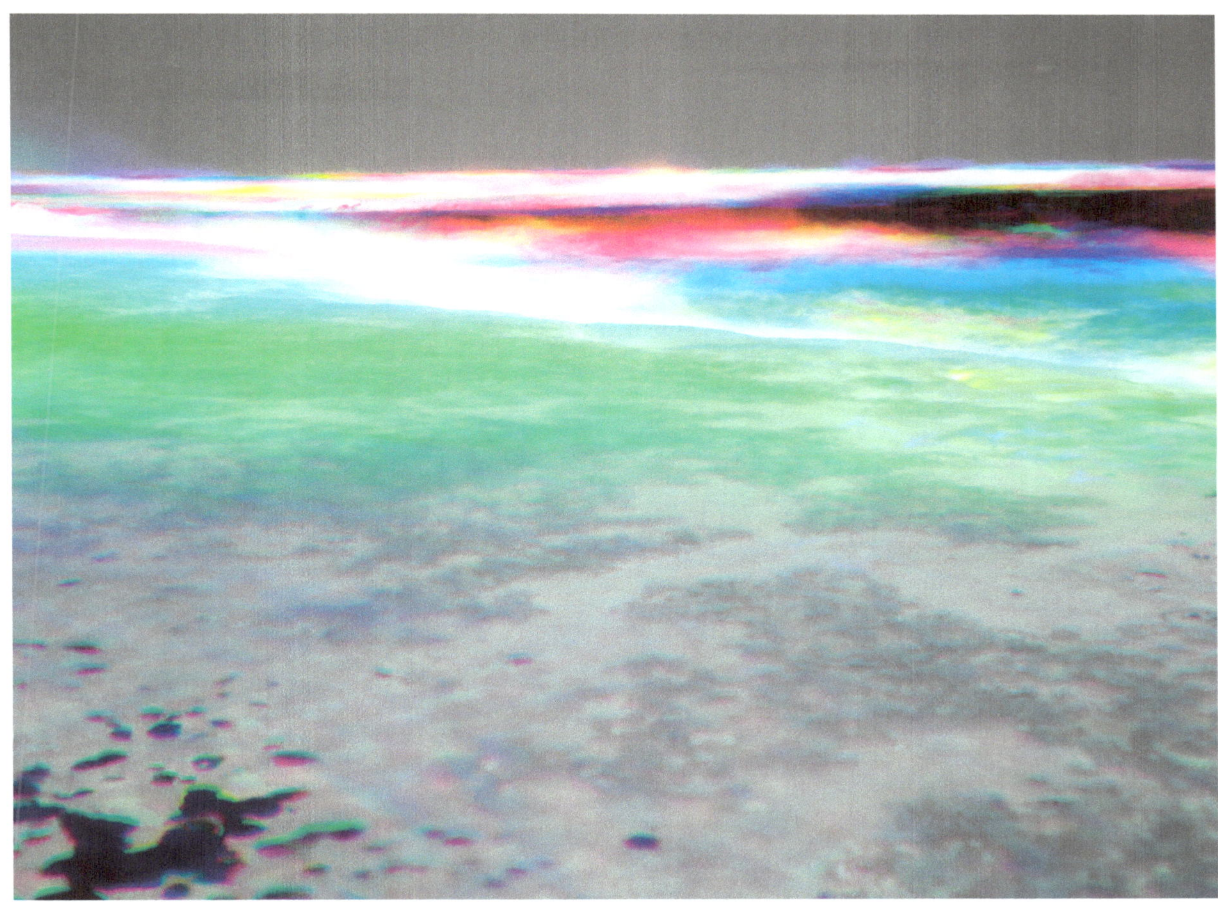

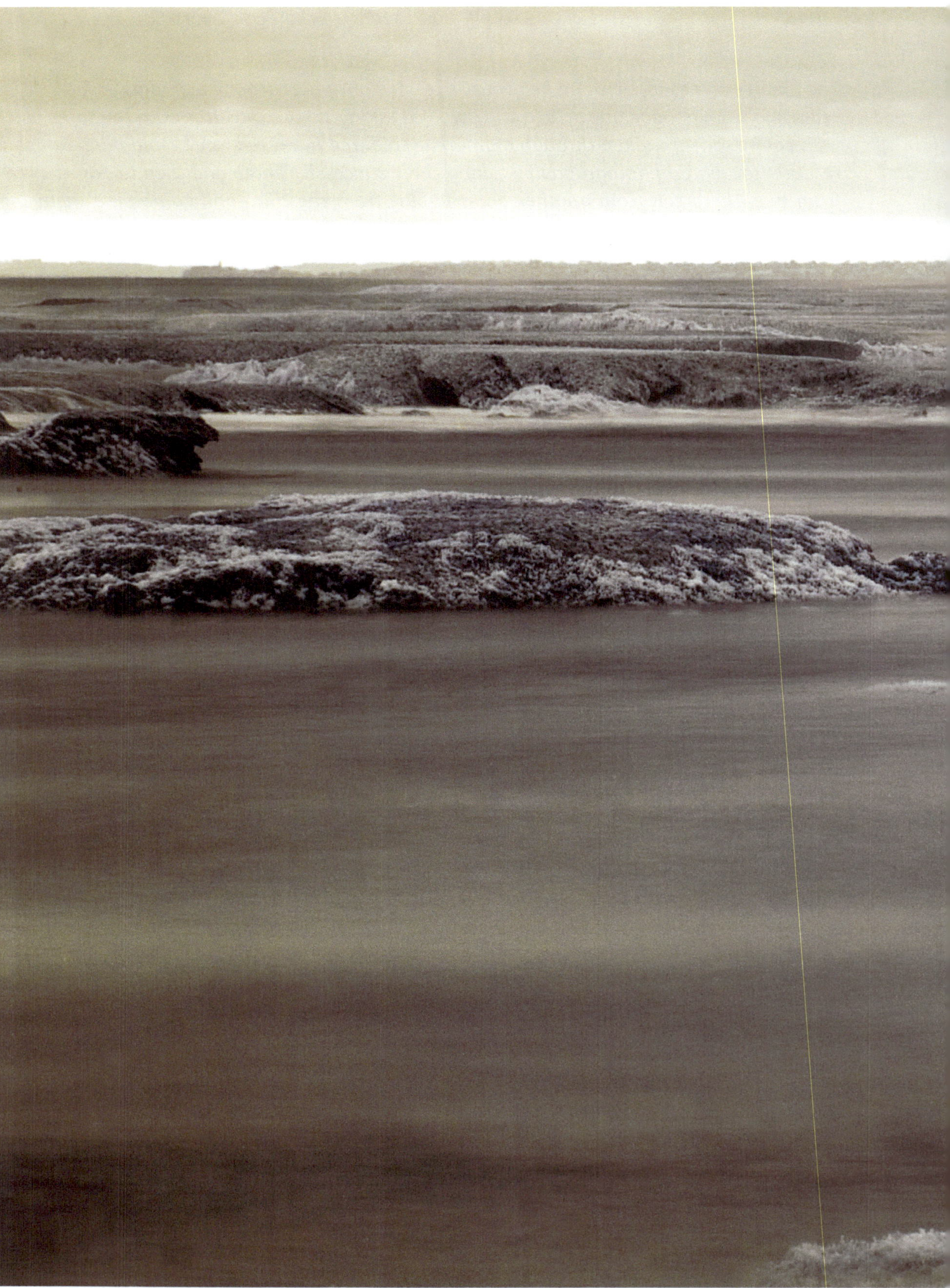

Shoot

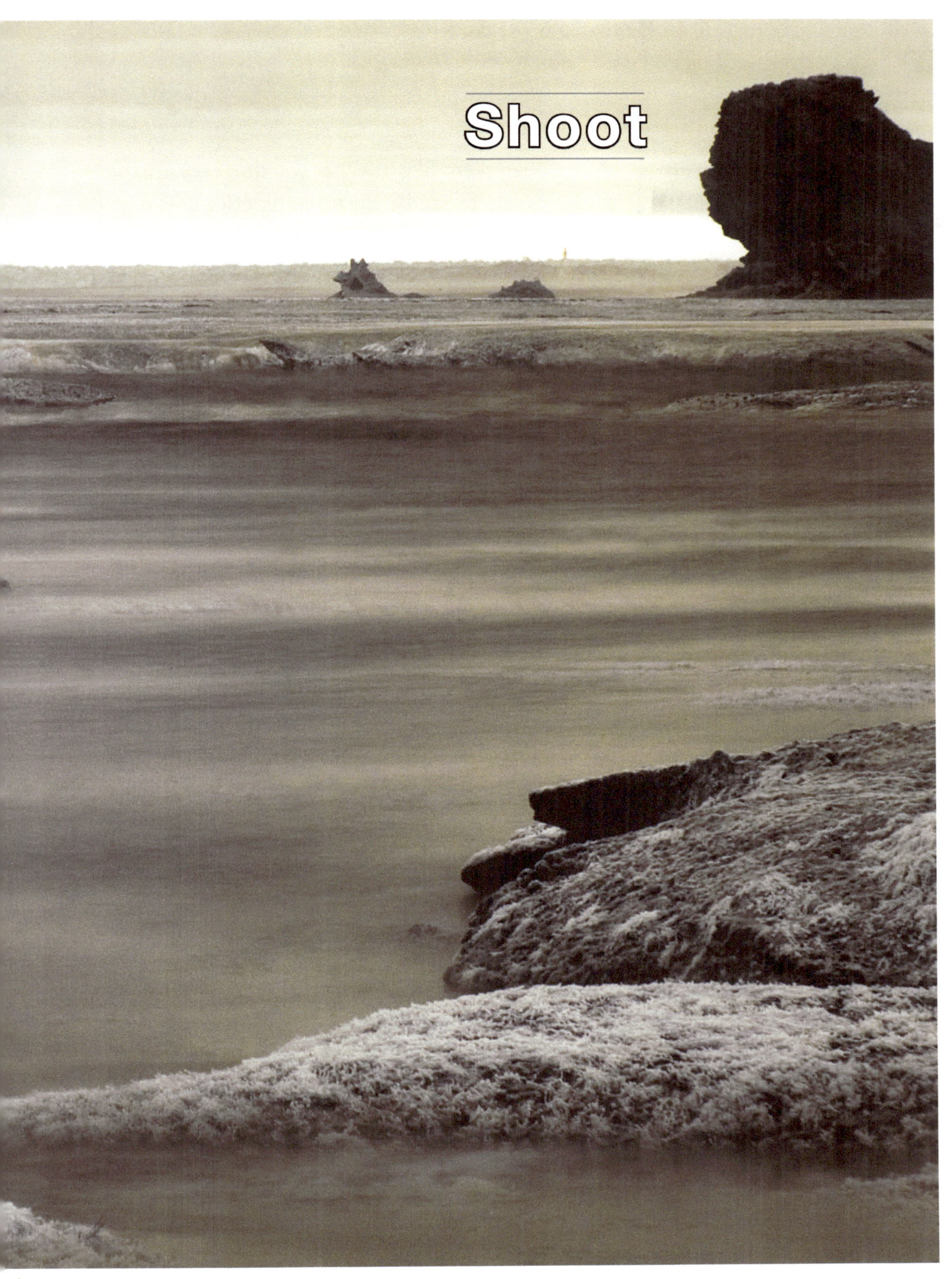

31. Shoot More

Practice makes perfect some of us were told as kids. Well, it is certainly true in photography.

Like many skills, photography requires practice, practice and more practice. Recent research is presenting a convincing case that our old ideas about some people possessing natural talent and genius are wrong. Sure, people may have a natural predisposition in certain directions, but hard work and practice are what makes for success, not just relying on the natural talent. All the evidence is showing that people with some natural talent will not reach their full potential, or even a tiny portion of it, if they do not practice and develop these talents. Likewise, the evidence is showing that even people with no outward signs of extraordinary talent can perform at the highest levels with practice.

Often talked about is the so called 10 year rule, that it takes 10 years of concerted, dedicated effort to excel. This is true in sports, science and the arts. Tiger Woods had a golf club in his hands before he could walk. Researchers go through years of preparation of their undergraduate and doctoral studies before they start doing their life's work. Most artists don't make it overnight, though sometimes it can seem like it. What you don't see are the years of study, learning, practice and poor work that is often destroyed by the artists themselves. Jackson Pollock's early work is really not very good and would be of no real interest if it weren't for Pollock's later drip paintings, for example.

Others have expressed the idea that there is some number of photographs you need to take before you become any good as a photographer. Some say 10,000, others have said 100,000, it is a similar idea to those in art that suggest you need to do a certain number of drawings or paintings before you are producing good work.

So we should not expect things to come easily or even quickly. We need to be prepared for a sustained and focused effort. The old principle of carrying a camera everywhere you go is not a bad one. If you have a camera with you, you start to see the world through a photographer's eyes all the time. This means that you will see more interesting subjects to shoot and, in fact, start to see interesting material for your camera where previously you might have walked right past without a second thought. Also, if the ideas of having to take a certain number of pictures are correct, then having a camera with you all the time may mean that you get to the magic number more quickly.

So the trick is to make photography part of as many things you do as possible. This might be time out with the kids, at work (assuming you can do this without problems), when travelling, shopping or whatever. The fact that most peoples' mobile or cell phones have a camera really does mean you always have a camera with you. So make use of it. Sure your better camera will take better images, but it won't if you don't have it with you.

Activity

Set yourself the duty of shooting some set number of images a day or at least a week.

Use slideshow or presentation software to allow you to easily run through and review the images you shoot. Too often we shoot and never look at what we have done and criticize them.

If you use a piece of software to organize your images that allows the rating of images, such as Aperture, Lightroom or Bridge, use it. Then go back a review your ratings every so often. You will usually find your standards rise over time.

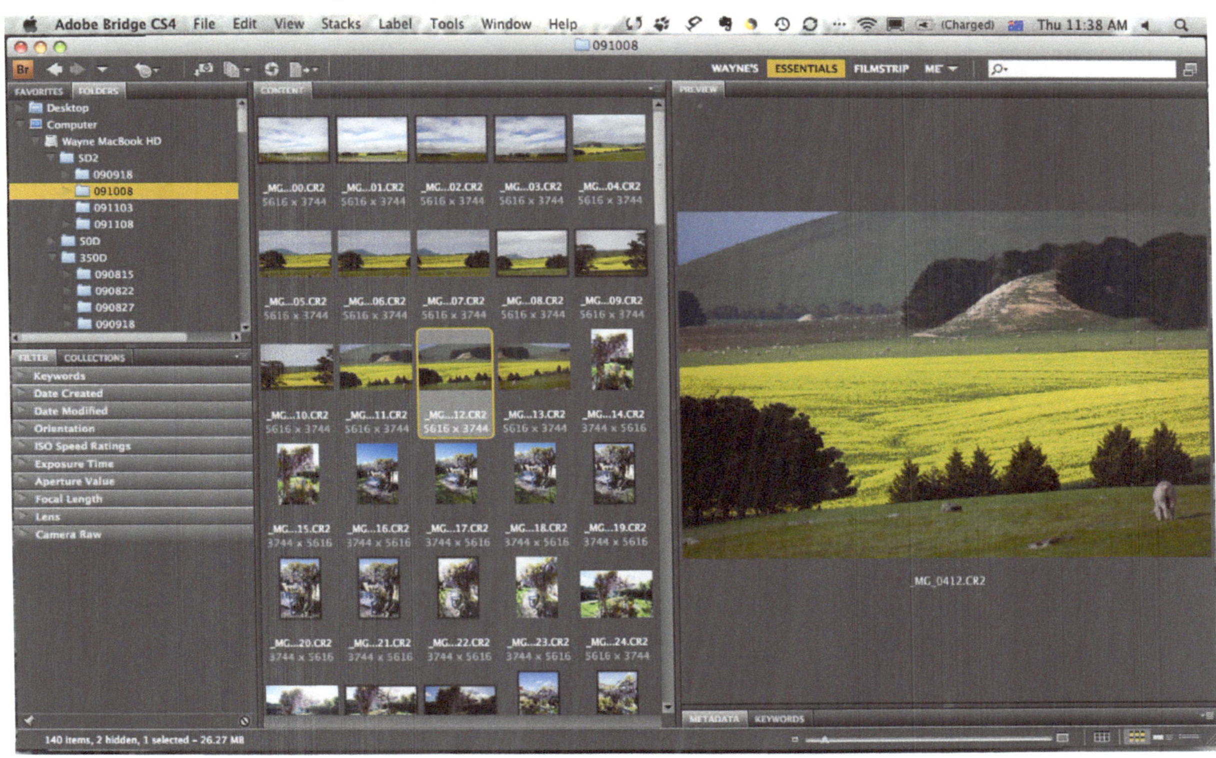

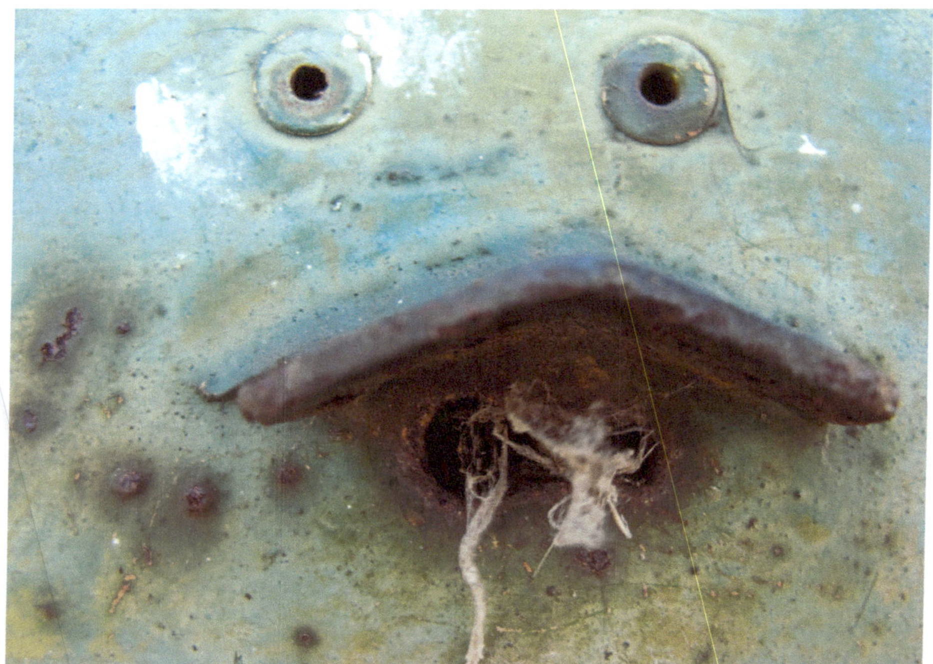

There are an infinite number of photographs to be taken in whatever location you are reading this, no matter how small the room or space or how plain it may seem. The question is whether you can see them or not. Anywhere you are you can find subjects to photograph.

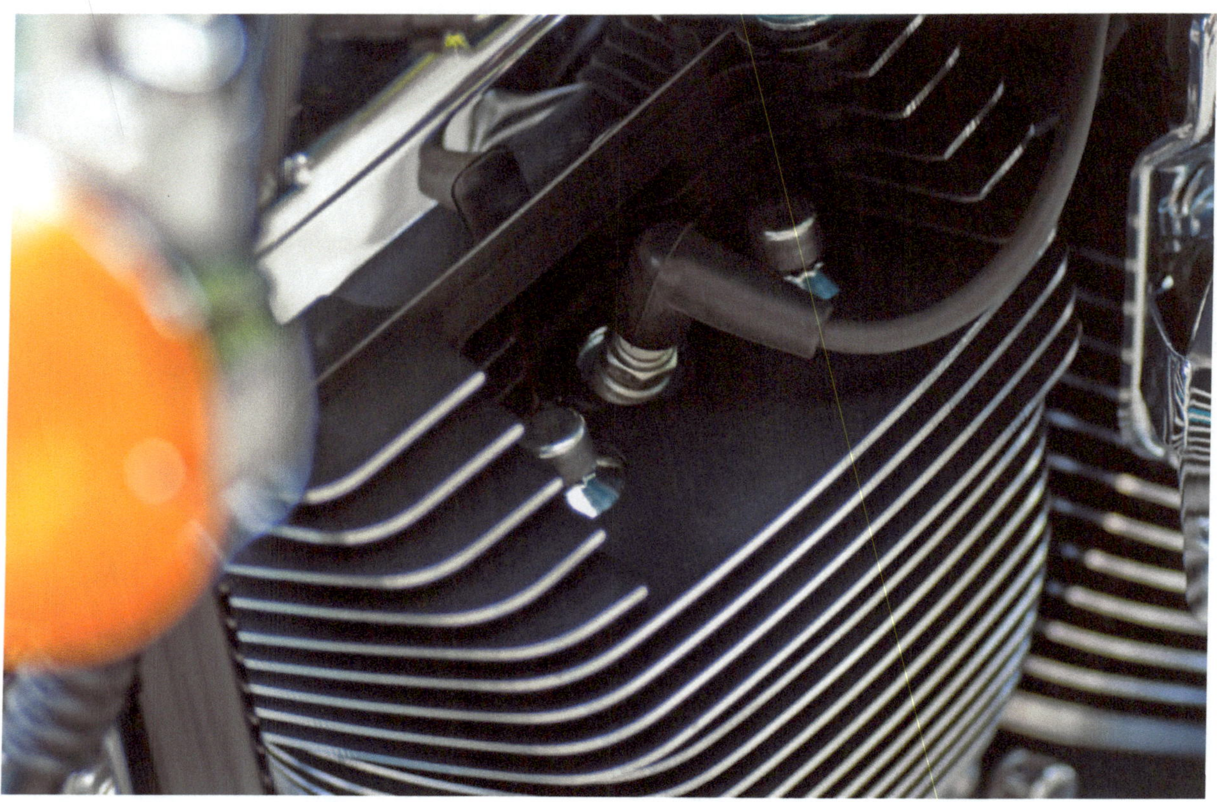

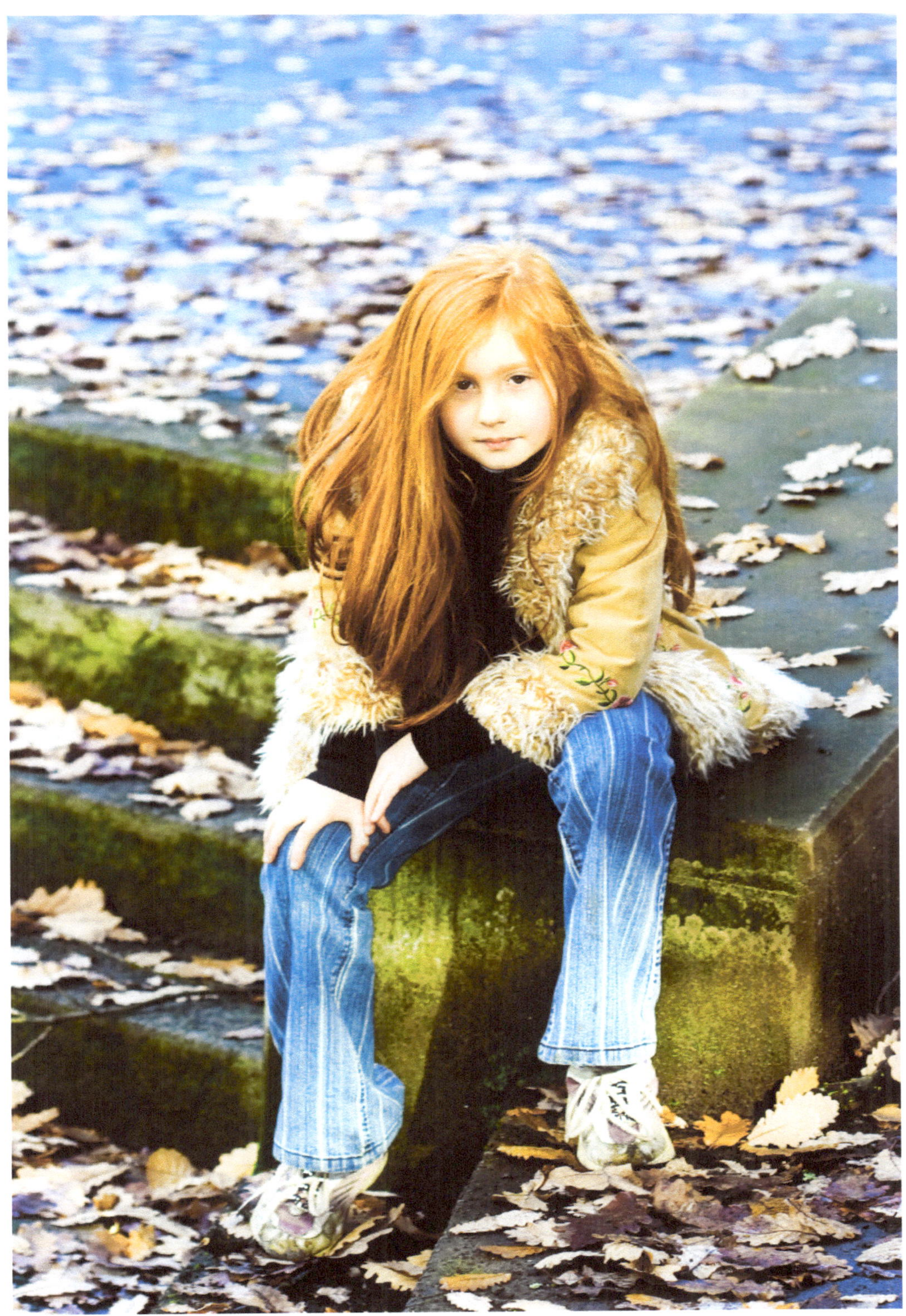

32. Shoot Different

Lack of movement is one possible sign of death. This can apply to your photography.

It is very easy to settle into a rut. This is a normal but regrettable state of affairs. It is regrettable because it is so easy to do and so many ideas in our culture teach us that stability is actually good. Stability, perhaps yes, but stagnation, no.

Any stagnation needs to be shaken up on a regular basis if you want to progress as a photographer. Try varying at least one thing about the way you shoot, from the lens to the subject matter, at least once a week or month, depending on the intensity of your photographic activities. This will keep you fresh and whilst you may never want to continue an approach you try this way, you will at least have gained more experience. Plus, you never know, you just might hit the key that becomes the focus of your mature work.

And maybe even stability is not good. One concept is that life is change, constantly, and that stability is either an illusion or death. Certainly this can be the case creatively.

So it is very important to try different things. Don't just be armchair photographers. When you read something that resonates with you in some way, go and try it. You don't have to wait until circumstances are perfect to try something.

Now here is something else to think about. A school of thought in the personal development movement says that it is the very things that you do not resonate with, that do not appeal, but in fact repel you strongly, that you should pursue for maximum growth. It is effectively saying that when you strike something that provokes a very strong, negative response that this indicates that you have hit an internal block. This is a tough path to follow, but perhaps a worthwhile one. The theory goes that it is the things we resist the most that will help us to find out the most about our creativity, our art and ourselves. It does not mean you will continue to do it, but that the process of confronting this block will unveil interesting things about yourself and help you to grow.

All the above are things I do on a regular basis across a range of areas of my life, from my photography and art to my spiritual beliefs. I will take on a different, often very confronting idea and wear it for a few days, take it out for a test drive, if you like. I'll pick ideas, techniques or photography subjects that I react against and give them a road test. At the end of a couple of days or a week I may decide they are not for me, but I will have learned something useful about myself in the process and have expanded my experience, my photography or my thinking in the process.

Give it a go and see if it produces results for you.

Activity

Like a New Year's resolution, take a resolution to try something new in your photography at regular intervals, such as monthly, depending on your degree of photographic activity. It is a balance of frequent enough to keep things interesting and you developing, but long enough so that you get a good chance to integrate and explore the previous approach, while also giving you time to work in the modes you are already comfortable with.

Find an image you react to and try to reproduce it, if not exactly then at least in style and subject.

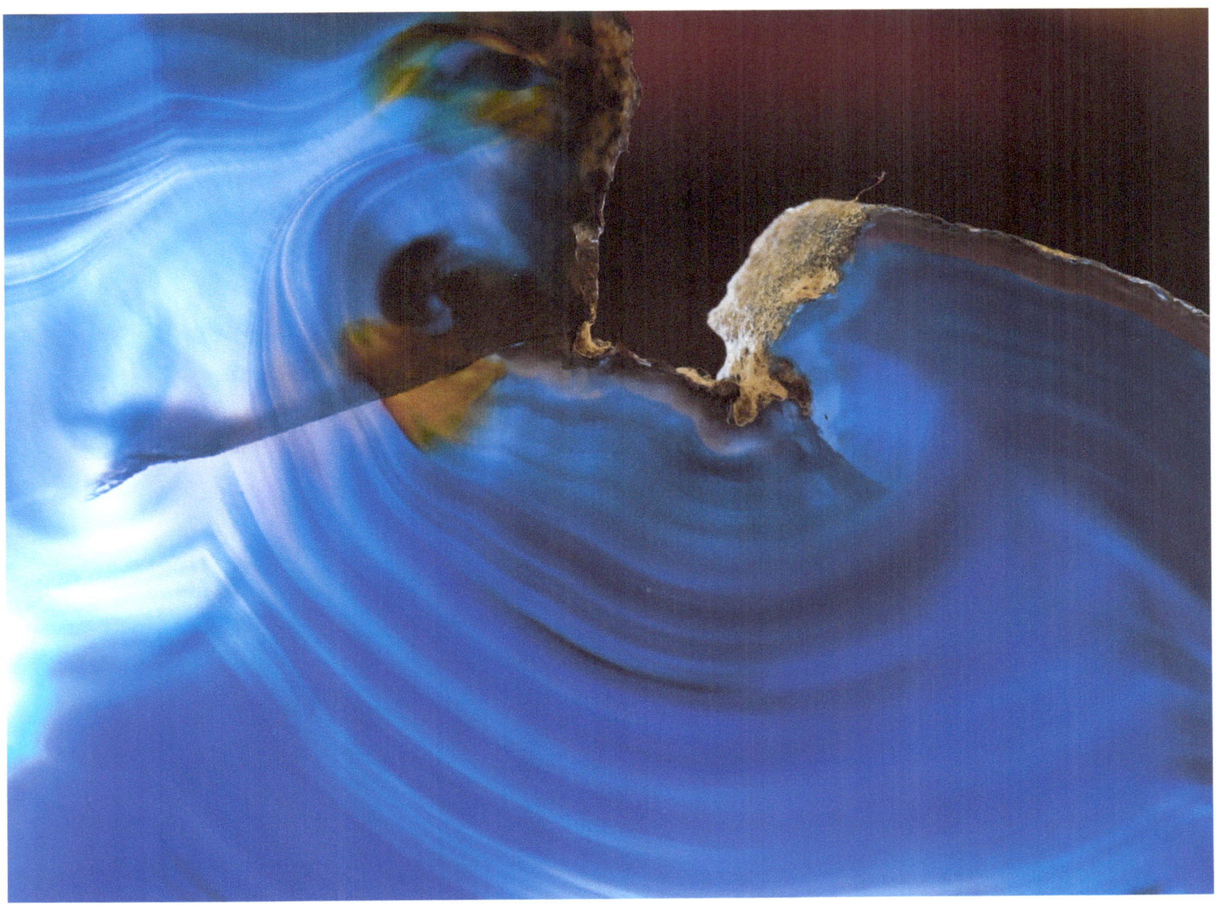

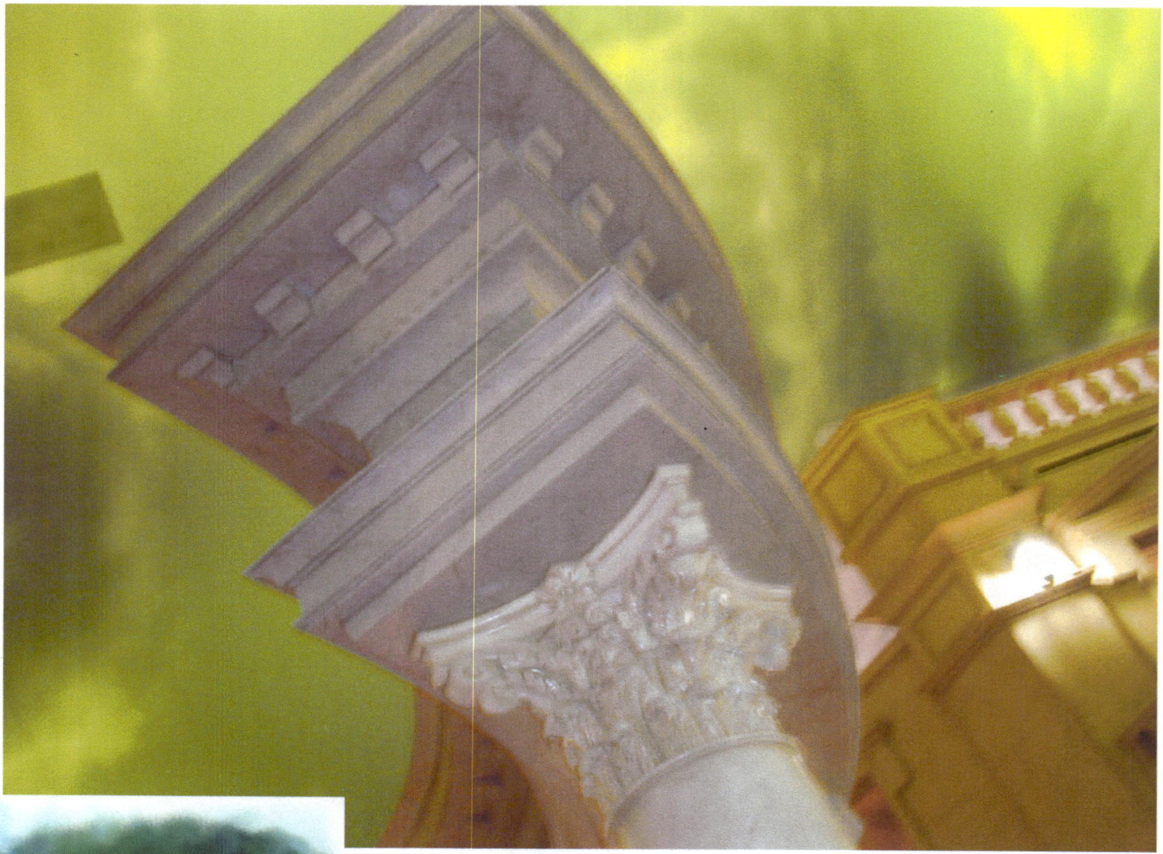

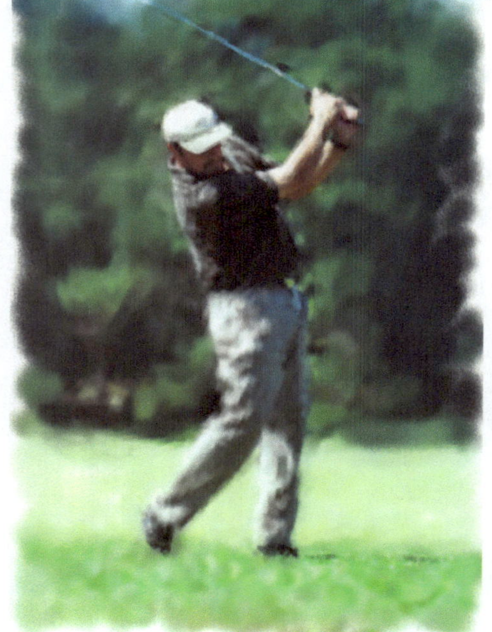

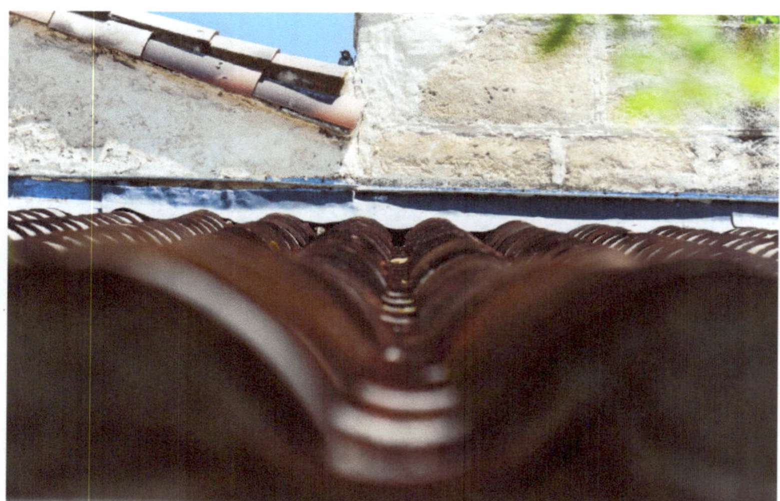

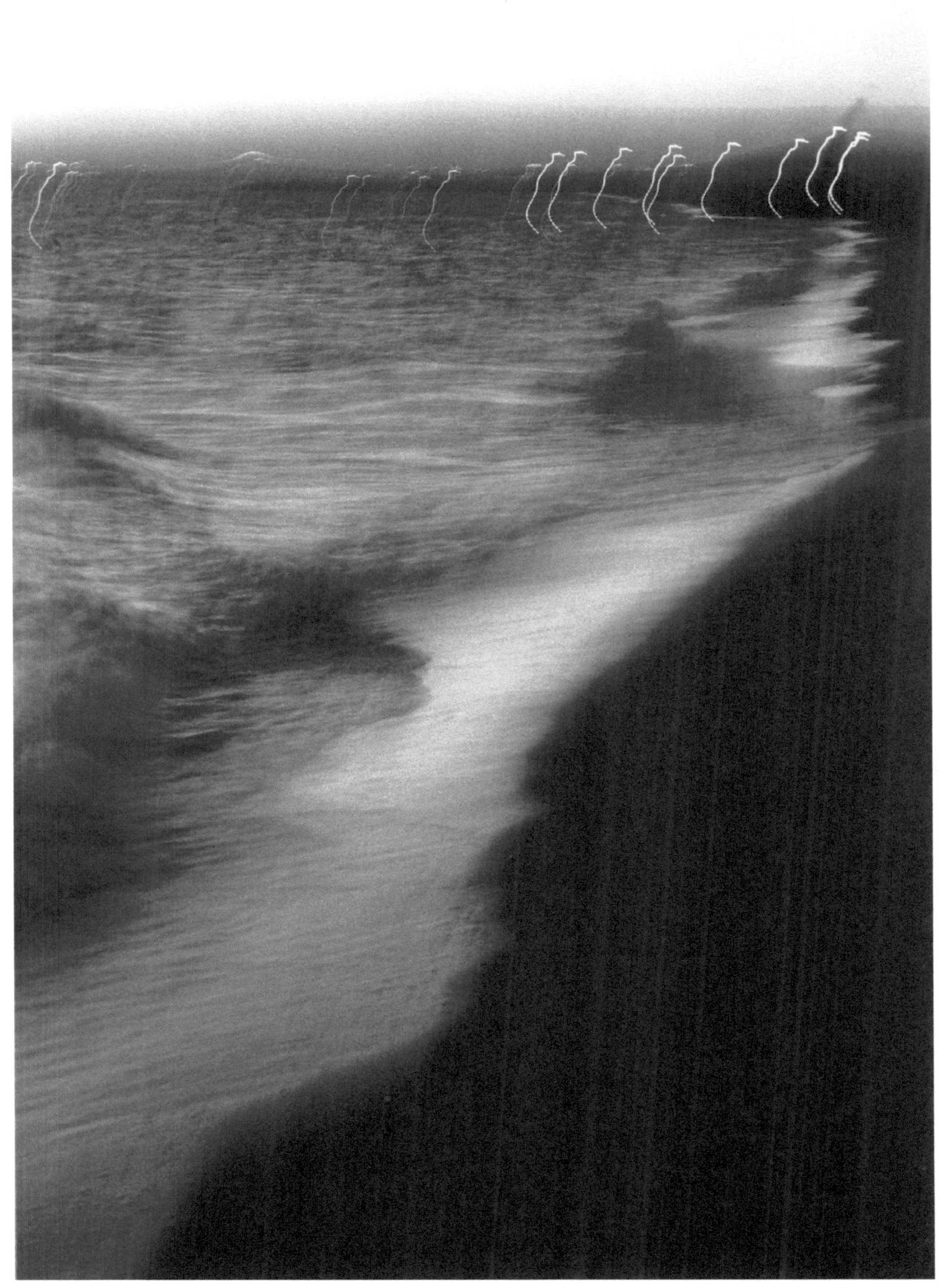

33. Shoot Always

Finding ways to shoot whenever and wherever you are can greatly expand your shooting experience and also open up new opportunities for your photography.

Linking this with the first suggestion means that you don't always have to use the same camera. In fact there are many times when carrying your normal camera gear would be a major problem. I would not always be willing to carry my normal dSLR camera with me on many occasions. Which is why I also have a number of other digital cameras in various sizes and capabilities, from my mobile or cell phone to a small 7 Megapixel compact digital that makes only a little bulge in my pocket. We sometimes get so over concerned with quality that we become blinded to other options.

There are many times when lugging our heavy dSLR gear and lens collections around are not practical. Yet we can always carry some sort of camera. Indeed there are major advantages to using other types of camera. A compact camera can fit into small spaces, allowing you to shoot subjects your big dSLR might not reach. Many compacts have much better macro capability than most common SLR lenses. Indeed some will focus to the surface of the front of the lens. Some offer built-in intervalvometer functions to allow you to take timed exposures in sequences over an extended time. With dSLRs this usually is only available with an optional extra. And how willing would you be to endanger your expensive dSLR in bad weather, at the beach or even underwater? A relatively inexpensive camera is more expendable and thus we can be more willing to experiment and also keep shooting in all the circumstances our life takes us into.

Having a camera with you all the time means that you always have something to do when you have to wait. You can not only scout out locations but document them too. There is no need to miss those great images you see when you do not have a camera with you.

Of course there is no reason to always leave your dSLR at home either. I commonly pick one lens and go out with my dSLR. Depending on the lens I put on, sometimes I will have to work really hard to find a way to shoot what I find. But isn't that having to stretch a bonus?

Activity

Put a compact camera in a ziplock bag and go out and shoot in the rain.

Put a compact camera in a double layer of ziplock bags and shoot from beneath the water. Better use an underwater housing for it.

Use a compact camera with a strong macro capability and explore your local surroundings from a different perspective.

Use the LCD screen on a compact to allow you to compose and shoot from ground level

Gaffer tape a camera to a pole and use the wireless remote that many compacts come with to shoot from up at ceiling height or from up in a tree

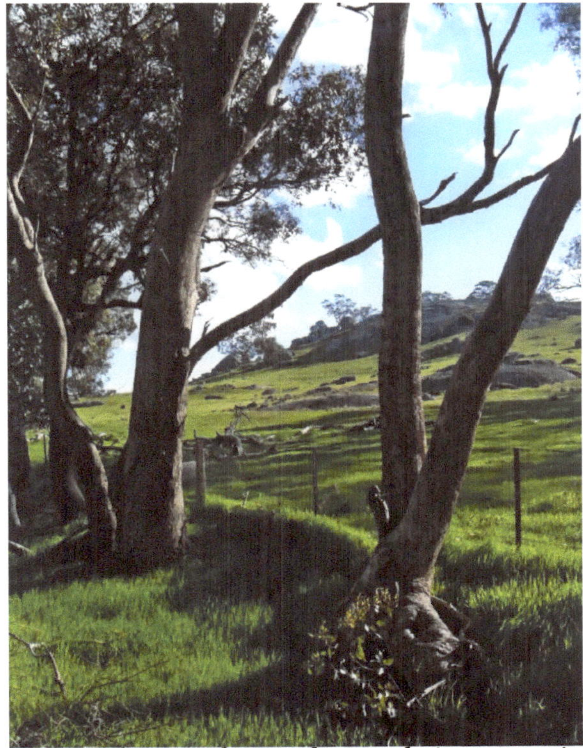

Shot with my iPhone, the result is a surprisingly good image after some noise reduction in Photoshop.

The shot below was taken in late dusk from a long distance away from Sacre Coeur in Paris with a very long lens and on high ISO film to cope with the low light. Everything said this was not the time to be able to shoot, since I had no tripod with me, but what I saw was saying to shoot anyway. So I did.

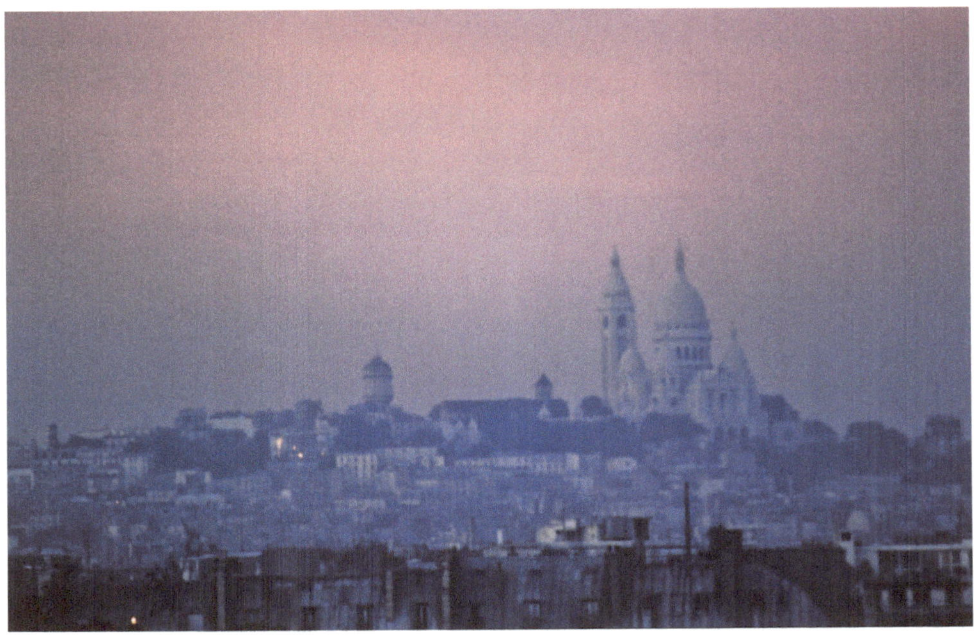

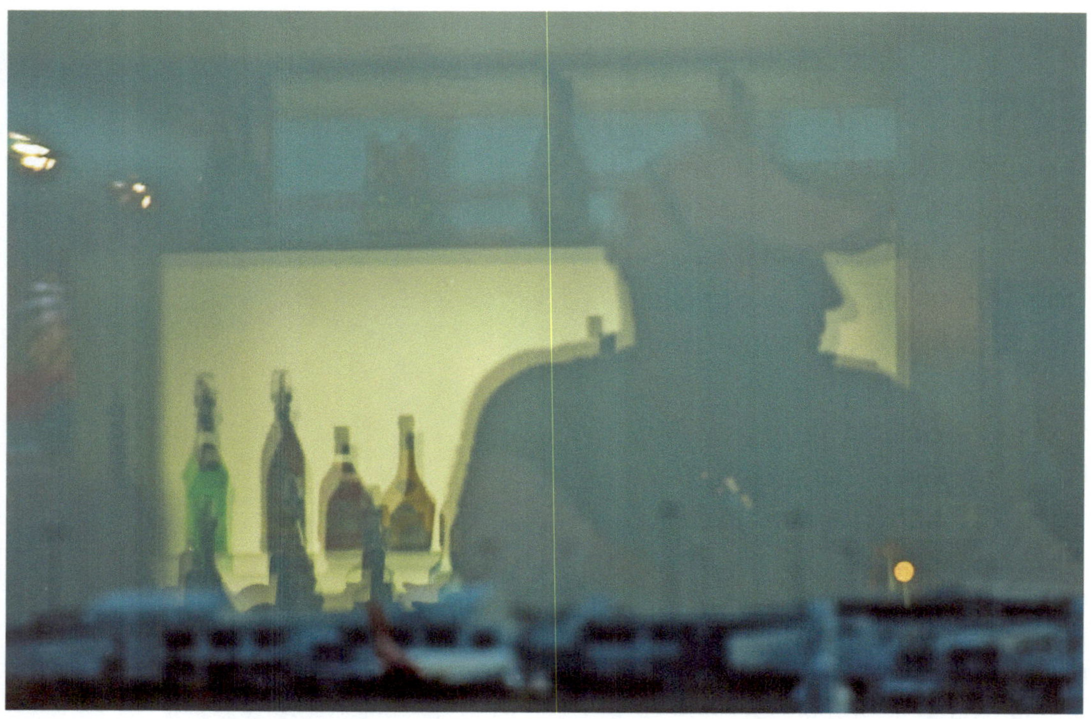

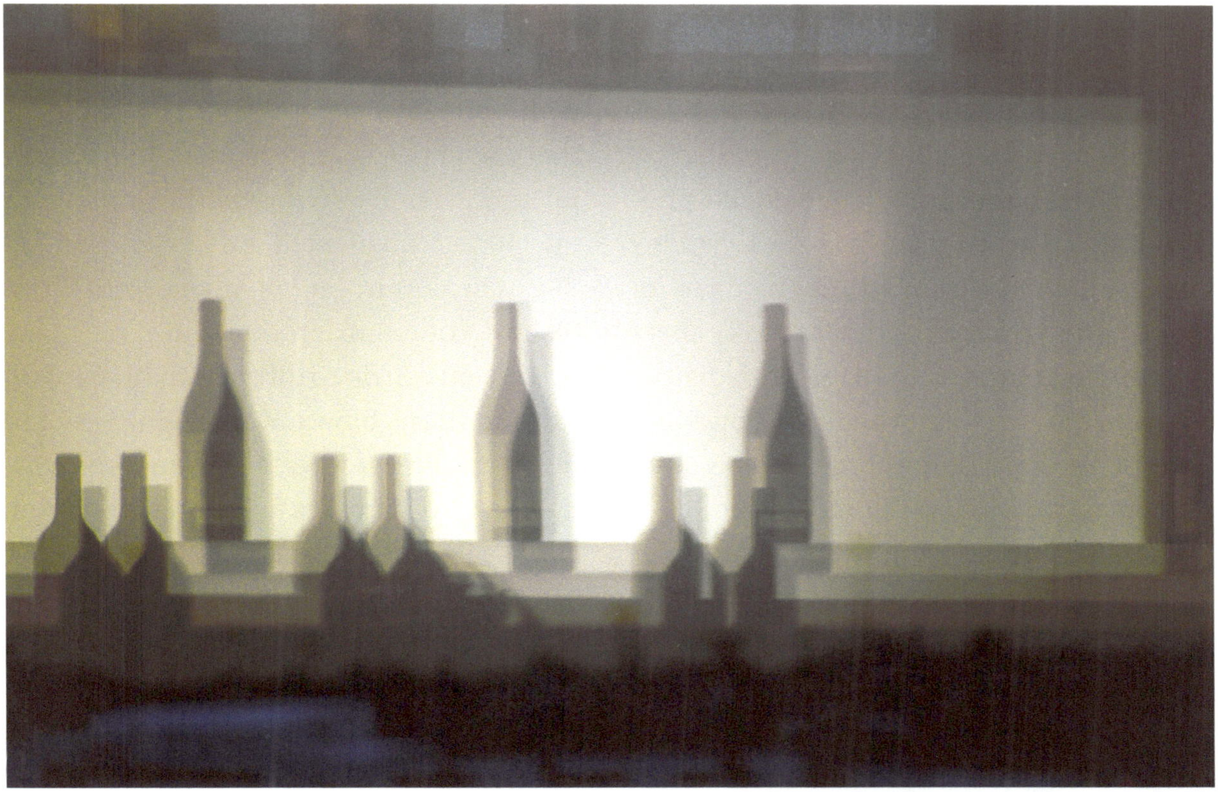

These three images were taken while waiting in an airport passenger lounge. The light outside was coming up and as it did I saw that I was seeing a blend of the outside view with a reflection of the bar behind me. Since the windows were double glazed the reflection was doubled. So over the course of about 10 minutes the light balance changed from the inside dominating to the outside dominating and producing the strange mix of lights and objects/people. They really illustrate the benefit of having a camera with you at all times and of being open to whatever opportunities present themselves. On the right is the very last image I shot before the magic had gone.

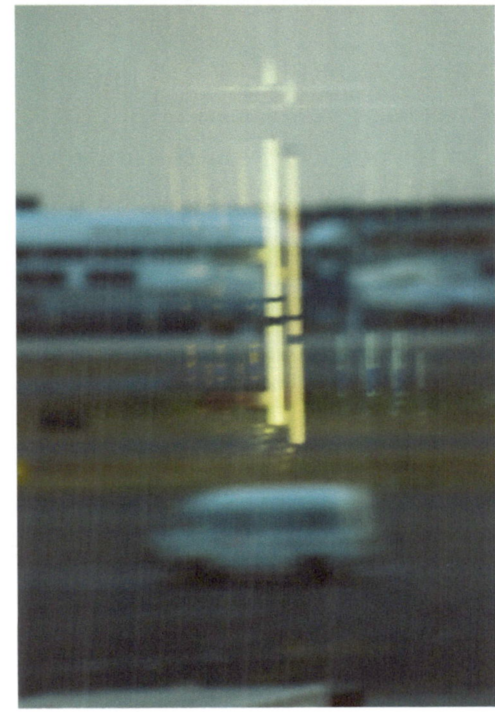

34. Shoot Dirty

If you think back to analogue photography, we often made use of very grainy film, soft focus, blur or rough forms of printing to create a particular look. There is no reason not to do the same with digital. There are lots of ways we can get down and dirty with digital photography. The obvious areas are in terms of resolution, lens, processing and printing.

We don't always need to shoot at the highest of resolutions. Lower resolution images blown up larger than theory suggests will have their own look, their own structure. You can take this to a great extreme and blow up so large that the pixel structure becomes a core part of the work. Alternatively you can take it up to a lesser degree but still allow the low resolution to have an impact on how the image looks. Related to this would be to deliberately over compress the image when saving as a JPEG, or even repeatedly so, to exaggerate the aliasing artefacts that this produces.

It is a sad fact that lens and camera designers go to great lengths to create crisp, high contrast images and photographers often like to dirty this up. But it is true. Hence the popularity of the Lensbabies, cheap, plastic lenses in a bending mount so that you can get blurred images with your expensive dSLR. The reality is that the imperfect image looks more natural, more handcrafted than the production line perfection of standard lenses.

Once you get an image into Photoshop (or similar) there are so many things you can do to dirty up an image. You can add noise, blow out the highlights and block up the shadows, exaggerate the contrast, apply scratches and brush mark layers, the list goes on and on.

Lastly in output you have more options for dirtying the image up. You can print on the wrong sort of paper, print on cardboard or handmade paper. Once the print is made you can take to it with sandpaper or steel wool, scratch it, crumple it, walk on it, splash water on it, apply paint over it, partly burn it, commit all sorts of transgressions by normal photography standards.

Perfection and sterility is not always the best breeding ground for creativity. It may be time to get dirty.

Activity

Try blowing a low-resolution image up massively, or do so to a small section of a larger image.

Try taking serious images with a mobile or cell phone camera.

Cover your nice, sharp lens with

crumpled up plastic food wrap and shoot through it.

Make your own Lensbaby or similar, using some cheap, plastic lens and a body cap with a hole cut in it to mount it on your dSLR.

Try roughing up an image in Photoshop to make it look aged or distressed.

Try all sorts of paper though your printer.

Once you have printed, try taking sandpaper or steel wool to it to roughen it up. Try other ways to 'damage' a print.

You need to be prepared to try anything and everything, because it is only if you have tried it can you decide if you like it for your work or not.

So saw a plastic lens off a toy camera and gaffer tape it onto an extension tube so it will fit on your SLR, or put a UV filter on your lens and smear the filter with vaseline, paint, butter or whatever.

Give it a go.

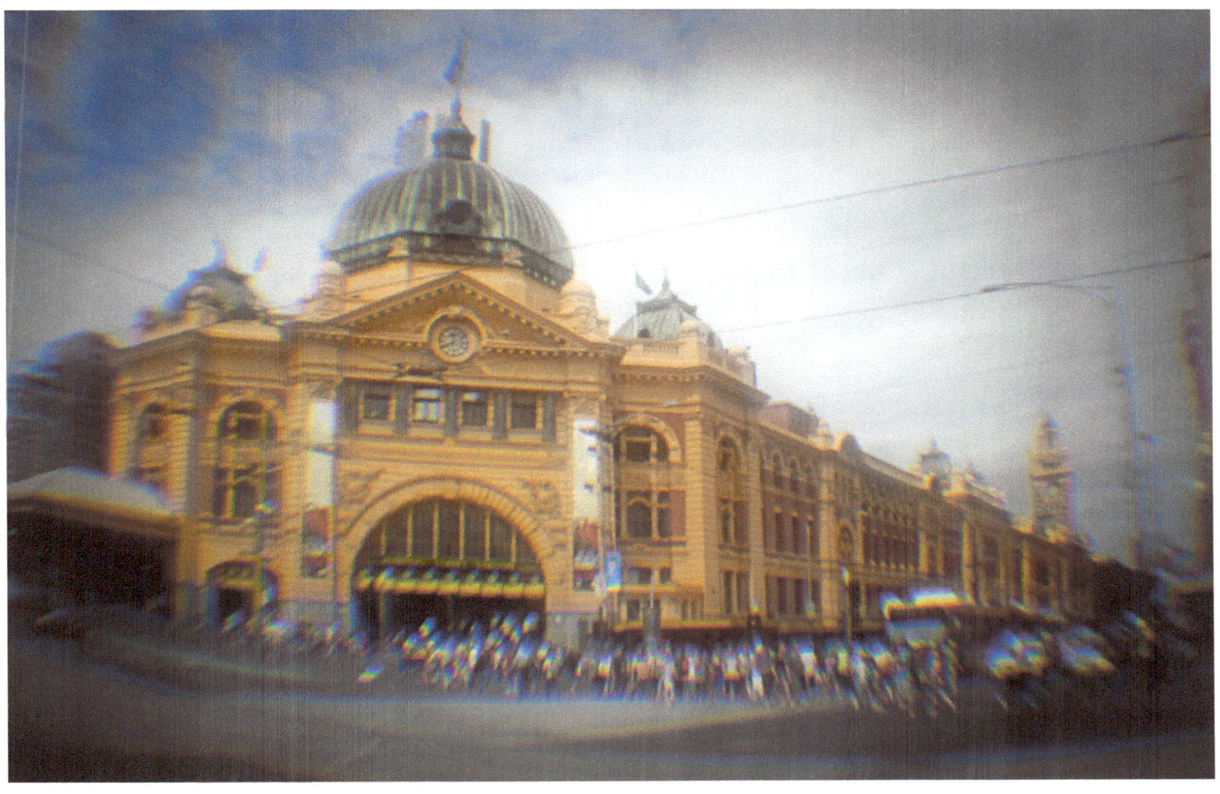

35. Shoot Anything, and See What Happens

We often have expectations of what we can and cannot photograph. Usually these expectations are not only completely wrong but they also hold us back in various ways. I had this made clear to me some time back.

We got away to the family beach house for a bit of R&R, which was desperately needed. One night we went to an amusement park that is set up on the foreshore every summer. I had my camera gear with me more for security reasons than with an expectation of shooting. But since I was there and I had my gear I decided to try out my IR converted Canon 350D. The results were fun and not bad, pointing to some more work I should do with it.

The resulting images have the now normal to me mixed warm/cool subtle colour tones and point to be being able to shoot such activities and get interesting results. Exposures were around f4 or f4.5, 1/45 to 1/60 second and 400 or 800ISO, depending on the amount of light present. I did notice that visible light levels were not always a good indicator of IR levels in this situation, so I let the camera decide.

In this case I overcame a preconception and learned something in the process. Now you may or may not like the results, and I may not choose to do more of it, but the key part is I tried something new to me.

As a photographer you need a brave and adventurous spirit, a willingness to try anything, anyway, and see what happens. Don't let other peoples' limits limit you.

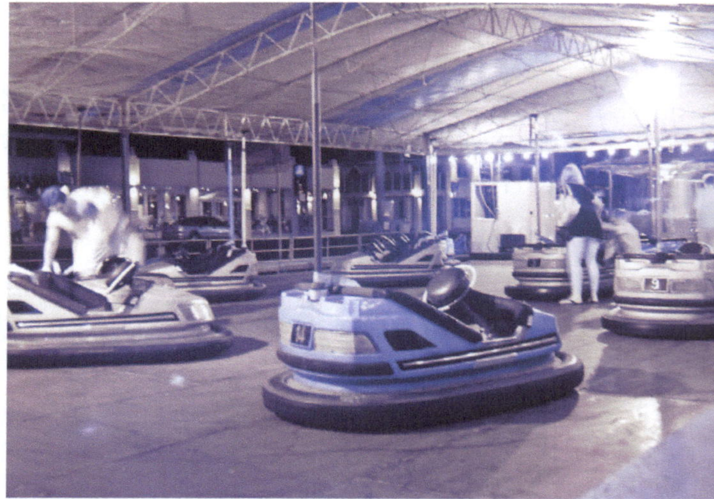

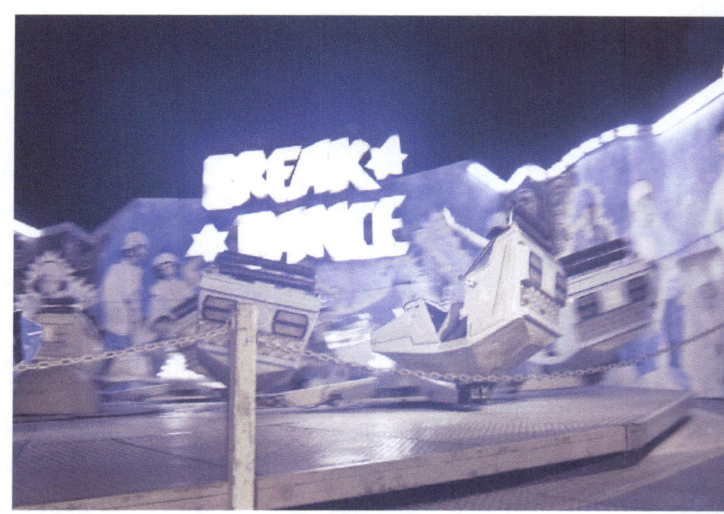

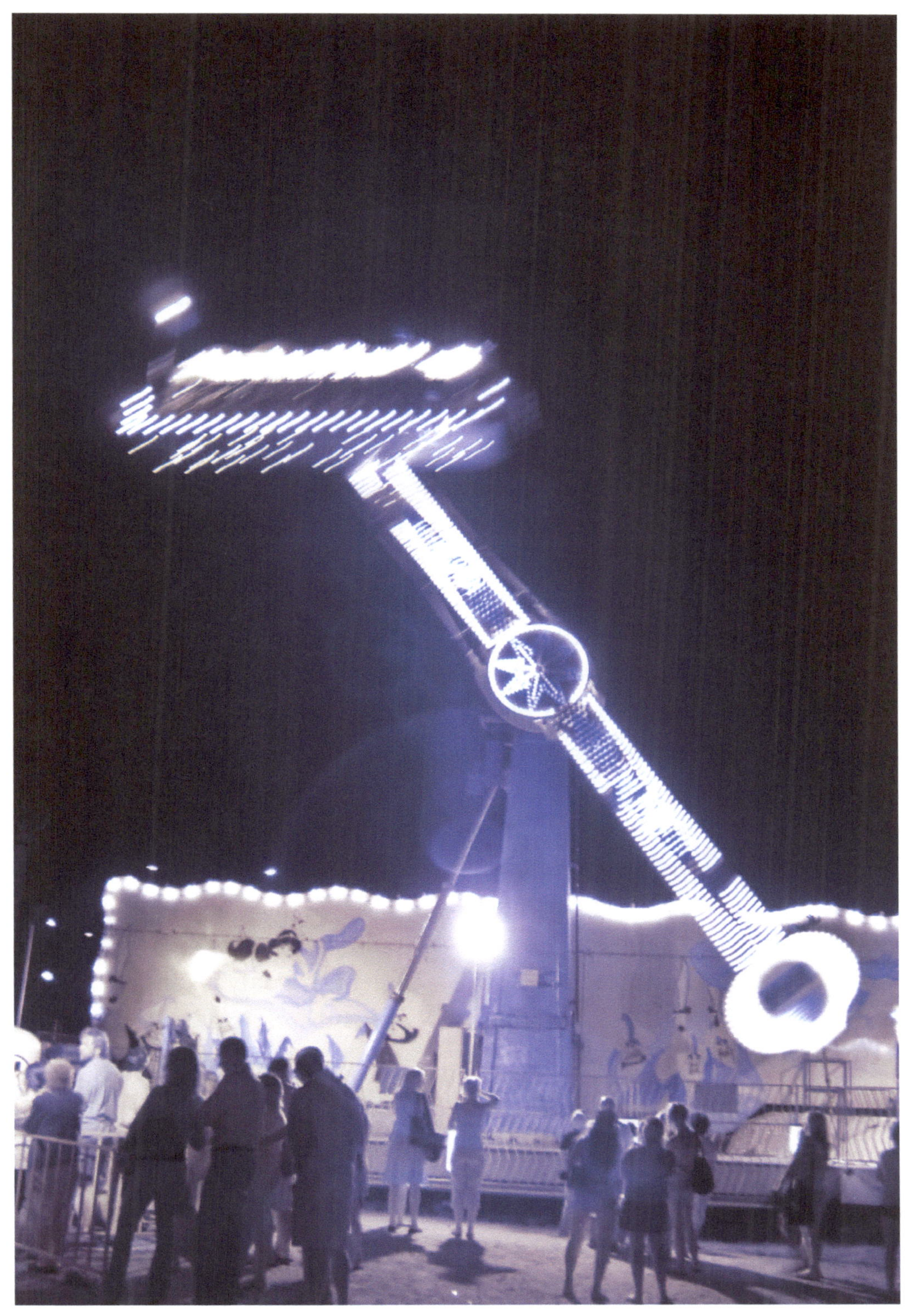

36. Shoot Extras and With Variety

They say variety is the spice of life and when it comes to photography, this is certainly true.

With film there is a financial advantage (superficially) to being frugal in our shooting. Film and processing costs money we may not want to spend. But with digital photography there are no such financial benefits from being frugal. Memory cards are fairly cheap and can be reused over again. Portable disk units that will download your pictures in the field are available which minimize the need for extra memory cards. And sometimes having a laptop with you in the field is a great idea.

You can never predict in advance exactly how you will use an image. Your images can be a resource well into the future and what will you be using your images for in 20 years time? Can any of us know? I know if I compare what I am doing now with my images to what I did 20 years ago there is no resemblance at all.

It thus pays to shoot a great variety of shots of each subject you find. Verticals, horizontals, wider shots as well as details are all great to take. In basic photography courses we were taught to crop in camera, but this was in the days of film, and especially transparency film, where there was little opportunity to work on an image later. But with digital, working on an image is natural, so having a wide variety of shots is hugely useful. Let me give you one practical example. When I was editing Digital Photography & Design magazine we were always looking for cover images, as all magazines do. Readers would send in great cover images that were cropped tight in camera with the subject filling the frame. However, magazine covers typically need space for the magazine title and for the all so important cover lines that promote what is in the issue and attract potential readers when they sell on the newsstand. It was sad how many times we would find a great image sent in but with too much of the scene busy with the main subject. We would contact the photographer and ask for a wider shot and guess what, they would not have it. They had cropped in camera and only taken that single shot. Or they had sent in a landscape shot (a horizontal) and we naturally needed a vertical, yet because of the shot we could not adequately crop one from the supplied (and usually only) image.

So if you view your photographs as a resource you will benefit from shooting a variety of images of a scene.

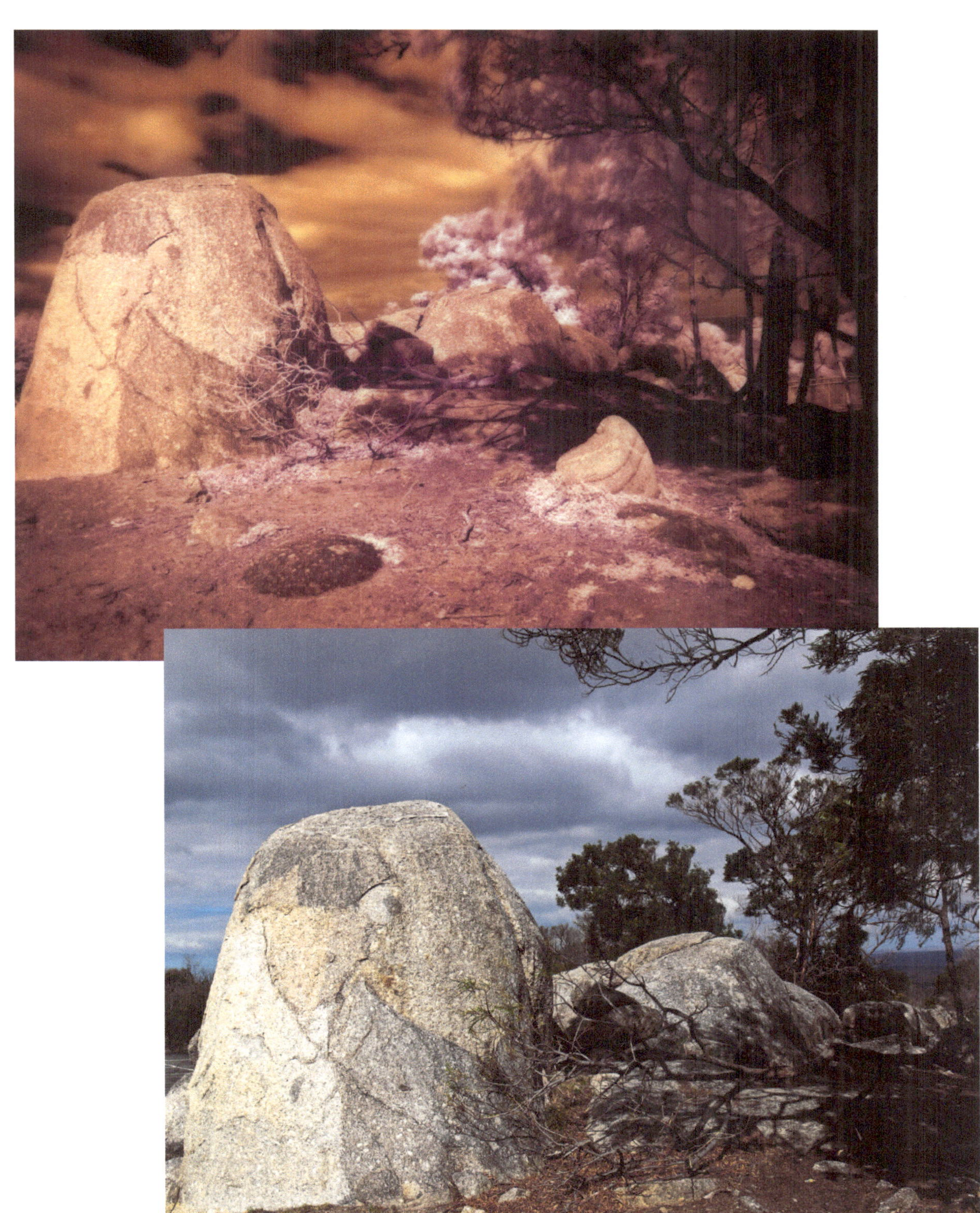

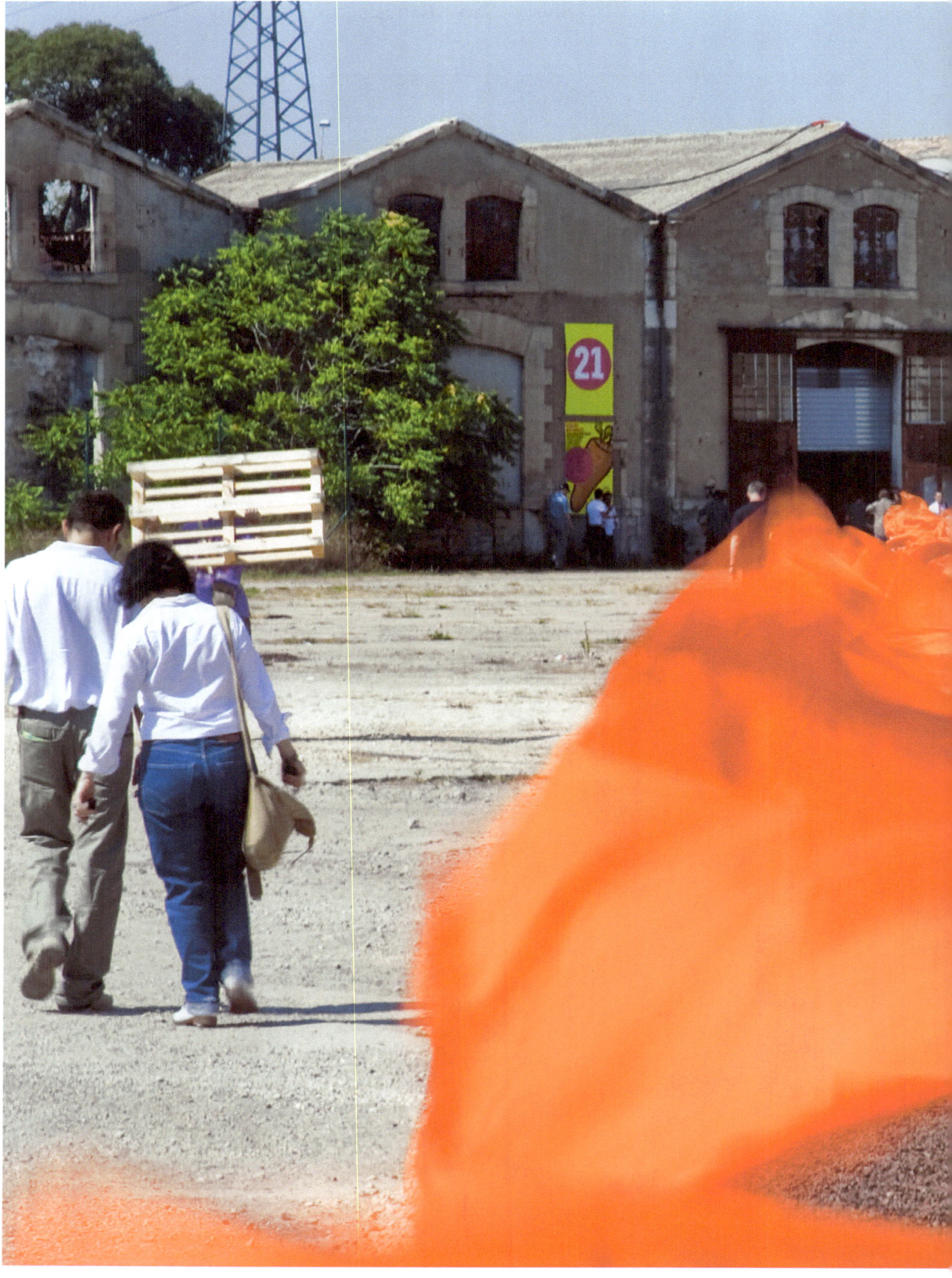
21

Observe

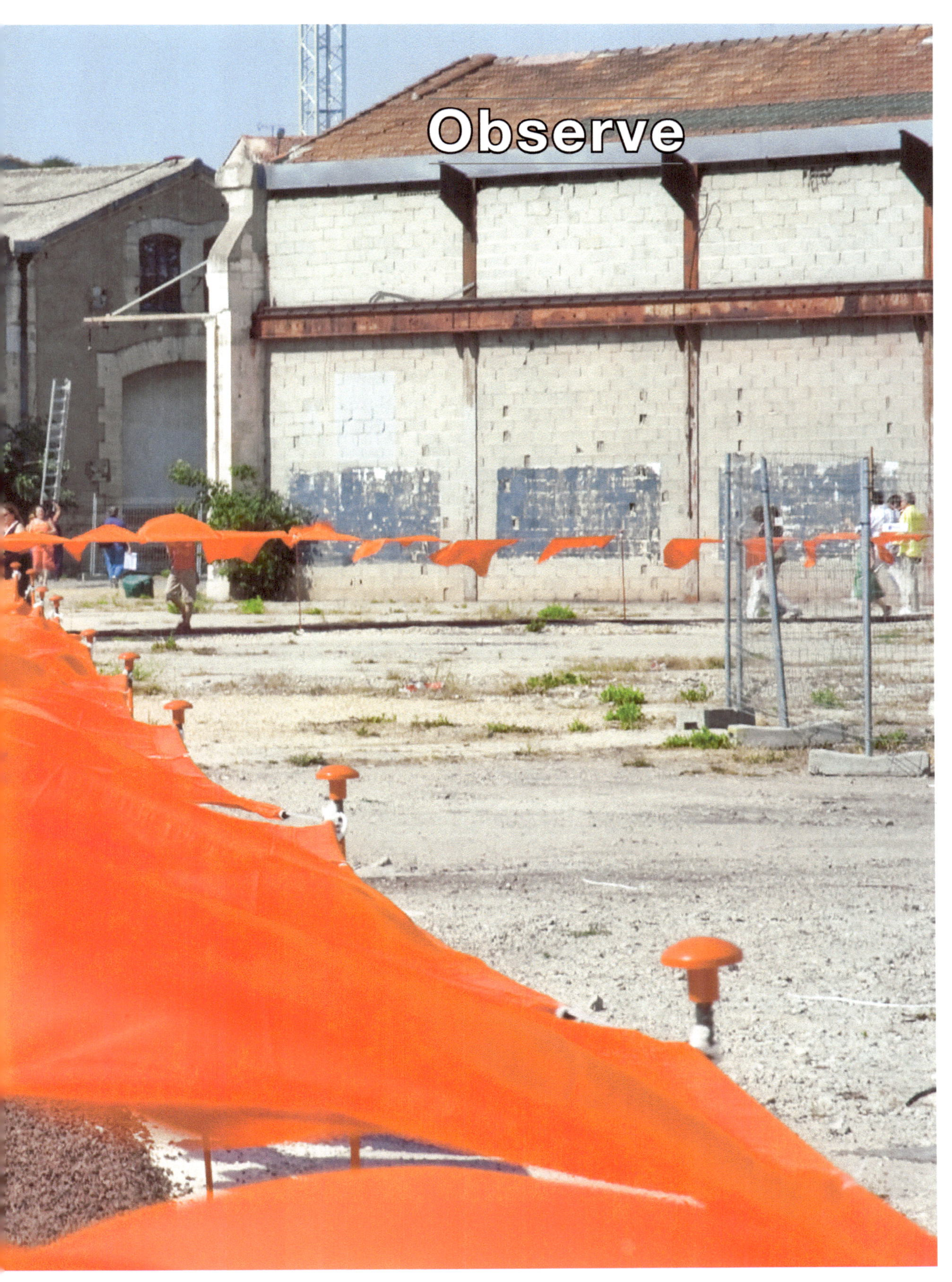

37. Work a Scene to the Max

There is always another picture that you can take, another angle you can try, another tool at your disposal or another variation in the camera controls you can try.

It is very important to take your time with a location or subject to see if you can milk any other strong images from the scene. It is worth remember that there is never a shortage of images you can take, only a shortage of the images that you are capable of seeing.

In the case of landscape photography, it is worth returning to the same location over and over again. It will offer up new images under different lighting and weather conditions, from different shooting positions and with different equipment.

Working a scene to the max also includes taking a great variety of shots, from the wide to the tightly cropped, verticals as well as horizontals (many people call this portrait or landscape orientation of the camera).

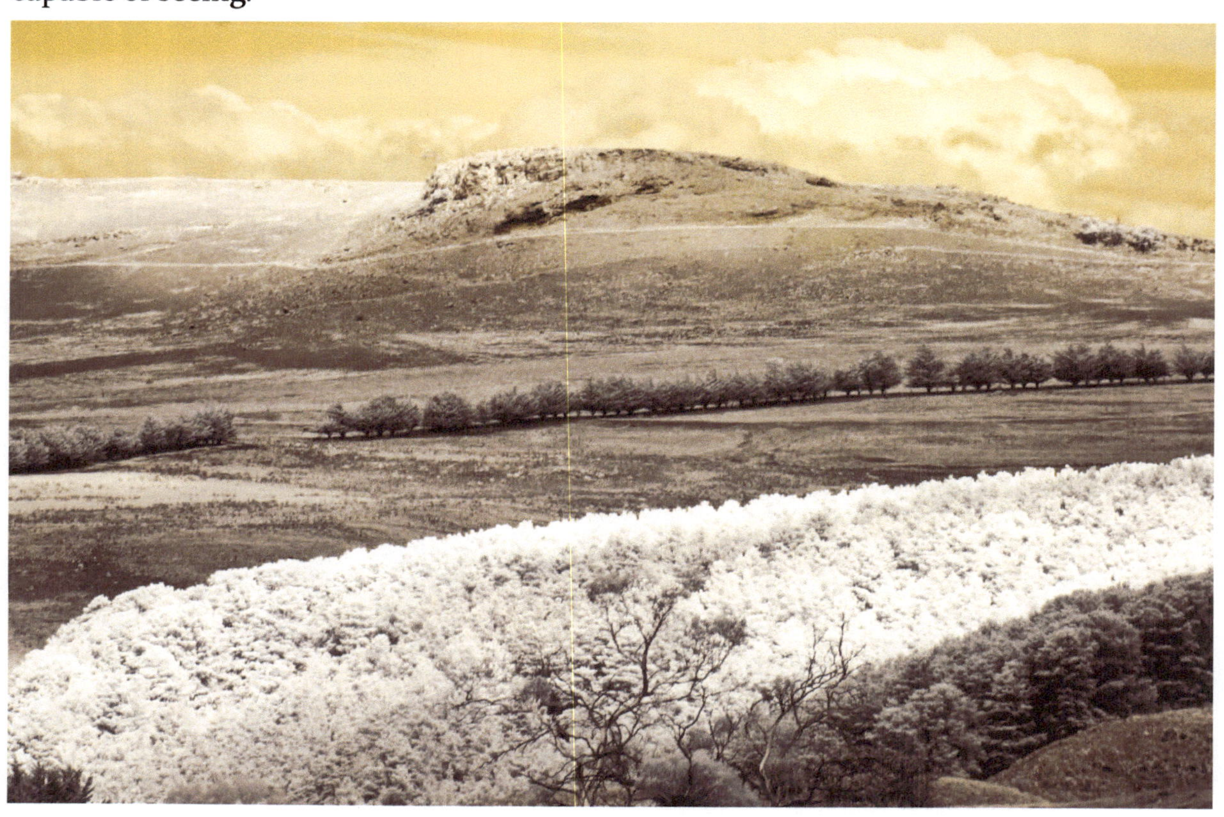

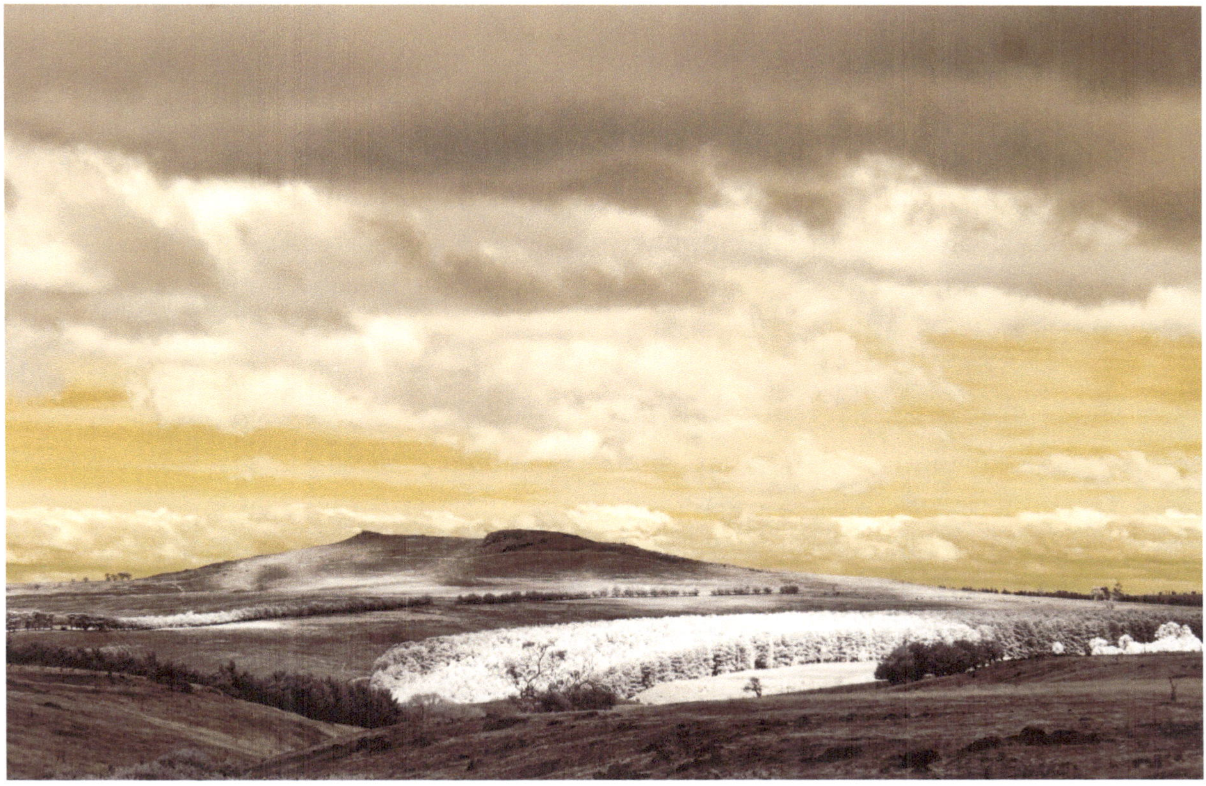

Activity

Find a subject or location and set a time limit that you will stay there and keep shooting for. Refuse to leave till the time limit is up and try to keep shooting for the whole time. Start off with a short but reasonable time limit, like 15 minutes and then gradually increase the time as you try this many times with different subjects and locations.

It is also worth gradually reducing the scope of the location or subject that you are shooting, so that in the beginning it won't be too hard to find stuff to shoot for the whole time, but, as you become more experienced with this technique, you push yourself to work harder and shoot more creatively.

Try shooting a location you know well from a different perspective or at a different time of day. I set my students the assignment of shooting their own house interior only from the floor level, making them crawl around their homes and see it, possibly for the first time, from this perspective.

Rather than time limits, you can also set yourself the assignment to shoot 100 images before you move location, or some such limit.

38. Look Carefully

Careful observation is what separates the professional and serious photographer from the snapshooter.

Focal Length Seeing

Remember that you see the world somewhat as a 50mm (on 35mm) lens does. Not quite, because we also have peripheral vision, but our main area of attention is roughly equivalent. That said, if you were out shooting with a wider choice of optics, you would benefit from working at being able to see the world as your other optics does.

At the telephoto end I sometimes carry a small pair of binoculars with me. They allow me to determine shooting possibilities more comfortably (using two eyes) than by using my telephoto lens. Using both eyes is much less tiring for extended viewing than one. In addition a compact pair of binoculars will be less tiring on the arms and may be less attention attracting, keeping the big lens away until needed. This can sometimes be very important where you want to capture people behaving naturally rather than tense or posing for the camera.

For wide-angle optics, we have the equipment, our peripheral vision. What we need to do is practice, first viewing through the lens and then looking at the scene to determine how much of our field of vision is captured at which focal lengths.

Activity

Find a location that has decent detail over a very wide field of view. Go there with your camera and all your lenses. Set the camera up and then for each lens and each focal length look at what the camera sees and then look at the scene with your own eyes. Get an idea of how that particular focal length looks with your own eyes. Practice.

Then reverse this. Pick a scene and estimate what focal length will cover the area between two strong objects. Then try the lens and see how it compares.

Don't forget to look up.

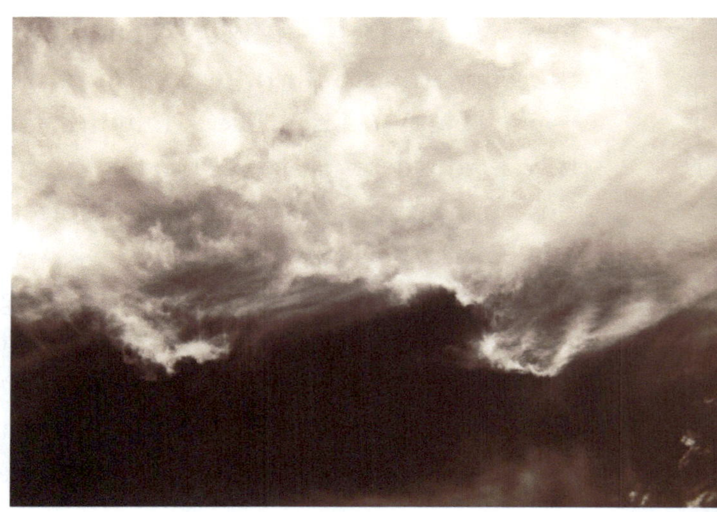

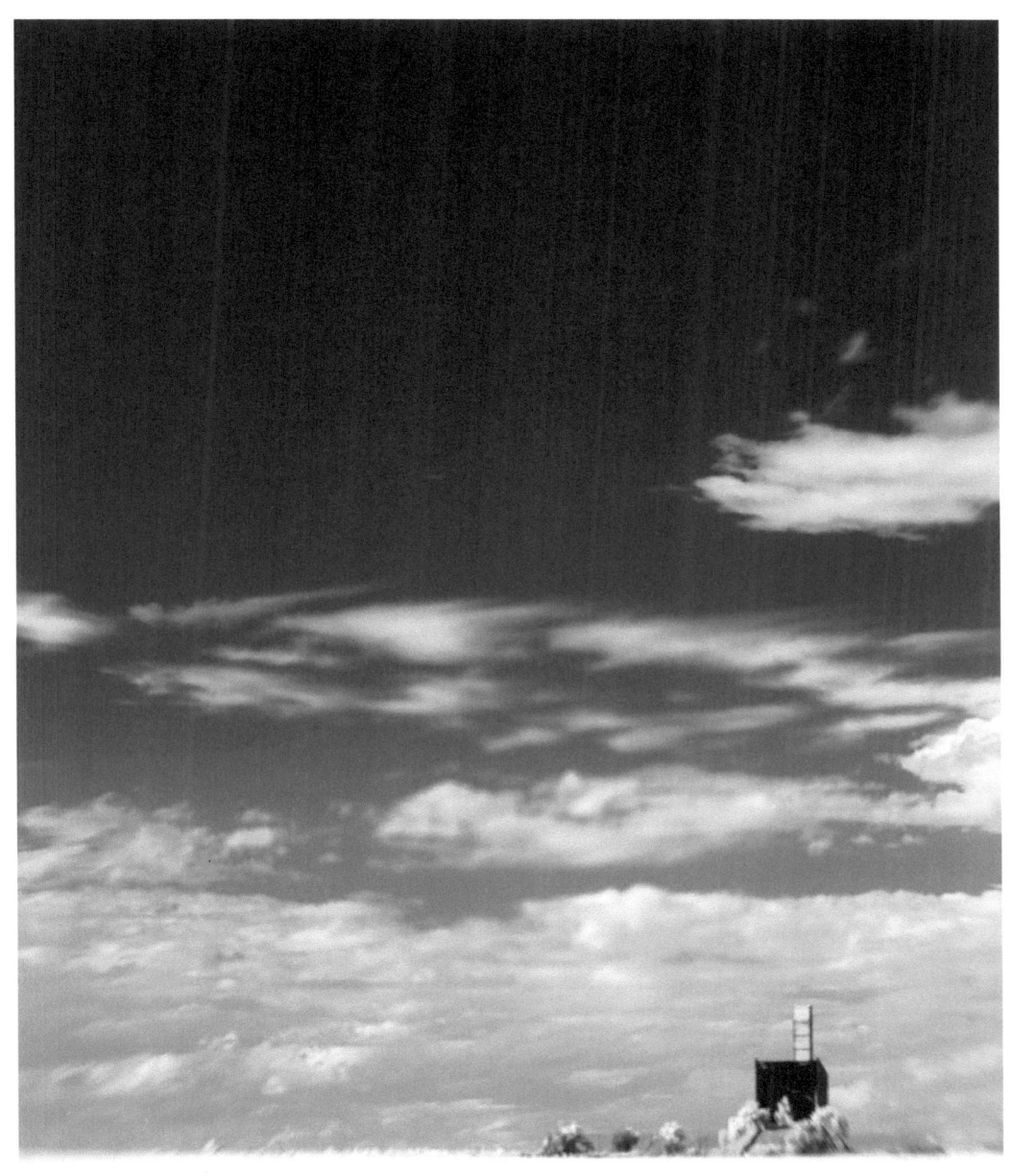

Always Look the Other Way

It is very easy when we are out doing photography to see something we want to capture and become so focused on what we are working that we fail to see something even better behind us. So it is very important to maintain what is called situational awareness. Sure, focus on what you have spotted, work it and get your shots, but be sure to have a good look around for something else. It is also worth trying to keep an awareness of spontaneous opportunities that may occur behind you. Try to keep your ears open even when your eyes are fixed on your current subject. I've seen photographers miss the most amazing opportunities because they did not hear activity behind them.

Activity

Explore your ability to maintain situational awareness at all times. In fighter pilot language, practice checking your six. In other words look behind you.

Develop your awareness skills by walking into a place you have not been before, taking a quick look around then shutting your eyes and building a picture of the space. When you think you have it, open your eyes, look around and check.

There's a favourite walkway in Melbourne connecting the Myer department store with the Melbourne Central shopping mall. The top level of this is all glass and exposed ducting which I often shoot. But turning around and looking down let me grab this shot with a Lensbaby attached on my camera.

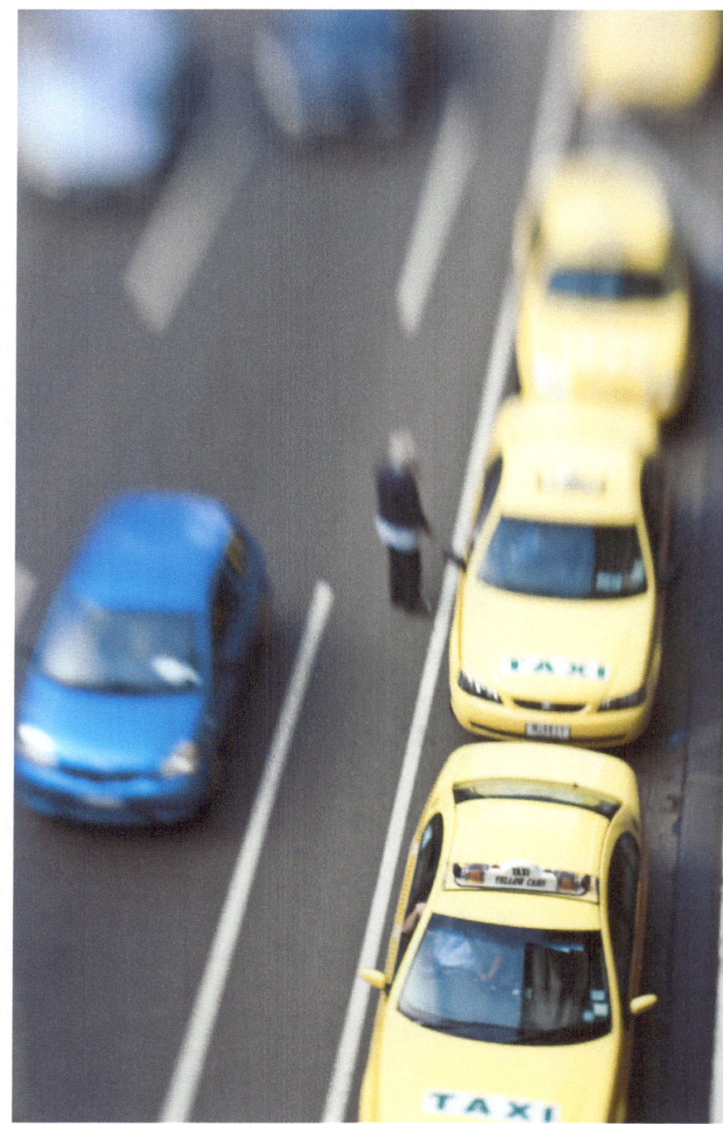

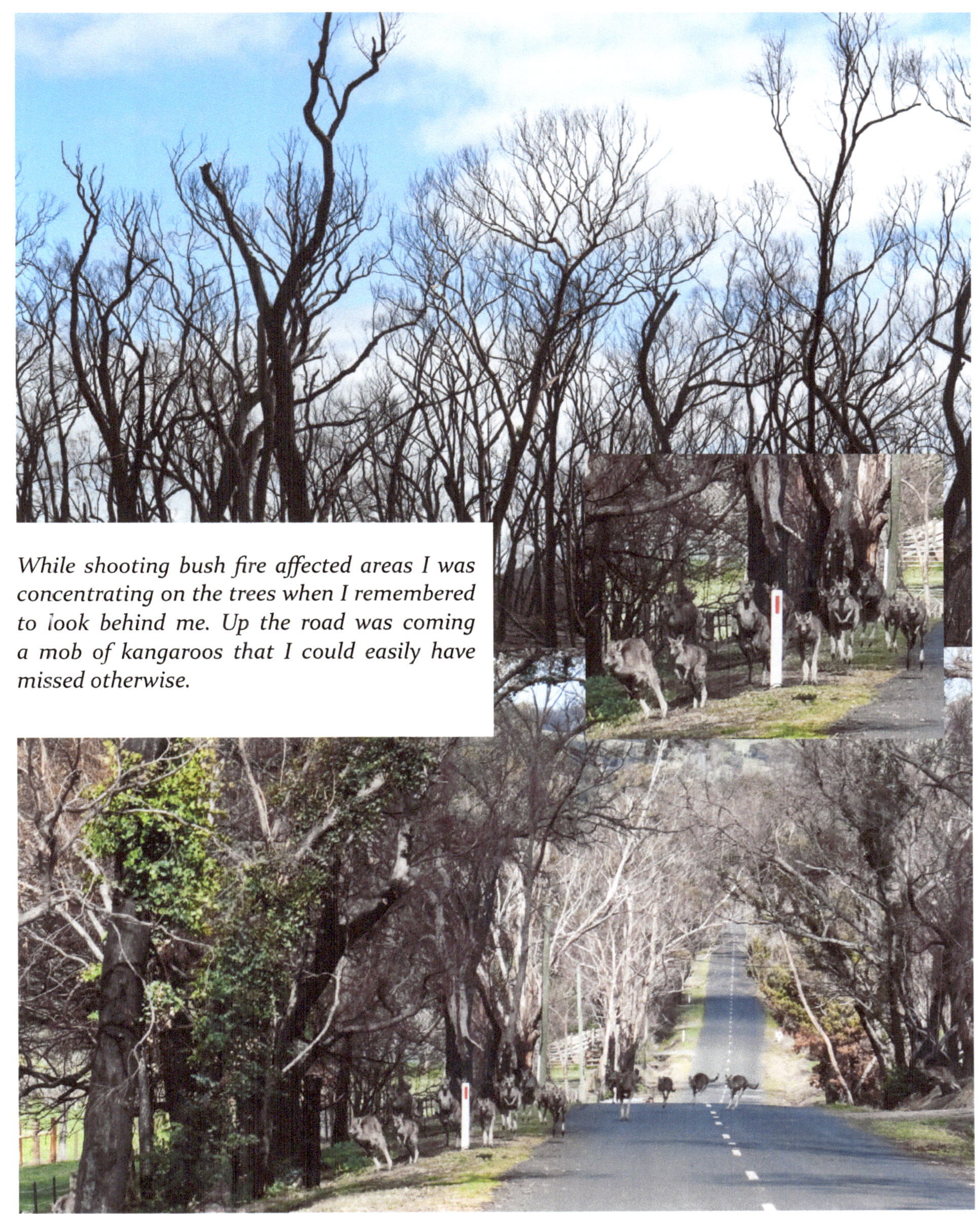

While shooting bush fire affected areas I was concentrating on the trees when I remembered to look behind me. Up the road was coming a mob of kangaroos that I could easily have missed otherwise.

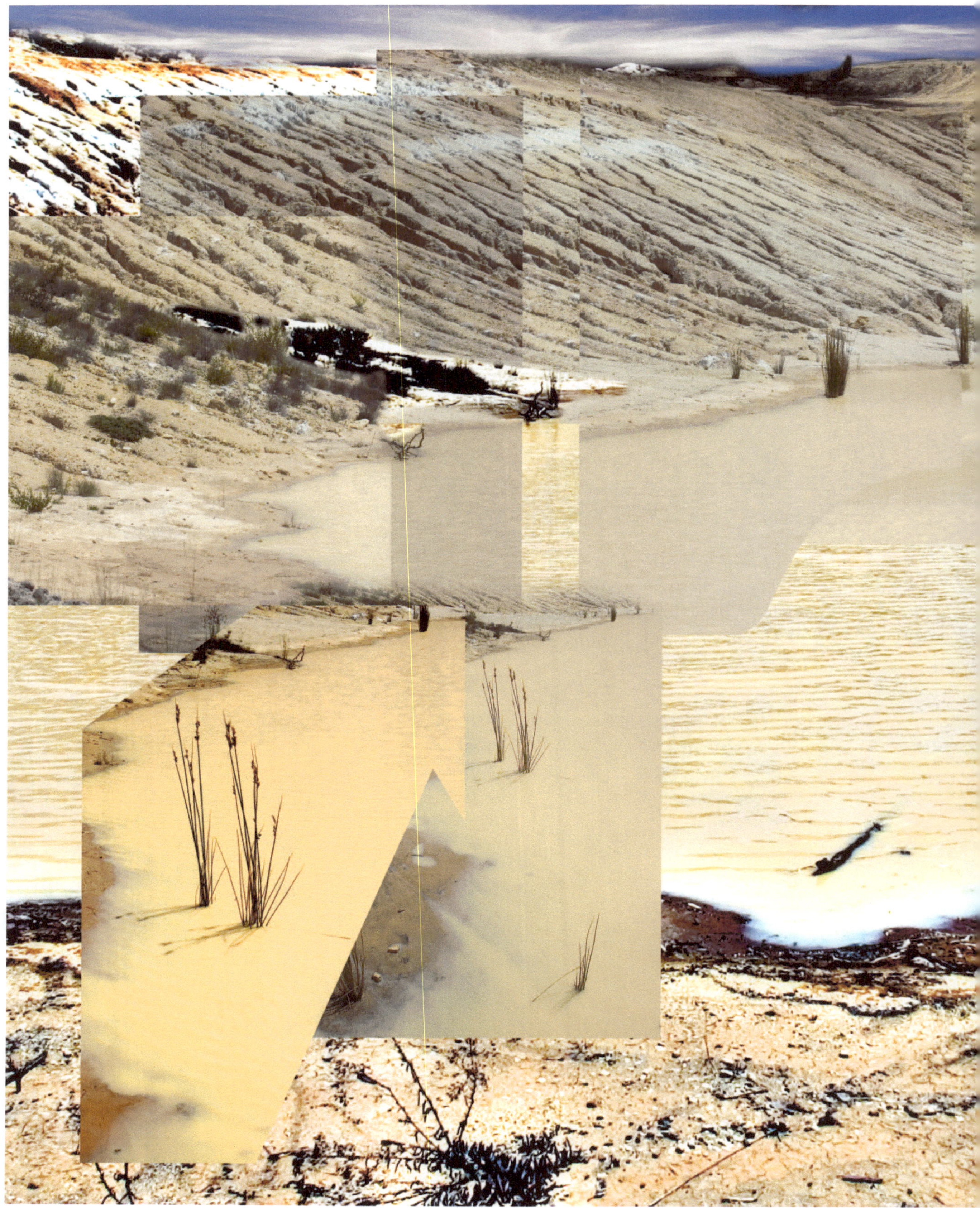

Create

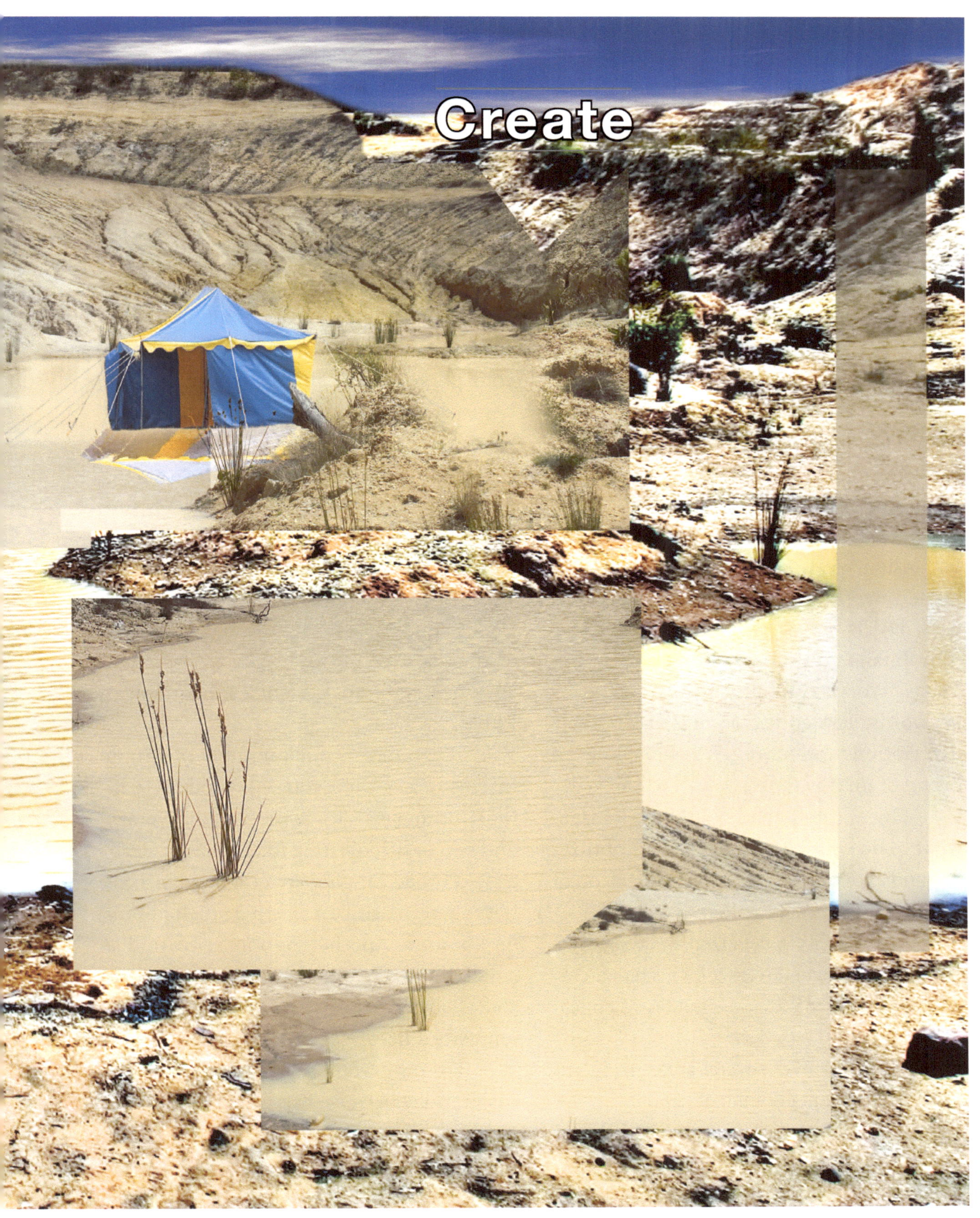

39. Your Own Library

If you have been doing your stuff right, you will have accumulated a great big library of images of all shapes and sizes, on a huge range of subjects. Now the key is to find ways of using your library.

To be able to find and use things in your library of images you have to be able to find them quickly. This requires organization and, these days, it requires software. I prefer Extensis Portfolio but other programs like Canto Cumulus, ACDsee and others will do the trick. They will catalogue huge numbers of images stored on CDs, DVDs and hard drives and retrieve thumbnails and preview versions of your images. You can organize your images by keywords, categories or tags, searchable descriptions and more. They will allow the rating of images too.

Once catalogued you can look to what to do with your images. Your options depend a lot of just what your collection of photographic image holds:

- Is it highly specialized and represents a dominant coverage of a small area?
- Is it a wide-ranging and broad collection?
- Does it cover several areas in significant but not dominant depth?

If you have a specialized and dominant collection then you can do what you want. You can approach a large stock library and do a deal. You can also set up your own stock library and build a comfortable business. Perhaps one day you sell it to one of the big players for a nice lump sum and retire. Being highly focused in your photographic interests is certainly a key to doing something like this. You need a real passion for your single subject area.

A broad ranging but unfocused library may not be the best start for your own library. However you can probably successfully place many of these images with various other stock libraries, providing the quality is great. You have a choice of the big stock libraries, like Getty, or the smaller micro-stock agencies, like iStockPhoto.

If you have a small number of strong interest areas then you will produce a library of images with some broad coverage and two or three strong focus points. Here, as in a broad ranging collection, your best bet might be with an existing stock library or libraries. Another option is to find a small group of similar photographers with shared interests and form one or more joint stock libraries.

Forming your own stock library is easier today because there are ready-made software solutions for the Internet side of the business. Like all businesses though, you need a solid plan, good research and some money behind you. It will almost certainly take longer to show a real return than you expect. Getting your images out with existing stock libraries is a low cost but lower return option that is perfect for those people who would rather shoot than run a business. Indeed you can also make use of the existing libraries while you are building up your own.

But there are other uses of your own library of images than direct stock sale. If you are a collage artist, as I am, combining many images to create a new composite, then your own library is a great help. Likewise if your business extends into areas like graphic or web design, having your own images on tap can be a real benefit. Just remember to charge for the use of your images.

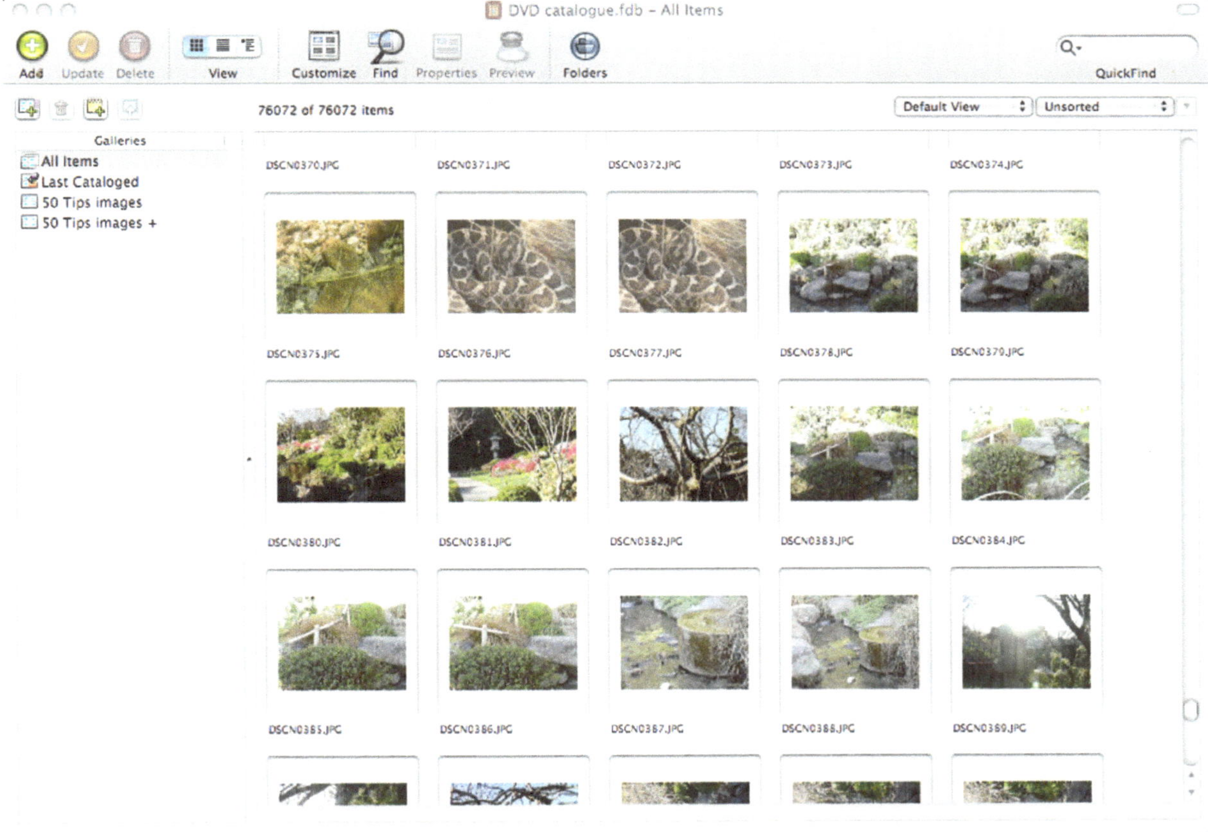

Extensis Portfolio is a great program for cataloguing your DVDs of images so it is easy to find what you want.

40. Every Image Has a Story

Summary - When it comes to selling your photography and art there is one great aid. Make sure that you have a story about or involving each image. People love a story.

It is easy for those of us who are serious about making images, whether photography or art, to forget why other people buy images. We are focused on the beauty of the image, or its symbolic meaning, the process used to create it or whatever, so we often forget to see things from the buyers' perspectives.

So why do people buy art? Well there are, of course, many reasons, perhaps as many as there are buyers. But broadly we can say that some will buy purely for their own enjoyment, some from a collector's mentality and others to enhance their surroundings.

No matter the personal motivation, most people who buy art will, in some way, share it with other people in their lives. It may be a conversation with a friend over coffee, down at the gym or while picking the kids up from school or at a dinner party. Describing images is a challenge for most people. But telling a story comes naturally to many. If the artwork has a story attached to it, it makes life much easier.

At gallery openings I have a tendency to watch the artist. I guess all photographers are voyeurs, but I find it very enlightening. Many of the artists and photographers that I see doing very well from exhibition sales know how to spin a yarn. As they chat with potential buyers they have an interesting story about every image in the show, "You know, when I shot this..." or "I have to tell you this about this image, I had a proof hanging in my studio and ...". You can see the way it changes how the potential buyer views the work. Now I am sure few are directly thinking "Wow, if I buy this I will have a great story for my next dinner party", though some will. For most, I think that it draws them into a deeper engagement with the work, adds depth and interest and increases the feeling that they just must have that image, that their life will be the lesser if they have to let it go. This same idea holds in other venues than galleries: it is applicable at art fairs and markets, online and in a portrait or wedding studio (helped here by the buyer's own stories about the images). Obviously the length of the story and how much time you have to tell it needs to be different in these varying contexts, but the idea is the same.

Selling is still selling and it is easy for artists and photographers to lose sight of this about their work. Sometimes people need just one more reason to buy. Make sure you give it to them.

My image Road to Elysium (p. 144) took six months to produce because when I came up with the idea it was not when the wheat was growing. I had to wait to get the shots I wanted up to six months.

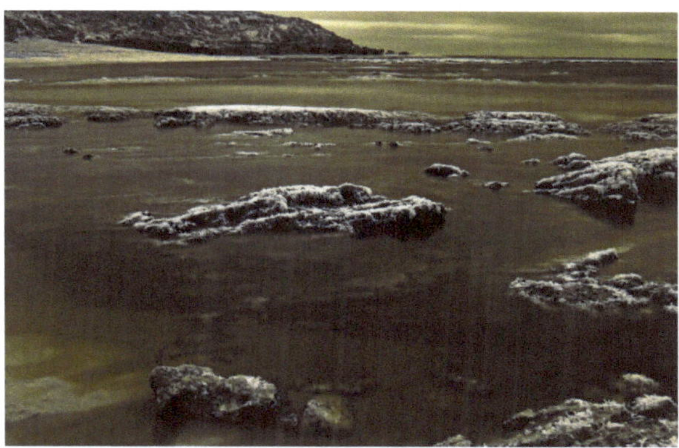

For this image the story is not only how my small torch was used to paint by light the seaweed on the rocks but how this little torch was essential to stumbling my way back over the rocks in the pitch black to find the car.

Activity

Pick a couple of images and create stories for them. The stories can be real or made up, but real ones will always work better as you will tell them better. Find a couple of people as a test. Show them these images with stories and a pair of similar images that have no story. See which ones the subjects like the most.

Implement a system to capture these image stories while they are fresh in your mind. Five years later when you decide to exhibit it you may have forgotten the funny thing that happened when you shot it. Ideally integrate it with your image cataloguing system.

You can use the meta data facility of Photoshop to add a text note to an image, use a notebook that is keyed to the image number (you do have a sensible numbering system for your images, don't you?) or add it to some other filing system.

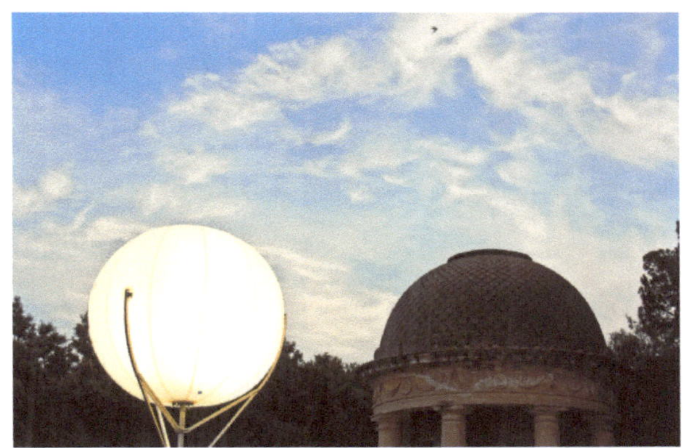

This image has a story of a magic night of alfresco dining with a group of friends in the park in Barcelona. Stories don't have to be elaborate, they just add interest.

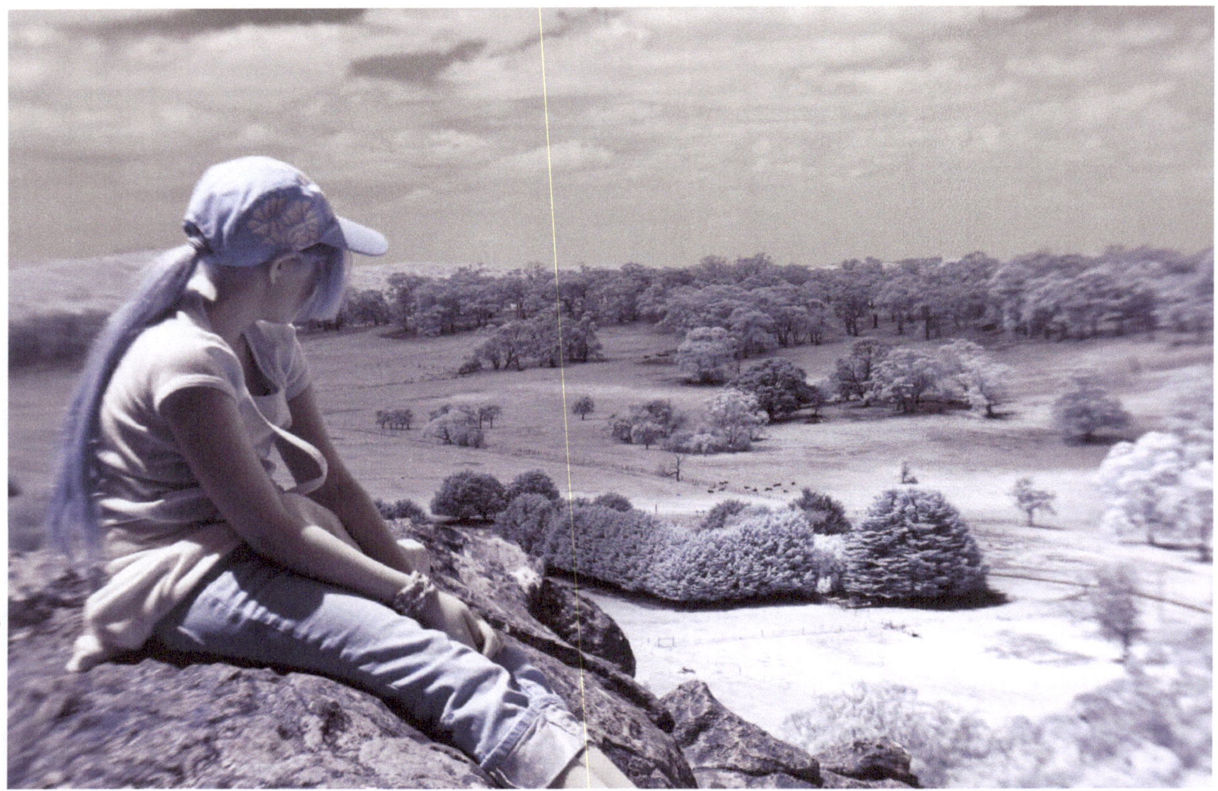

This image, and ones from the same shoot, have the story of how I have ALWAYS become lost when at Hanging Rock, a place in central Victoria made famous by the movie Picnic At Hanging Rock. Seriously, every single time I have been there I have become disoriented and lost, ending up finding my way back down by some strange path. This started with a school trip there in my early teens and has continued up to the present day with multiple trips there for photography.

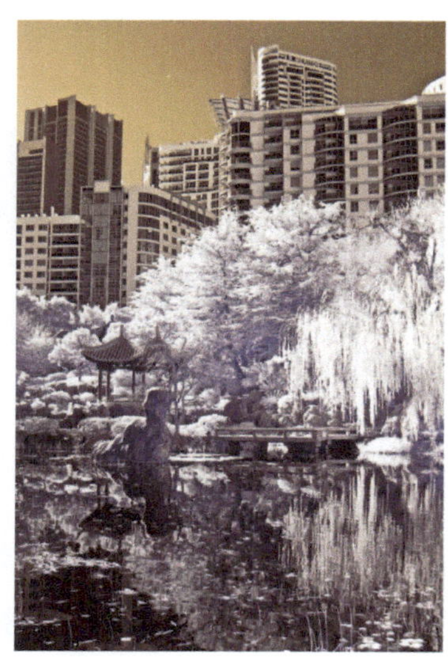

The image at left has the simple story of how this particular location, the Chinese Garden at Darling Harbour in Sydney, is a favourite place to shoot whenever I am in Sydney and how I always find its peace and serenity recharges me after a usually hectic time doing whatever has brought me up to Sydney.

The shot at right taken in the bush fire ravaged areas of Victoria comes with the story of how strangely quiet the bush was, unnaturally so in fact, with so much wildlife either dead or pushed by the fire into other areas.

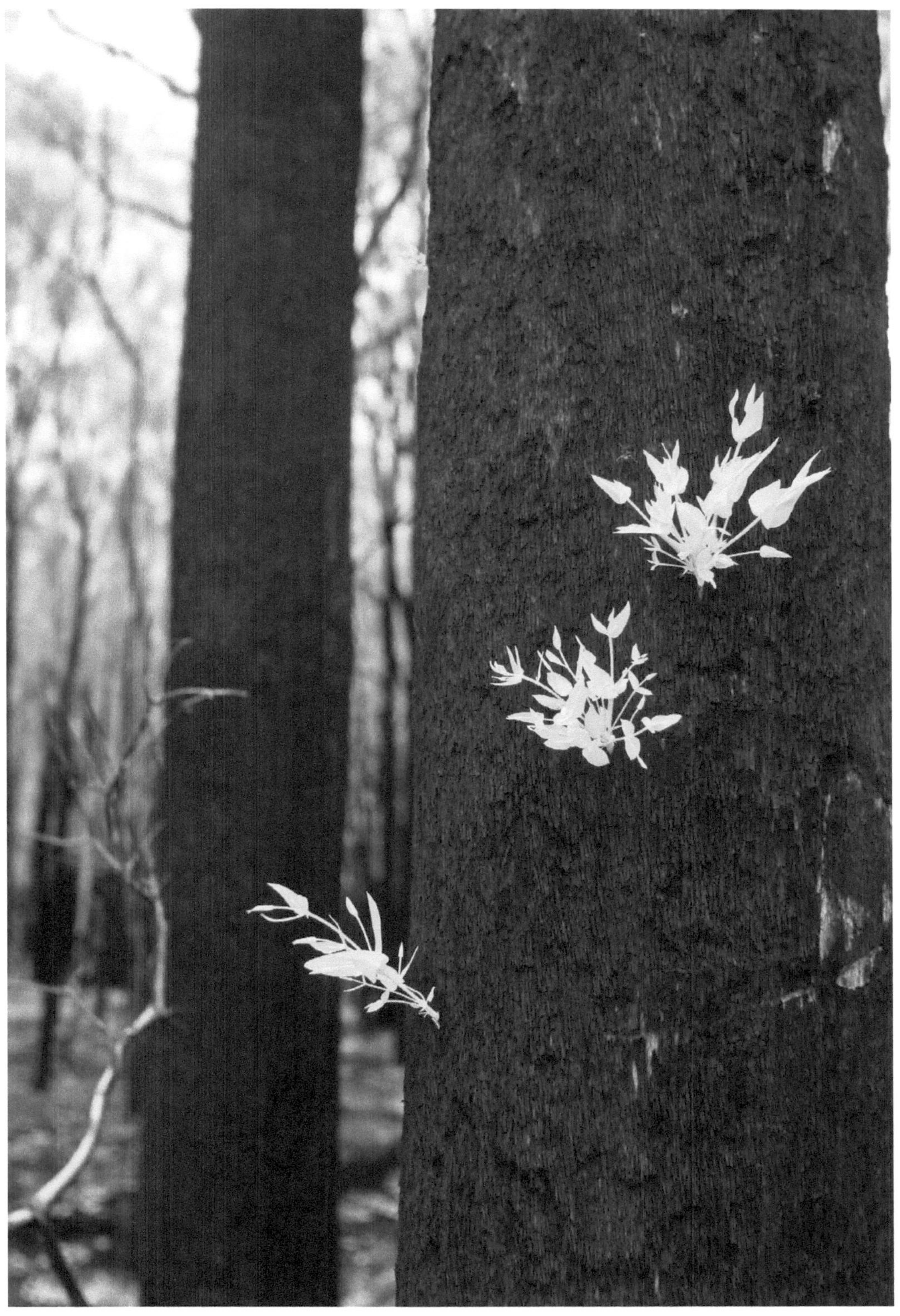

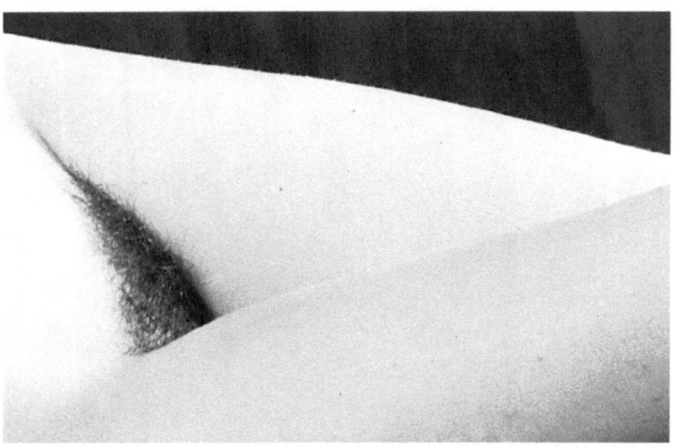

41. Strong Emotion Is Powerful

Shoot what you love and what you hate.

Anything you are ambivalent about, leave.

Emotions are powerful and two of the strongest are love and hate. When you are passionate about something your emotions will be strong. The strong emotion you have (either way, love or hate) will eventually lead you to stronger images. When we have wishy-washy feelings about a subject we risk creating wishy-washy images.

We also want our viewers to have a strong reaction to our images. Love the images is great. Hate the images with a passion is also great, because we have made a lasting impression. If you are building a reputation in your photography, effectively branding yourself, awareness of your name is important. All the people who hate Andre Serrano's 'Piss Christ' did nothing to hurt his career and in fact greatly advanced it.

Strong emotional response is your aim, both yours when coming to the subject and your viewers when they see the result of your image making.

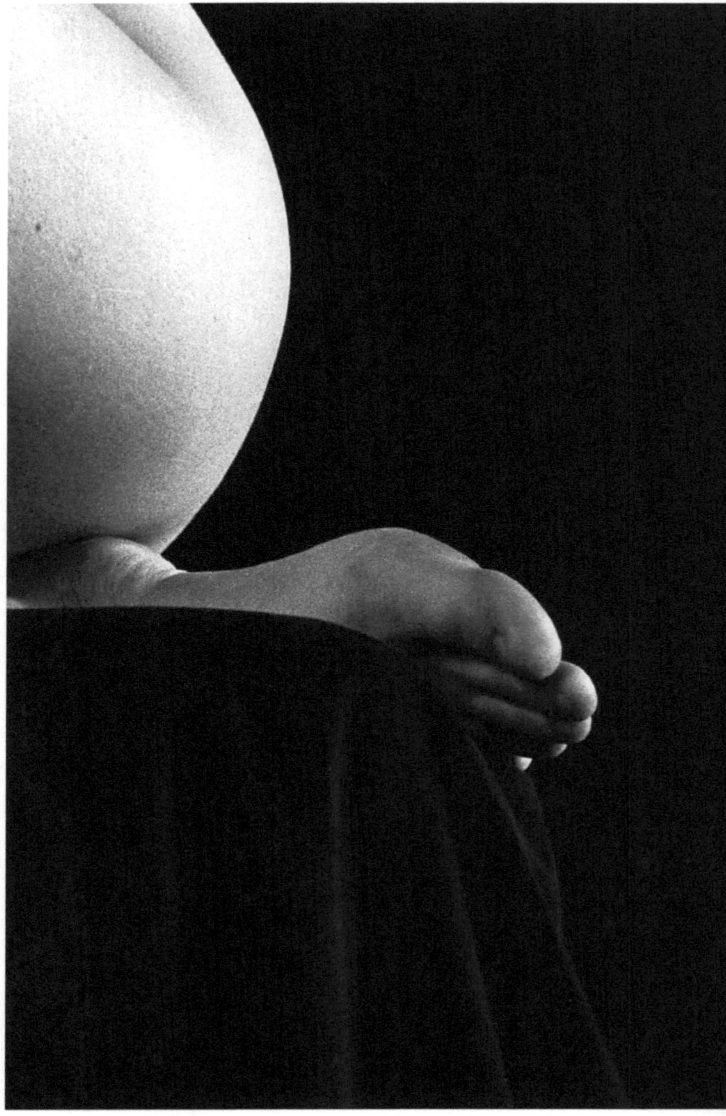

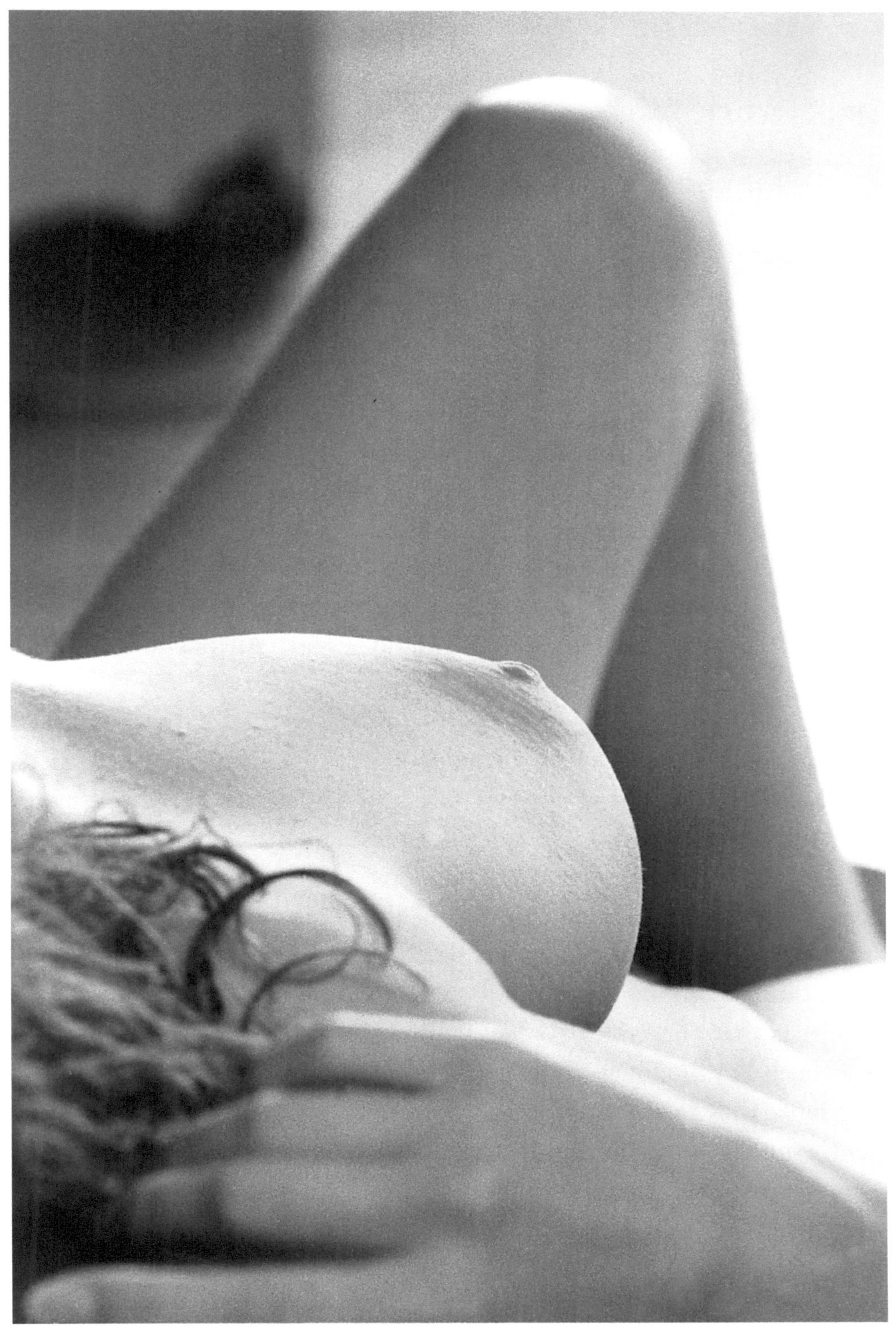

42. Work With Many Levels

When we start with photography getting our cameras to do what we want and produce a well-exposed image can be a struggle. Later though, we should be concentrating on the content.

Learning any new skill is a progression. In the beginning it is all tied up with the technique: whether it is driving or photography, we have to concentrate on getting the basic technique right. As we grow in our skills these basic techniques drop to the level of something you do automatically. This is great, because it frees you up to concentrate on new things.

One of the things that is often lacking in photography is depth. I don't mean depth of field or suggestions of dimensional depth and distance. I means layers and substance. You see many clever images, whether it is in books, advertising, from students, on lists or in exhibitions even. But the problem with many of these images is that once you have 'got it', there is little else in the image to engage you. In this sense they can be like a joke, once you get the punch line, you have a good laugh, you may tell a few people the same joke, but that is it.

Now think about what we might want from our photography, or think of what your clients might want if they choose to buy it (and here I am talking about fine art photography, rather than sport, editorial, etc). If I buy a picture to hang on my lounge room or office wall it is so I can look at it. It is so my family and visitors can look at it. It is, perhaps, so it can be a topic of discussion. I may intend to have that image on my wall for years and years. I want to be able to keep appreciating it, keep enjoying it, but also occasionally to find something new in it, discover something I hadn't seen before or for it to get me thinking in a new direction.

An obvious image tells you what it has got quickly. That's it. Thanks for coming, there's the door. It may be stunning or shocking, or amazingly clever, but that it is. It may be kitsch or clichéd, overly romantic, overly dramatic or whatever. But it may not be lastingly engaging. Boredom can set in.

An image with depth rewards study, rewards careful contemplation over years. Is like a fine port and keeps getting better over time. Can surprise and shock you years later. Such a work is stunning and a great joy. Having it on your wall becomes an ongoing dialogue between you and the work, you and the photographer.

Depth can be in many forms. It can be depth of meaning, with layers of sym-

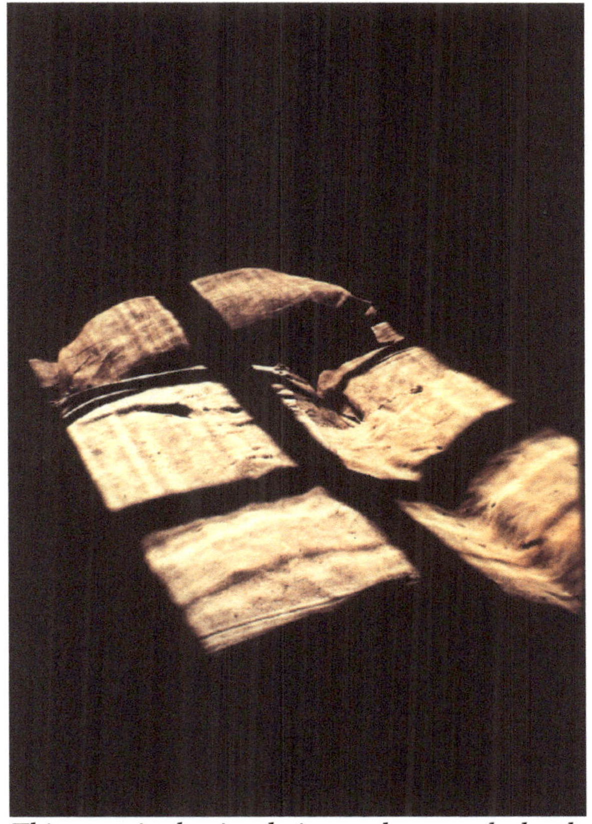
This seemingly simple image has much depth, from the meaning of the hessian sackcloth covering the bed to the inverted cross in the shadow. A photograph I took at Auschwitz.

bolism that you only access as your understanding advances. It can be layers of recognition or identification with some aspect or someone in the image that can change and develop over time. It can be the image acting as a mirror into which you can project and slowly recognize your changing self. Or it can be a crystal ball that allows you to have a number of spiritual experiences with yourself and the world. All this and much more.

This is no easy thing to achieve and there is no simple recipe or magic Photoshop plugin for it. And sometimes it is not obvious that you have done it. This is one reason I recommend printing and living with an image for sometime as you are evaluating it. But it is, I believe, always something to aspire to.

The image "Road to Elysium" on the next spread is the first image in a series of the same name. This is a constructed image, since it only ever existed in my head. Constructed from about 30 images that were shot specifically for it, the concept and layers of meaning came first, the image second. At its top level, Road to Elysium is about the choices we make in our spiritual path in life. The two doors signify the traditional Western choice: the left handed path that may be considered dark or even evil and the right handed path that is open and positive. As we dig deeper in the image we find more meaning. The strands of wheat showing over the wall above the left doorway shows that either path may lead to the same destination. The trapdoor shows that there is always a third way, though it may be less obvious. The worn track in a circle shows that there are times when we seem to just be going around in circles, and the bench illustrates that there are times to take breaks. Even the fact that the ground you must cross is gravel suggests that all is not easy going and there may be stones in your shoe along the way. The tree draws in references to Norse mythology, Buddhism and the Jewish Kabbalah. And so it goes on and on, adding lots of room for the viewer to read into the image as much or as little as they want or can do based on their life experience and knowledge.

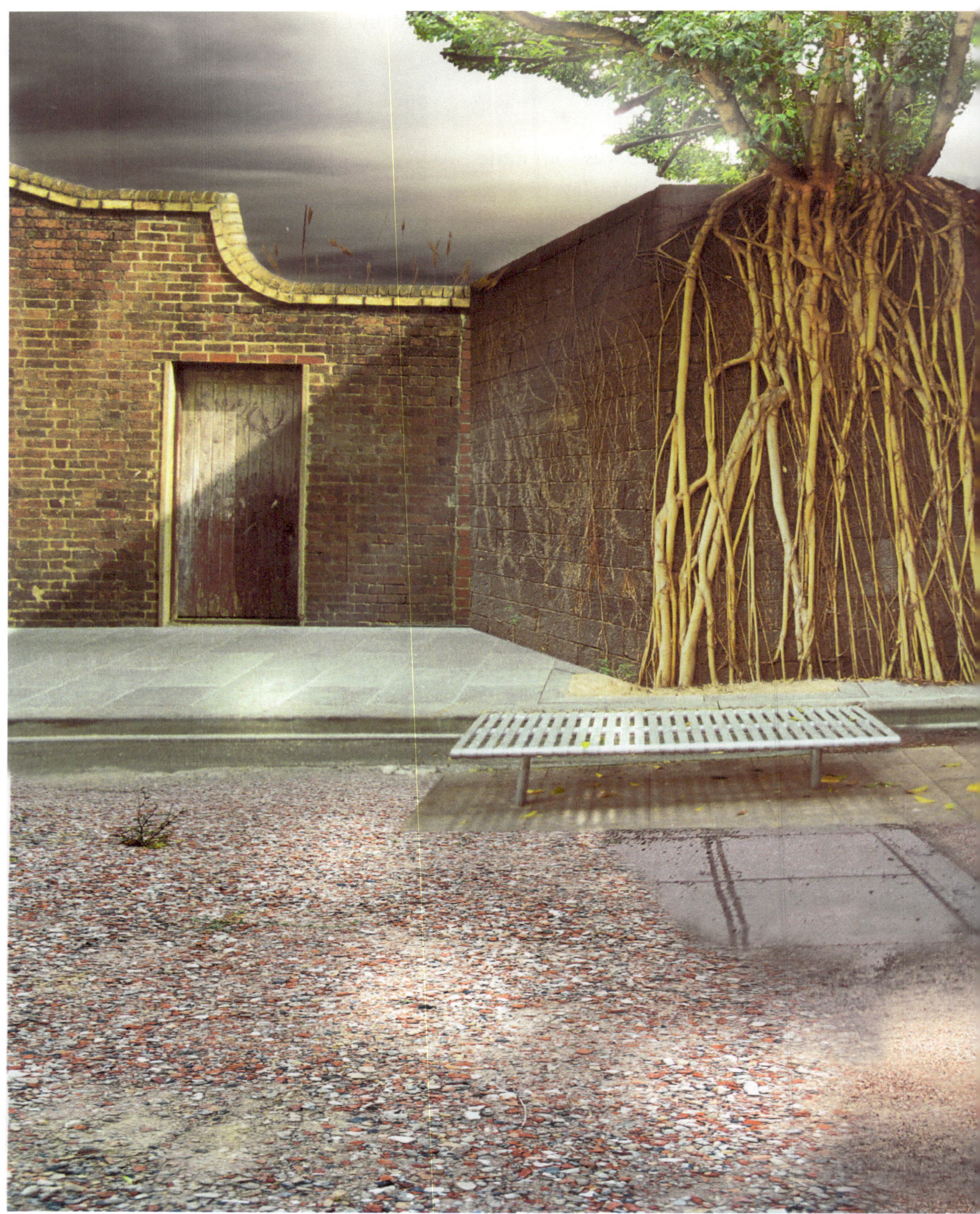

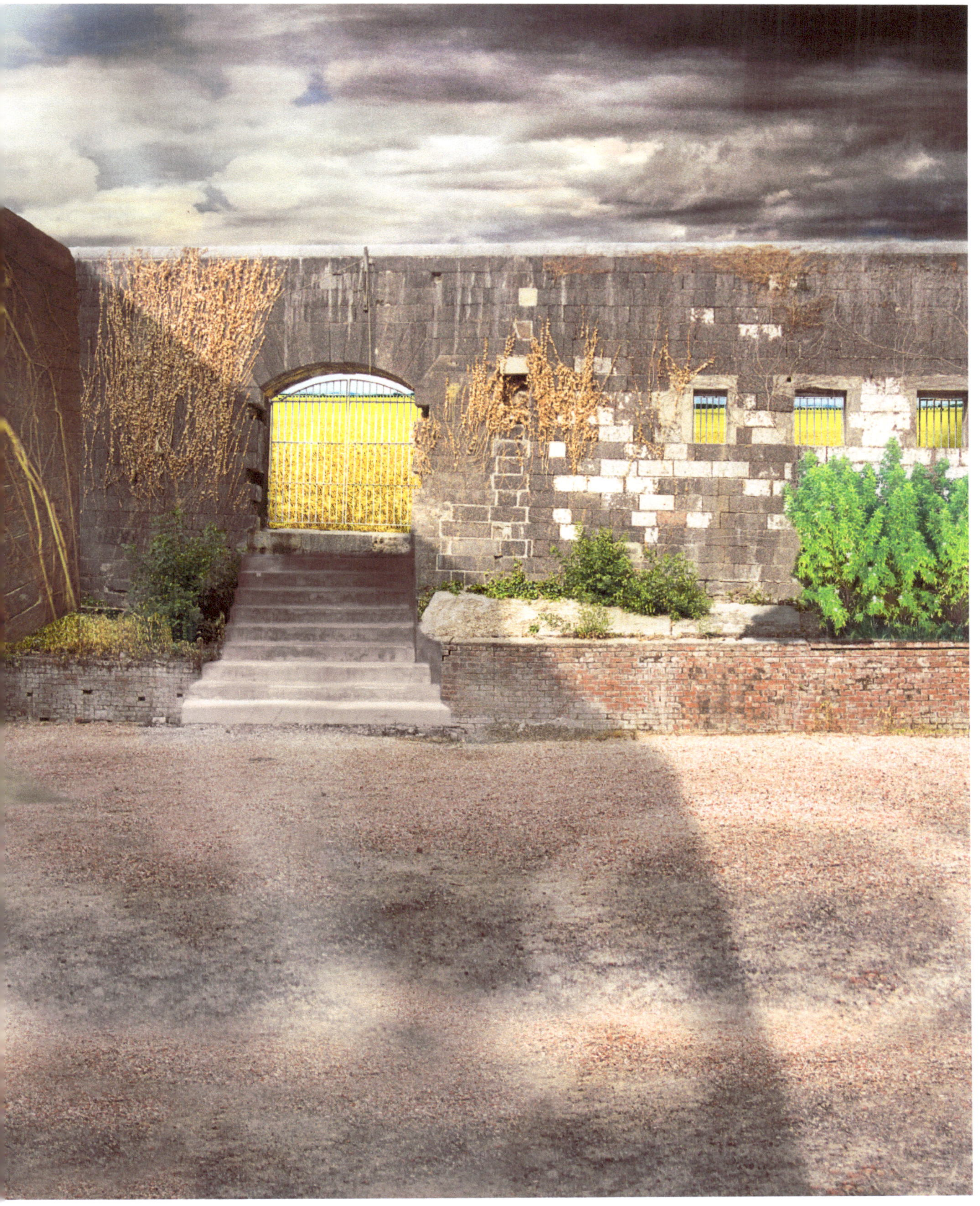

43. Construct

Photography need not only be found, it can be constructed or crafted. The collage has been a part of photography since its beginnings and offers great potential to take your work to new levels, if this direction appeals to you.

For inspiration of just what is possible, look at the work of the American photographer Jerry Uelsmann, who invented a whole way of doing amazing collage images in the darkroom and still works in this way, yet his images look Photoshopped.

The key to successful collage work is having something meaningful and deep to say. Sadly, you see a lot of digital collage work that is shallow and superficial, even if well executed. It does tend to give the whole domain of collage a bad reputation. in some circles.

When the collage has something meaningful to say, has depth and complexity (of meaning, not of image content) and is striking to look at, collage is a perfectly valid way for a photographer to work and can be a great way to take the work to new levels.

The trick is finding this meaning yourself. Now this can be triggered through play: taking some images into Photoshop and playing around with them until something emerges. This can be similar to the way a sculptor engages with a block of stone until the statue within emerges. But once you identify you are onto something then one needs to step back and ask yourself 'ok, I'm onto something, now how can I exploit this with meaning and depth'. An alternative approach is to plan the whole images out before you even start. I believe that something to aspire to with any image, whether a painting, photograph or collage, is a not obvious complexity of possible interpretation. Being not obvious is important so that people are puzzled and intrigued, so wanting to engage further with the work. Complexity of possible interpretation is important so that the viewer can connect personally with the work, finding not only some of what the image may have meant to the creator, but also their own meaning, understanding and enlightenment that might be a totally unique and personal meaning, but a meaning none the less.

Constructed imagery can be achieved in many ways, from long exposures and multiple exposures to double mounting slides, masking and multiple printing in the darkroom to layers and blending modes in Photoshop. It does not matter how it is done, so long as the result achieves what you want.

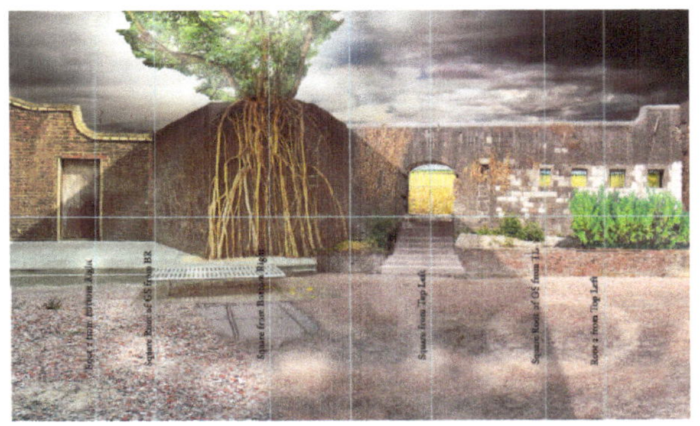

Road to Elysium, shown and discussed in the previous section, was constructed on a structure calculated using the Golden Ratio to add another layer of meaning to the image. A blank canvas was created in Photoshop of appropriate size and proportions, and guides were carefully positioned. The images were shot and opened up in Photoshop and then dragged into layers. Layer masks and adjustment layers were used to allow fine control and an accurate blending to occur.

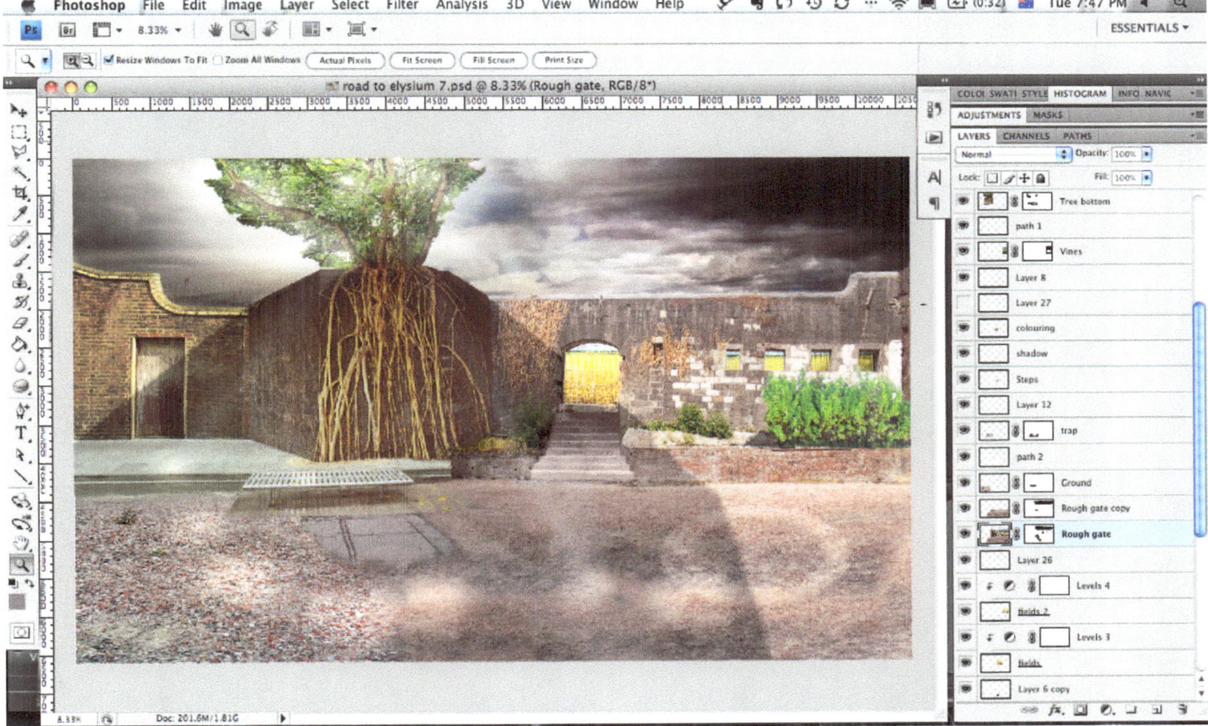

The image on the next spread, 'Introspection', is also from the Road to Elysium series. This time we explore Eastern ideas of quiet contemplation, meditation and inner change. The image makes reference to ideas in Buddhism, Confucianism and Shinto. A fractured rather than continuous blend was chosen for this image to show that many of these traditions have arrived at similar approaches from completely different origins, yet the uniform colour space of the image along with the common element of bamboo shows that despite unique origins there is a common feeling to many of these Eastern approaches.

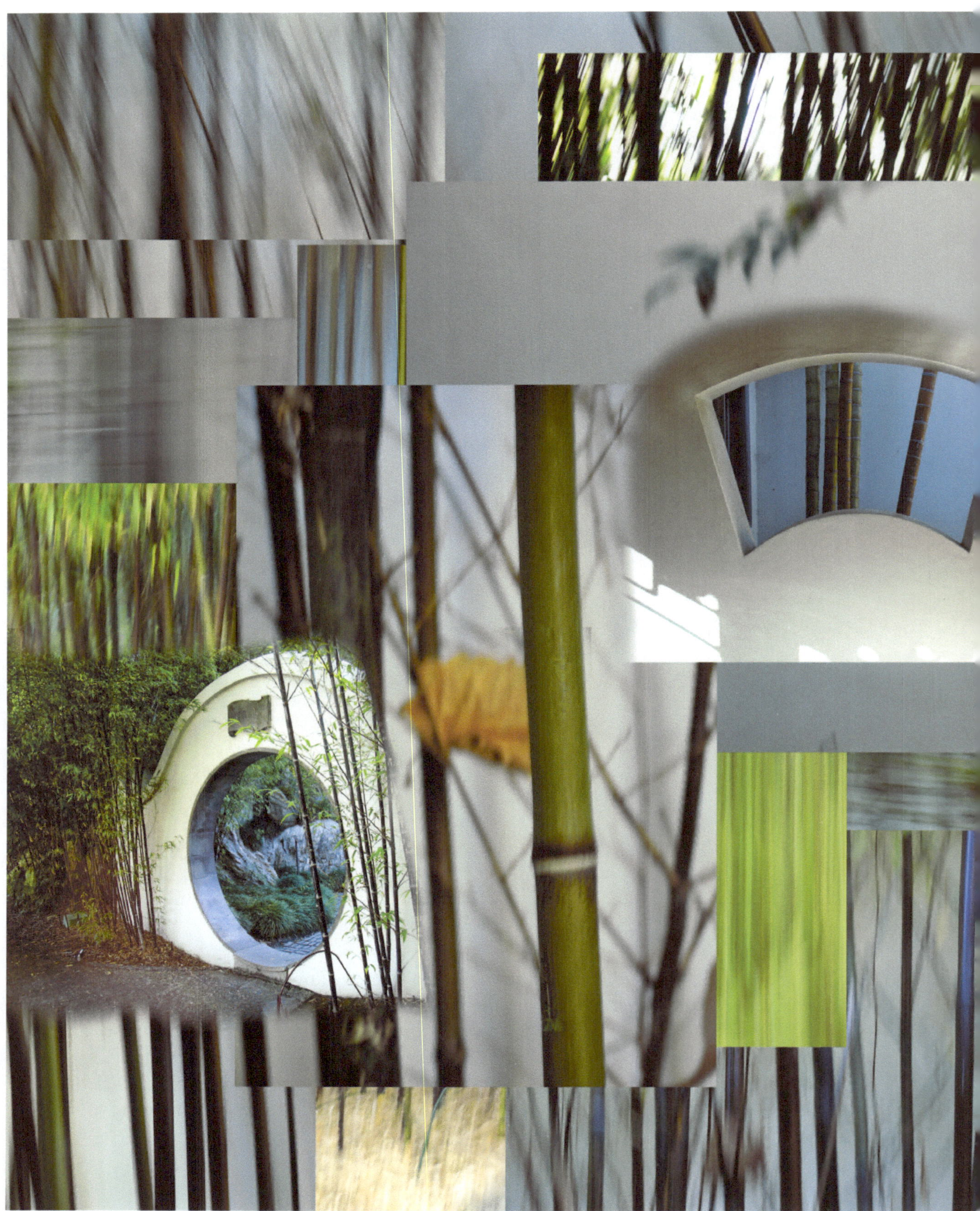

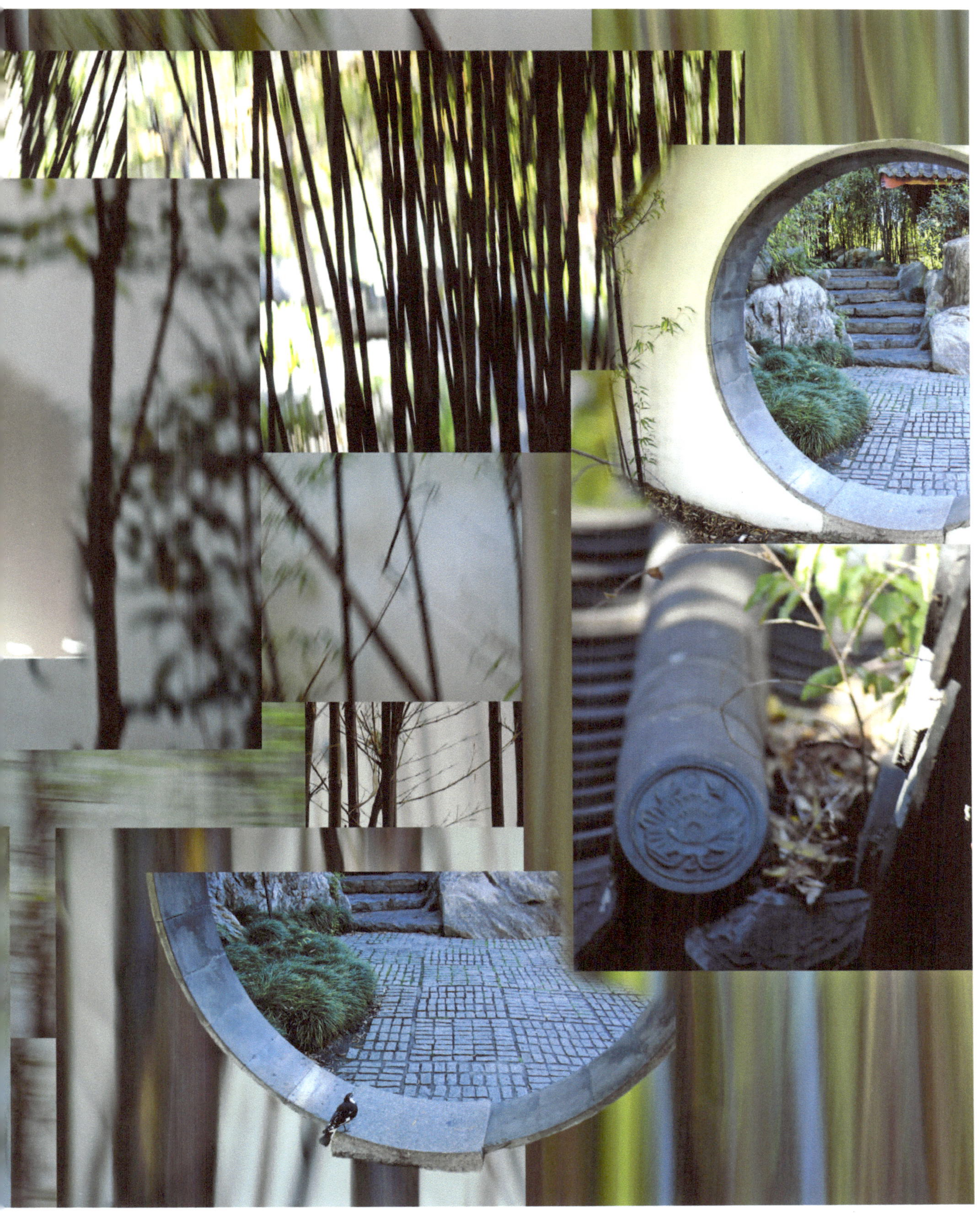

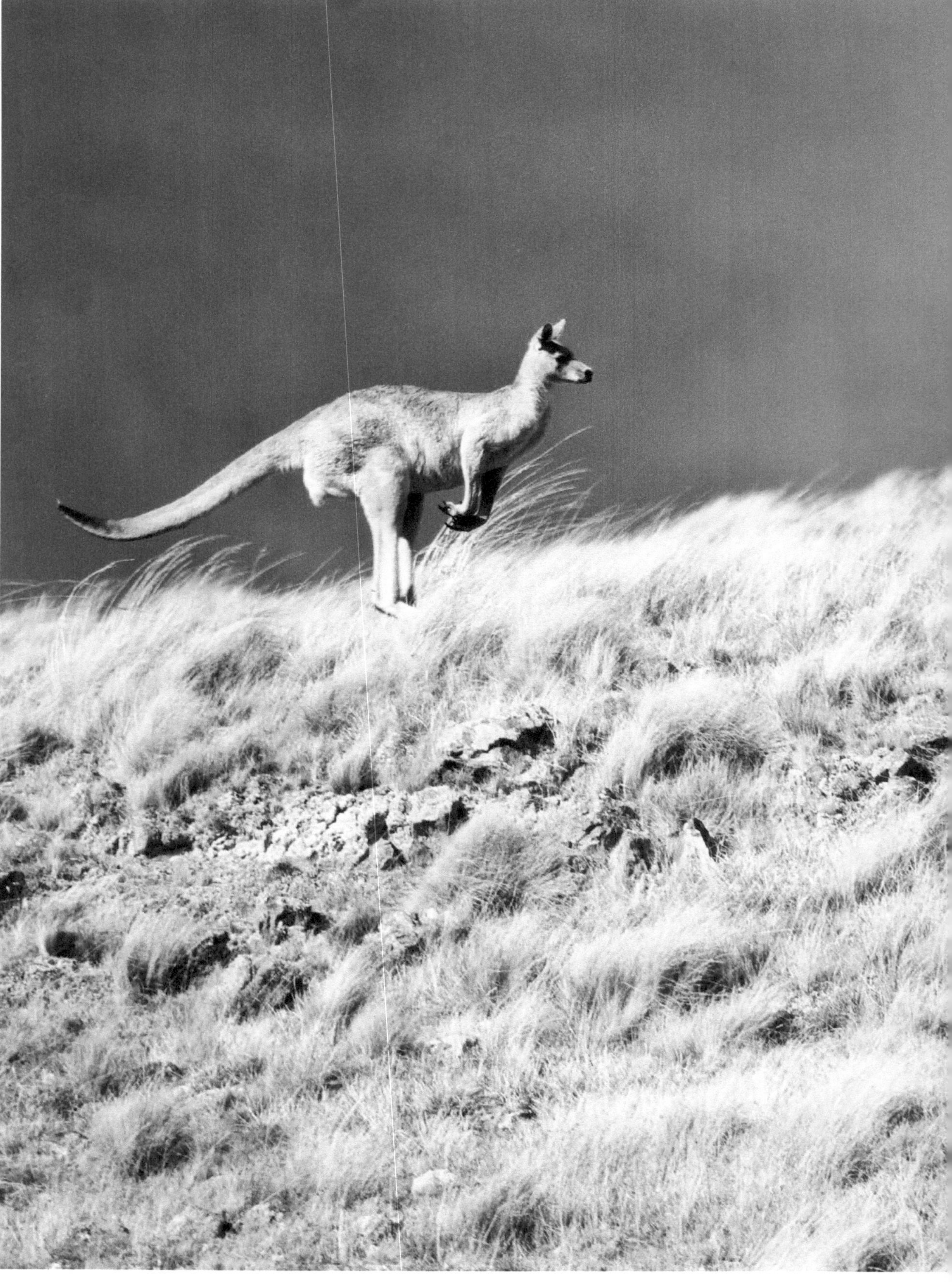

Make It Personal

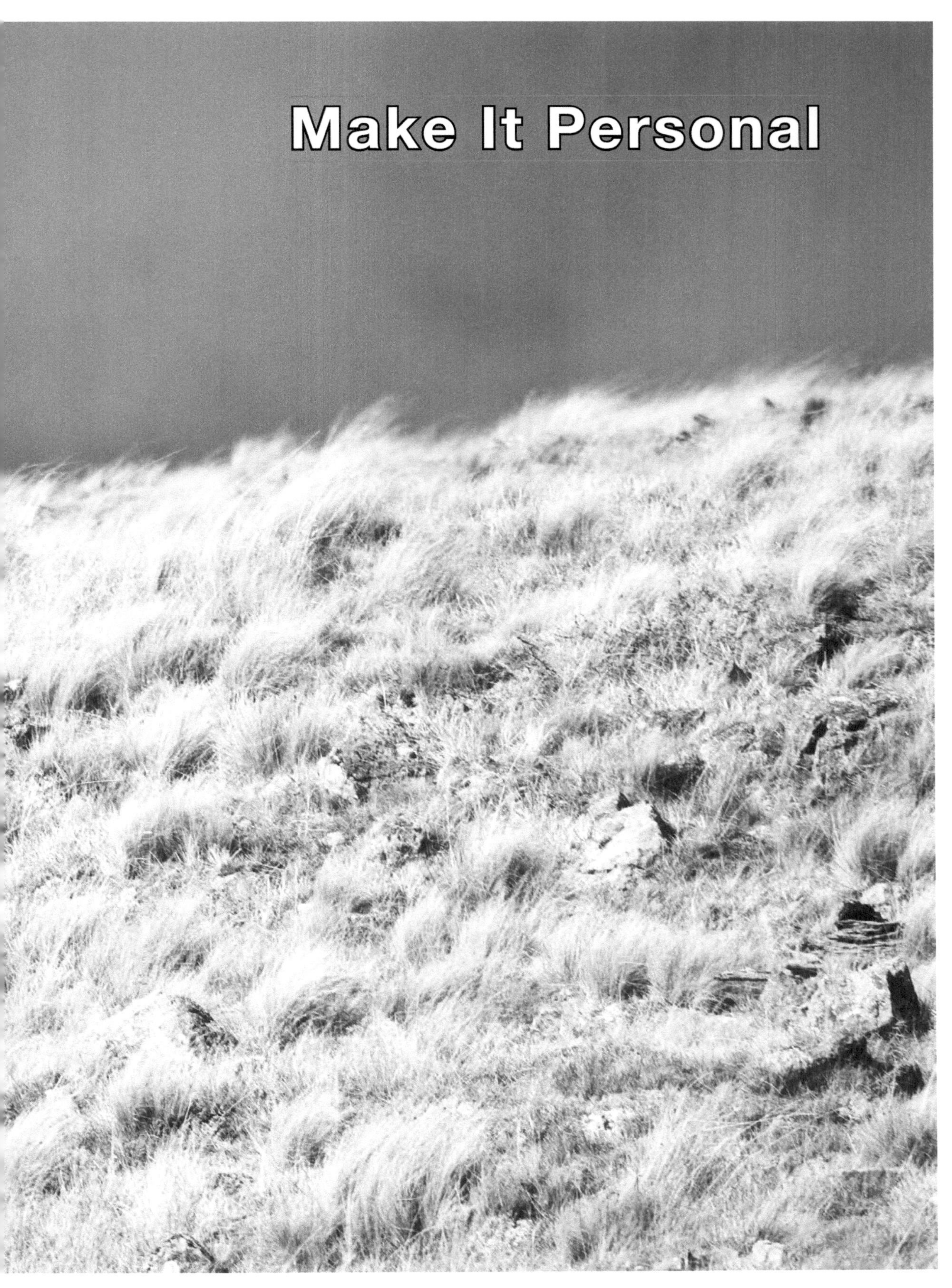

44. Seek Out Peers

While there is great value in the idea of the artist or photographer working away in blissful isolation, there is also a lot of value in learning from others.

One school of thought is that if you work in isolation that you will be free to create your own, completely personal and original voice as an artist or photographer. Now while there is some value in this line of thought, there are also major issues. Art and photography are an outcome of our social nature and as such can benefit from interaction. Likewise how will you know if your work is original if you do not have a good look at what is already out there. There is also so much to learn, doing so in isolation can be, for most people, less than ideal.

So if you are going to interact with others then how, why and where do you do it?

The opinion of family and friends about your work is good and valuable personally, but are often worthless from the perspective of making your work better. Family and friends will usually not be brutally honest about your work and often do not have the visual experience to provide solid, critical advice. What you do want is the opinion of other people experienced in your form of art or photography, and preferably more experienced. Seek them out, join groups or create them. Now you must use careful judgment, as there are lots of people who sound convincing but, in fact, will lead you astray.

Clubs and groups of all sorts have experienced a decline as people's lives have gotten busier, but they are still worthwhile. Face to face discussions can't be beat in many ways. Plus they provide the opportunity to see real prints, which is invaluable. The shared experience of doing photography or art together gives you the opportunity to observe different working methods and approaches, which can be key to your development. These positives must be balanced with the negatives of groups, such as requiring a time commitment, travel to and fro, plus the inevitable politics and personality issues.

The Internet and things like discussion groups and forums, bring the club into your own home. There are groups for all sorts of specific interests, from users of a particular camera model to people who shoot through a microscope. Now there are problems with online groups, but they can be worked around. You don't have the immediacy of looking at a physical print, but this can be solved with a portfolio circle that sends physical prints between members. Discussions can become quite heated because you can't read the body language online and people tend to be more abrupt online. You can also come across cultural differences that can get in the way, because the online community is really global, even between different English-language speaking countries. And you also get people with the 'big fish in a small pond' syndrome, which think they know much more than they do. But the benefits are that you can meet some wonderful people online who live too far away for you to ever meet them in the flesh and keep the dialogue going over a long time. Plus in the case of typed messages, you have a history of the discussion you can look back to, something I find invaluable. Online groups also usually have the benefit of not costing anything to join, making it zero risk to try.

A specific word about portfolio circles. In these at set of prints are circulated around the members of the group for comment. When you work online for too long you start to forget just how low-resolution email and website images are, and how limited in tonal range and colour. Seeing prints is a key to getting better as a photographer or artist. Now there is some cost involved in posting the prints around, but it is not huge and is more than offset by the great benefit that comes form handling real prints. I highly recommend looking into one.

When you look at the biographies of great people of the past they usually entered into lengthy and prolonged written communication with others of like mind. They were great correspondents, in the older use of this word. The online world is probably the modern day equivalent of this. The secret is in finding the right people. There are so many forums to choose from. The big places are Yahoo and Google, but there are also great forums run by the online magazine sites and many smaller, more focused, private forums. It is also very easy to start your own, although building them up can be tough. Online groups, like all such groups, virtual or physical, want people to participate. It is important to realize that everyone can learn from everyone else and your experience is as valid as others. So when you join a group, get involved in the discussions that interest you and do not let the loud mouthed ones put you off from contributing. What you want to say is as valid (and probably more sensible) than theirs.

One thing to watch out for is the time consuming nature of groups. They can soak up as much time as you want to give and are often used as a subconscious means of avoiding having to actually create work. So you need to balance your commitment with groups with your commitment to practicing your own art. But they are a fantastic way to learn and grow.

Activity

Look into whether there are any groups that meet within reasonable distance of you with similar interests. If so, make it a point to join. Give it a reasonable time, say six months, before you decide whether it is for you. Many people leave too soon.

If you can't find a suitable group, start one. Meet in a coffee shop, set a time and place for the first one and get local camera shops, clubs, community organisations and such to put up a notice or to include it in their newsletter.

Look online at one of your favourite web sites or groups.yahoo.com to see if there is a group that covers your interests. If you can, read the previous message traffic to get a feel for the group. Then join. Introduce yourself and get involved.

After some experience, a more interesting group may present themselves. There are some groups that are invite only and who look for suitable members in the public forums. There are also portfolio circles that send physical prints around. Try them.

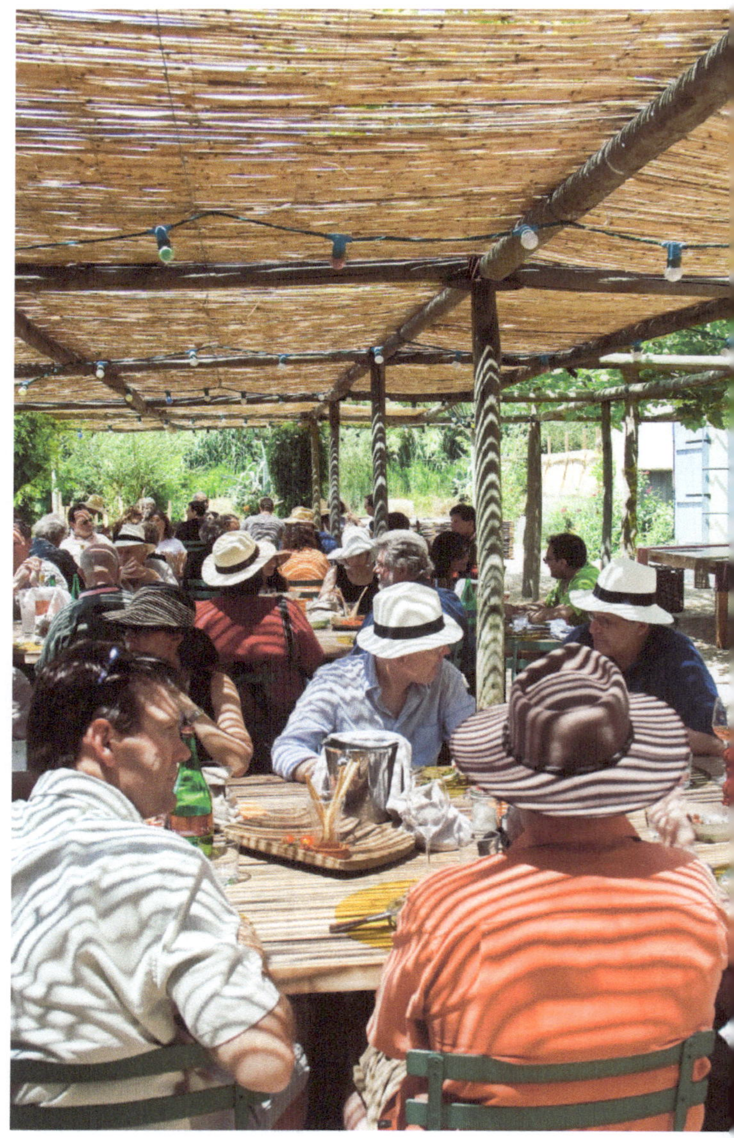

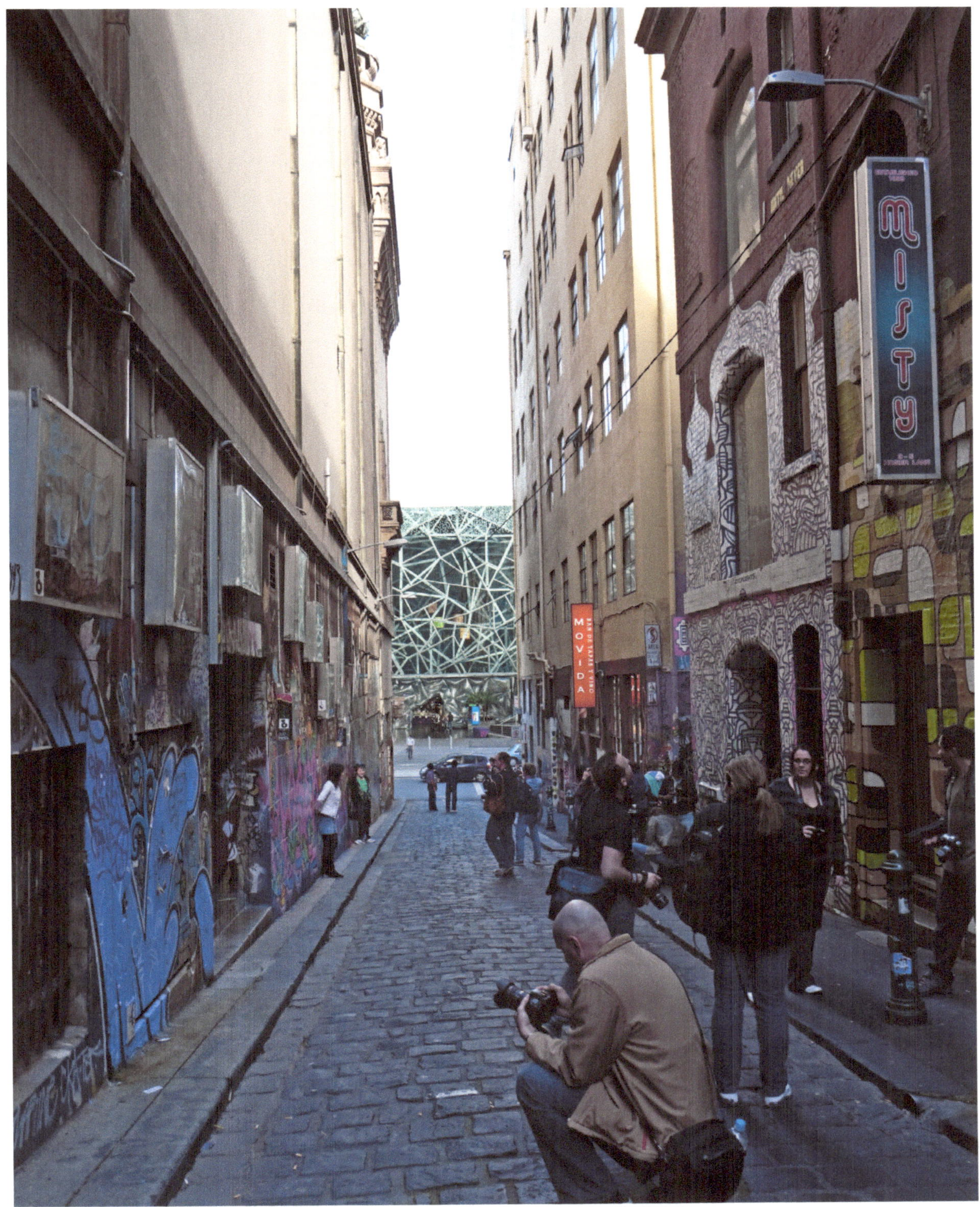
MISTY
MOVIDA

45. Trust Yourself

Too often we surrender our authority to others. Very often it turns out that the people we have surrendered to are completely inappropriate. Learn from this and don't be so surrendering in the first place. Especially in the visual arts, there is no such thing as right and wrong. The people who tell you that there are will usually be the ones you should listen to least. Frankly, I call this the camera club syndrome. It is not exclusive to them, and there are good camera clubs, but sadly I see it there all too often. There will be one or two loud, dominant people, who are often described as the camera club's pro photographer or who stand willing to always present an opinion. They dominate conversations at the club and use the words should, must and can't a lot, usually in conversations with the least experienced members of the club. These people are almost always wrong, but it is hard to see if you don't know more than them. And too frequently these people act as a break on the development of the members of the club.

There is a difference between self-trust and arrogance and you would be wise to watch yourself for signs of the latter. At the same time you need confidence to push your work out there into the world in exhibitions and competitions. Like all things, balance is required.

The thing about successful people in any area is not that they make fewer mistakes, in fact they may make far more. If you are scared of failure to the extent of not doing something then all you have done is made sure you will never find out. Sometimes this is a psychological trick to avoid the risk of failure and having our dreams deflated. But all success is obtained through taking a risk. Successful people take lots of risks, though well considered ones generally. Where they differ is how they react when they fall. A successful person picks themselves up, looks at what they may have done wrong, learns the lessons and does NOT lose faith in themselves. Un (or under) successful people beat themselves up over failures and, in the process, sow the seeds to future failures by nibbling away at their confidence. Many of us remember all our failures but are hard pushed to point out the many successes we have had. Sometimes this is the consequence of bad parenting that taught us that failures were more important than successes. Sometimes it was school or partners later in life. The truth is all of us have had far more successes than failures; it is just that we may not value them as much.

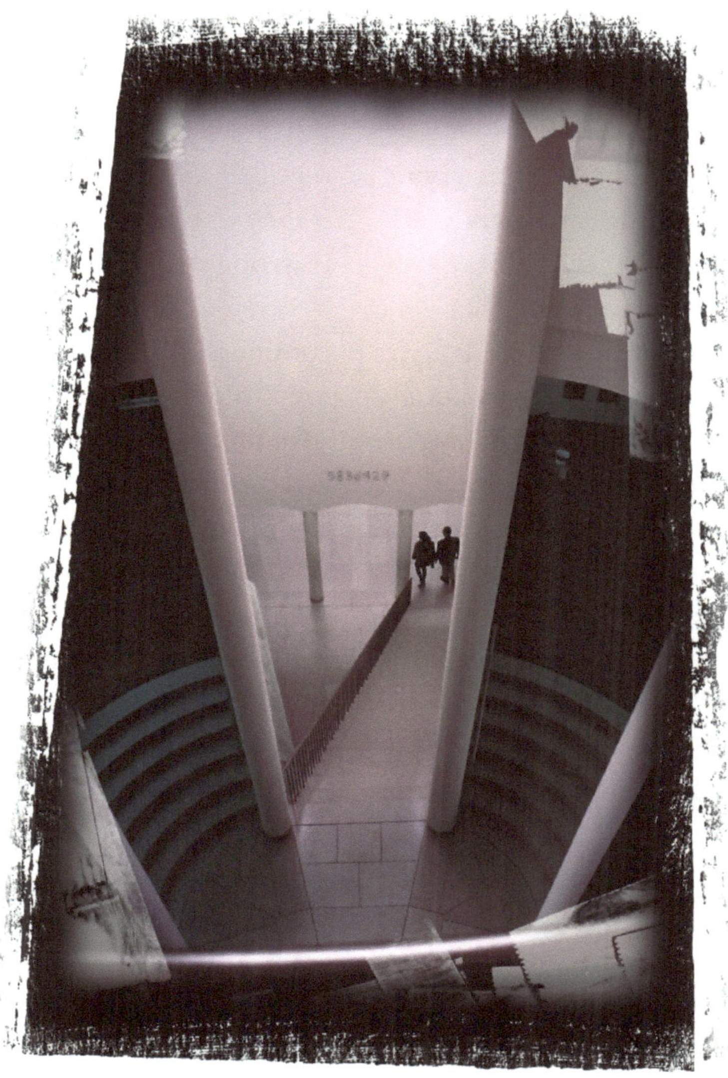

Activity

Think back in your life to the time of your first, big failure (at least to you). Write down at least ten successes that also happened in your life around this same time and don't leave the table till you have them. They can be anything, just something that you did well in some way.

Now do the same with whatever you consider to be the biggest mistake in your life.

Now write down the ten biggest successes you have had in your life.

46. Produce for Yourself

Do not fall into the trap of trying to produce what the judges in a competition or the market might want. Stay true to yourself and produce work that you love. The rest will follow if you are true to yourself and produce work of great quality. Now of course it is that last that is the issue. It is very easy to become deluded that we are producing amazing work when in fact it is very poor. Now that is the dilemma. How do we work out if we are doing really great work or not, especially if people do not understand it? This is where knowledge becomes important, as well as self-knowing and trust, and some of the rules mentioned above.

Remember that the people who manage to really advance an art form are usually not appreciated at the time. Think of Vincent Van Gogh in painting. It is possible for your work to be so out there that your peers will not appreciate what you are doing. That is possible. Of course, on the other hand, you could just have no clue and are producing rubbish. Sorting out which is which is hard and ultimately it comes to knowing yourself.

You cannot create photography (or any other form of art) for a fictional, ideal customer or buyer. You can only create for yourself. If you are not producing for yourself it will show in the work as a lack of integrity. Many people will pick this up, even if they won't be able to tell you exactly what is wrong with the image.

Now obviously if you are shooting commercial photography for a client you must please the client. That is a different situation and shooting to please the client is a core part of the job. And a job it is in that situation.

But when you are creating images with no single, definite customer in mind, you need to concentrate on only pleasing yourself. This is especially true of the fine art photographer and the hobbyist.

Why is this? Because one of the keys to creating strong work is maintaining the integrity of your images. You can't do this if you are second guessing yourself and trying to please someone else who may or may not even exist, and who you definitely do not understand as well as yourself. By the same token, don't create for your spouse, camera club judge, parents, friends or instructor. You must be true to yourself.

Activity

Make a point of critiquing your own work carefully. Compare, document, try to view your work from someone else's perspective.

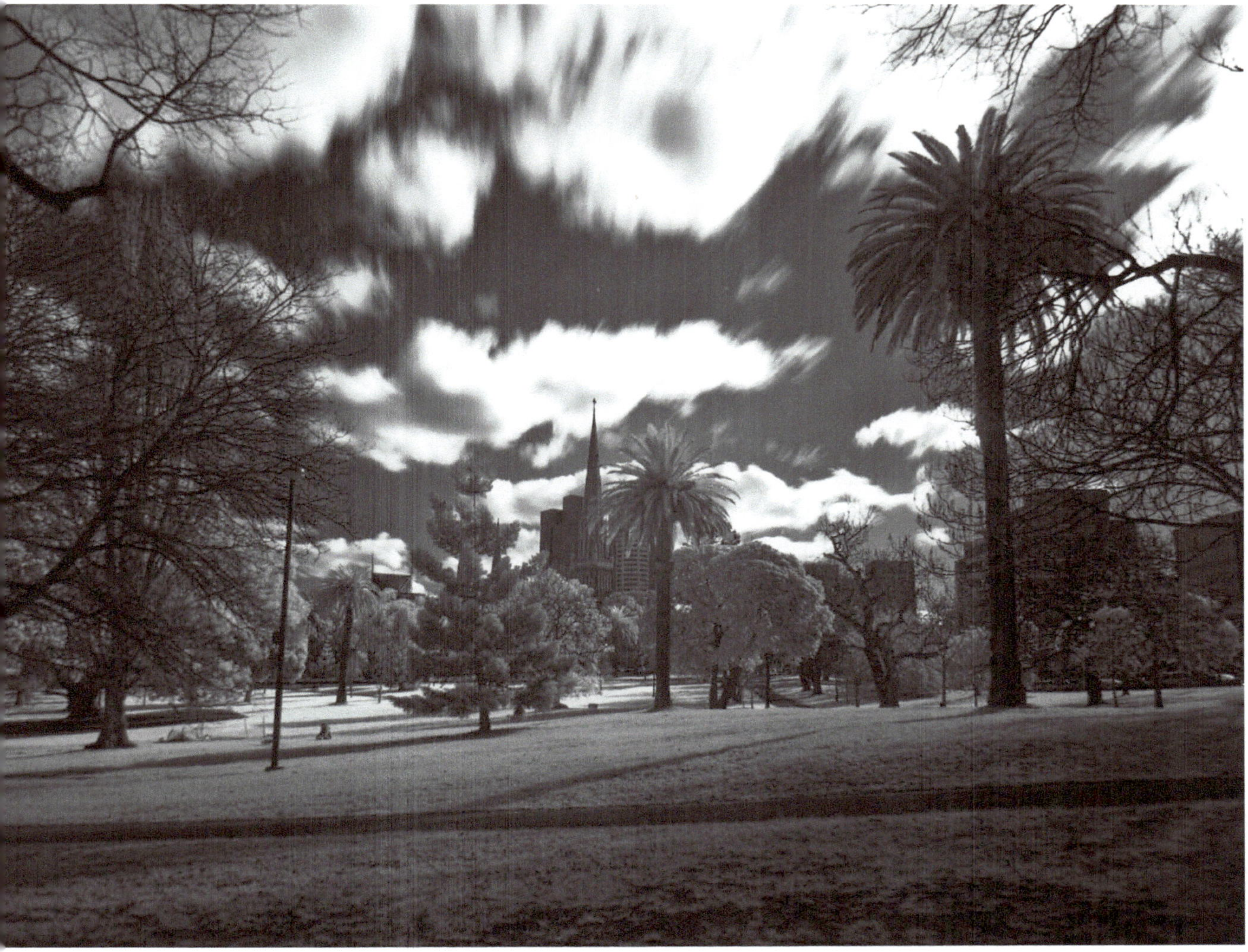

My personal passion is infrared photography, sometime I prefer to shoot in virtually every situation. IR is far from being everyone's favourite, but it is mine. So I shoot it every way and time I can, from long exposures , as above, with unconverted cameras, to very high resolution IR panoramas shot with a converted for IR camera.

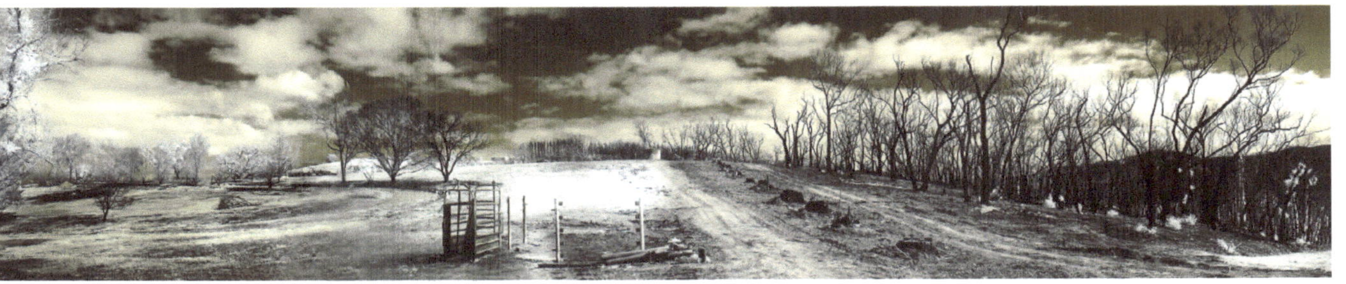

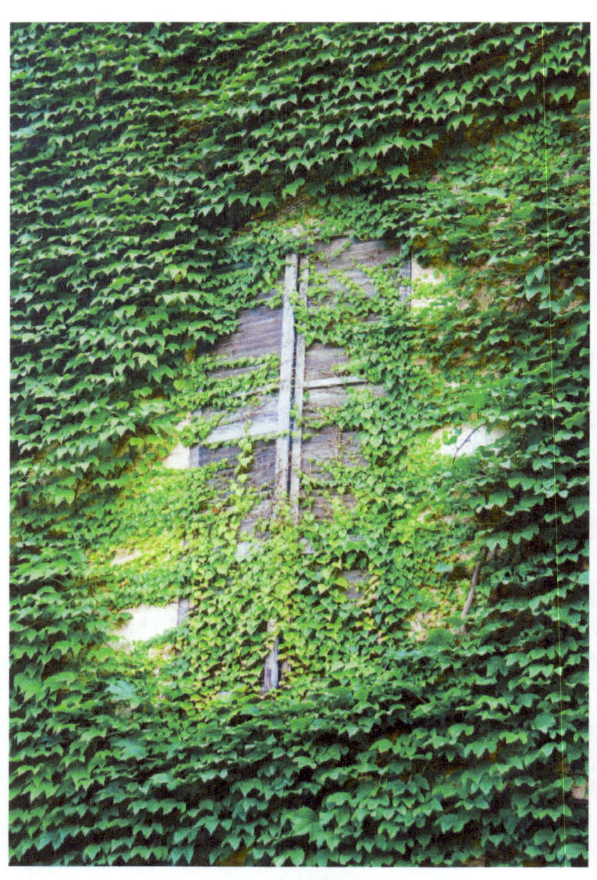

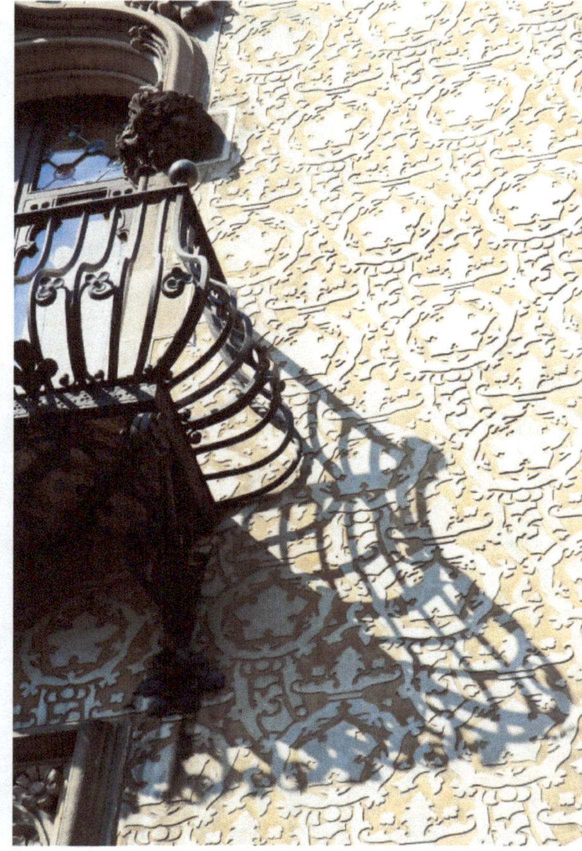

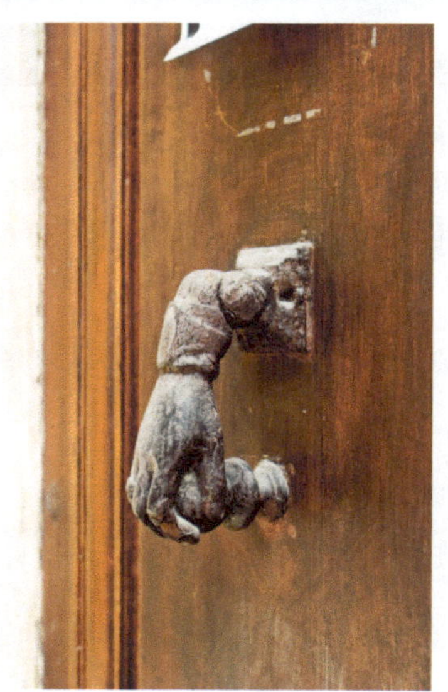

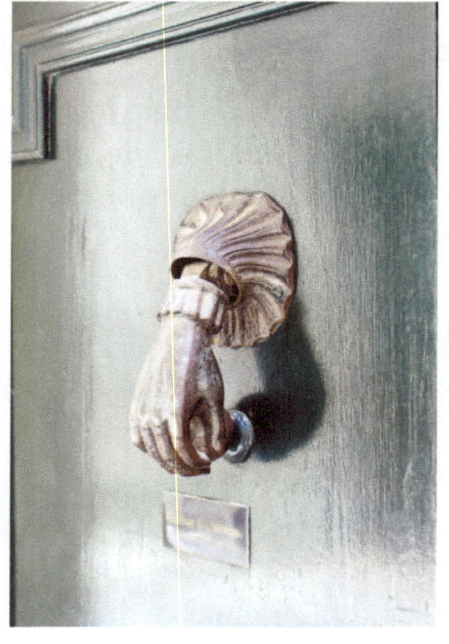

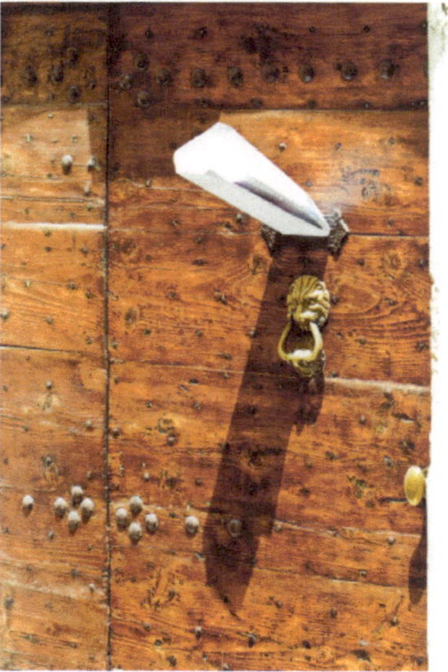

Collections

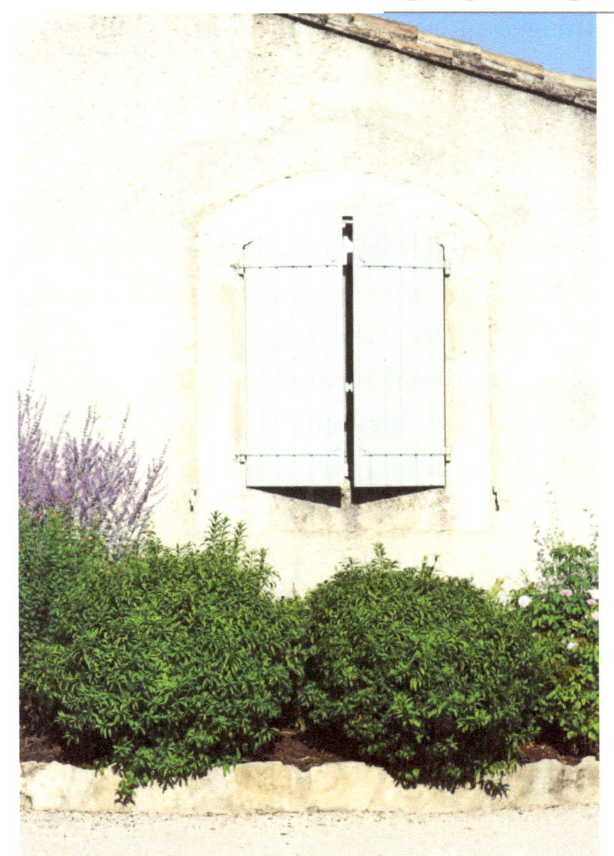

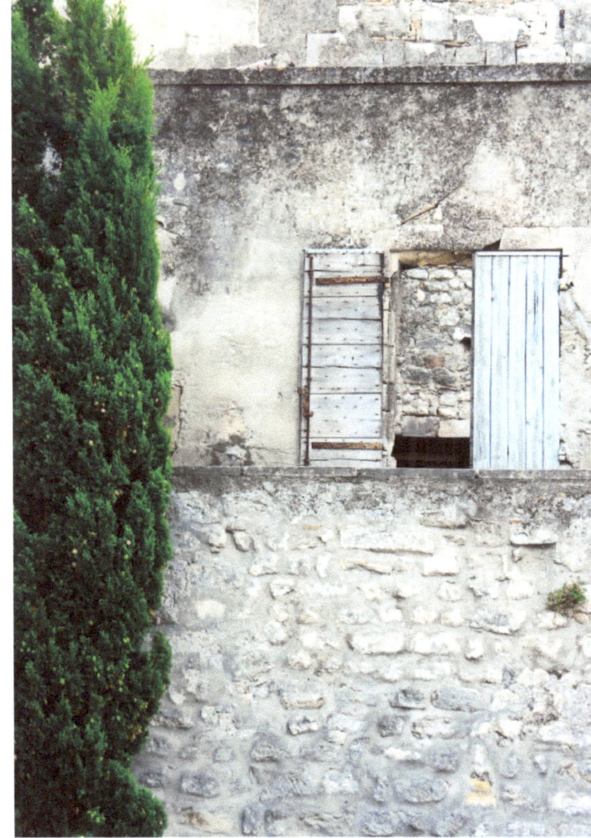

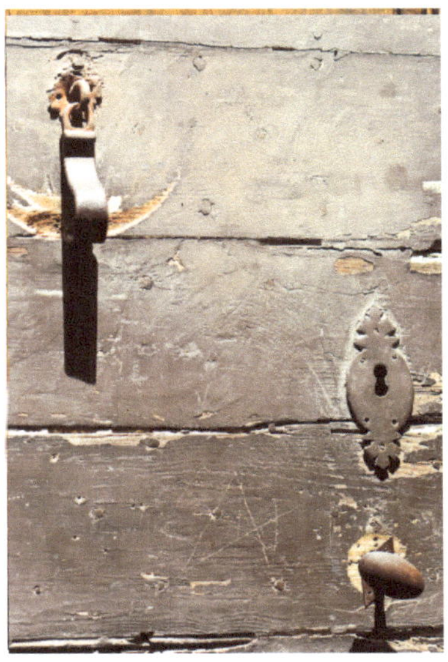

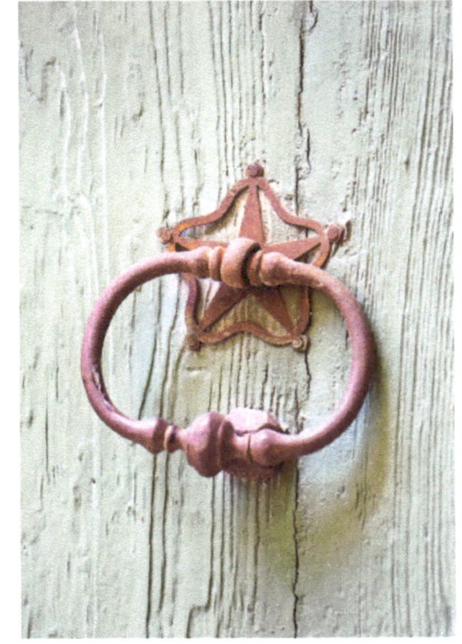

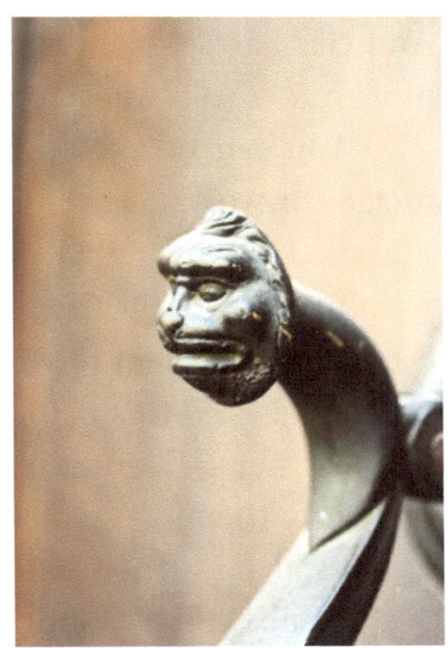

47. Think in Bodies of Work

Summary - As photographers and artists we are usually focused on the individual image or work. This is fine, as far as it goes. Indeed it is necessary for creating that stunning image. But it is not the only option.

We rarely use images by themselves. In an article there will be several, in a book a lot and in an exhibition many. So while as photographers or artists we often think about the single image, we will commonly use them in collections.

A collection of images or art works can just be a collection of images. But this would be to miss out on some of the real power that is possible in a body of work. And that last phrase is the key to getting more out of your images.

You can think about a collection of images or works as a single entity, a body of work, exhibition or series, whichever term works for you. You can do this after the making of the individual images. But you can also do this before and as you are making them. Taking this into account as you make the individual pieces allows you to expand on a theme you can't cover in one image, create relationships between images and develop narrative beyond what is possible in just one image.

A body of work will always be measured by its weakest image. So an otherwise strong series of images can be devalued by one very weak one. Now there will always be variation in the strength of works within a series, but you want to eliminate obviously weak members. Edit savagely. This can be very challenging to do, but very rewarding. Done well, a body of work adds to and enhances the individual images that make it up and allows you to go further than a single work would. It also pushes you to get beyond a single great image on a topic or idea, and to create a series of strong images. In the end, this makes you better at what you do.

The collection of images on the right and on the following spread are from a series called "Better to be a Wolf Than a Sheep'. It is a series that came out of thinking about religion, of all things, and how the Christian idea of a flock is mirrored with that of being a follower. From that thought I decided to think about how it was different to be a leader rather than a follower, yet whilst still being part of a community. This led me to thinking of wolves and from there the decision to create a series of images that explored what the world might look like to a wolf.

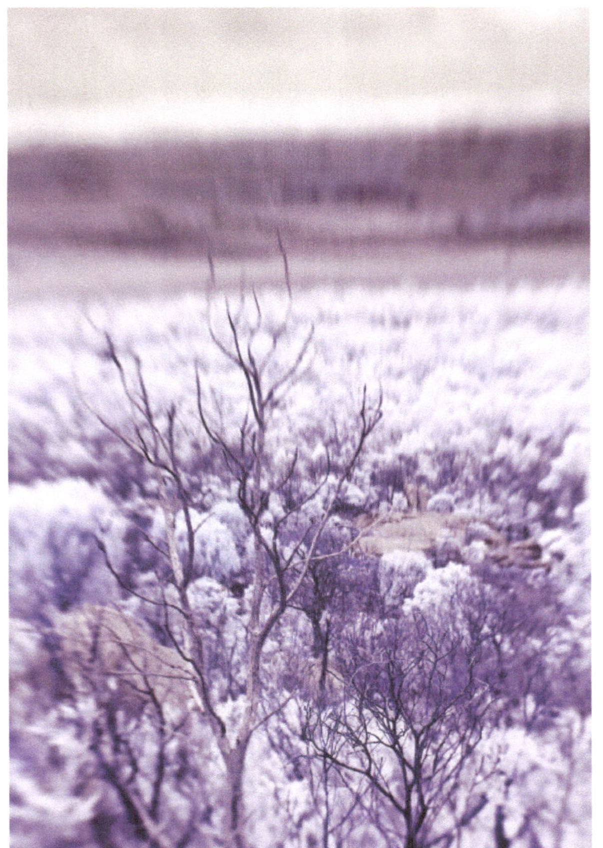

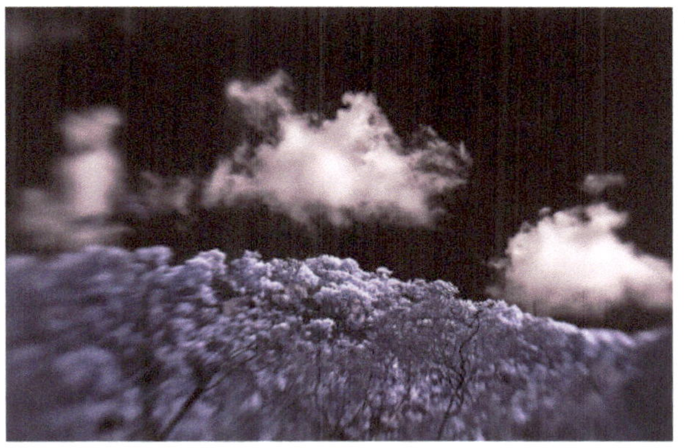

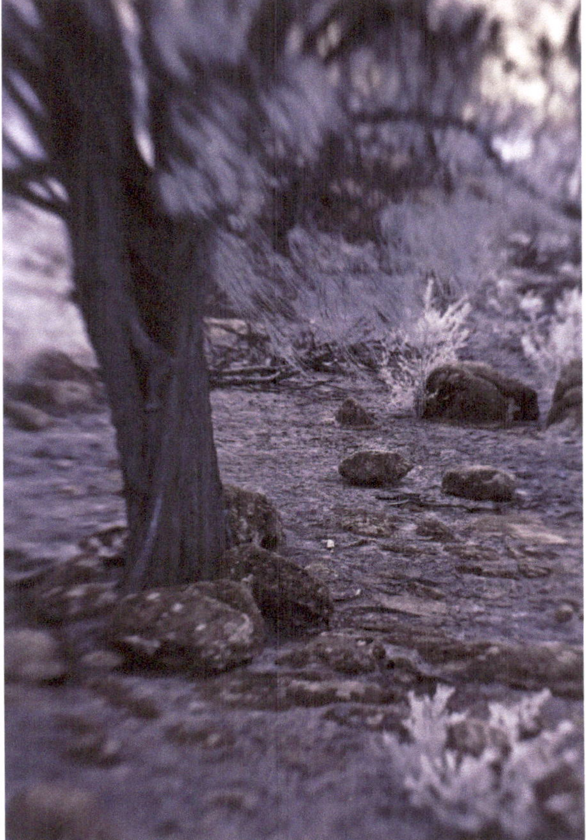

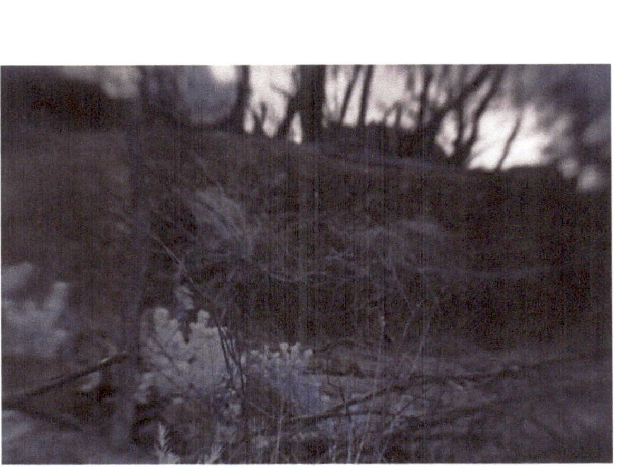

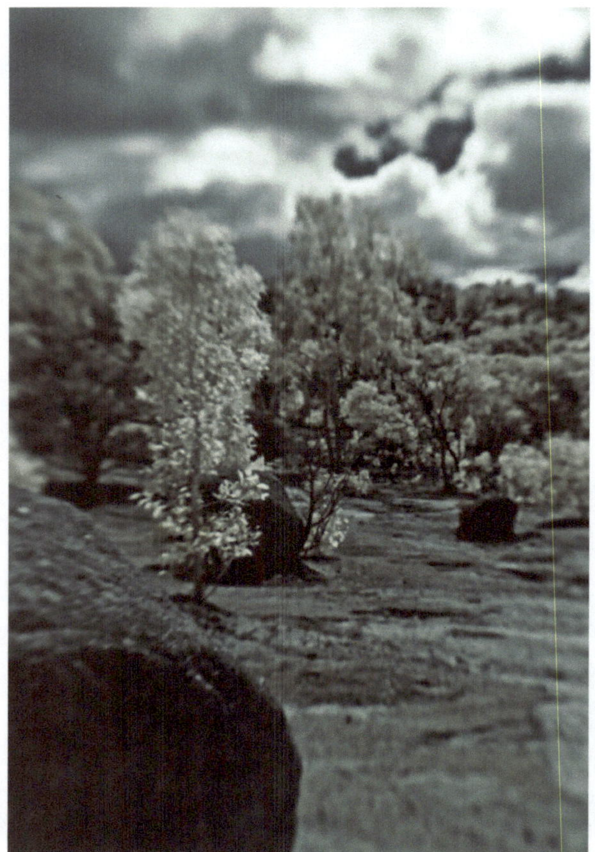

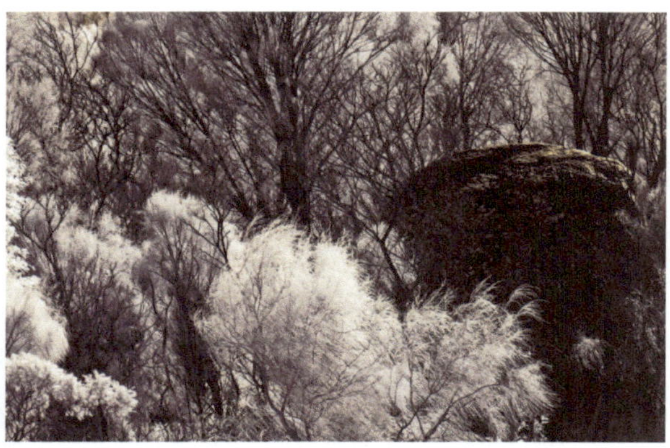

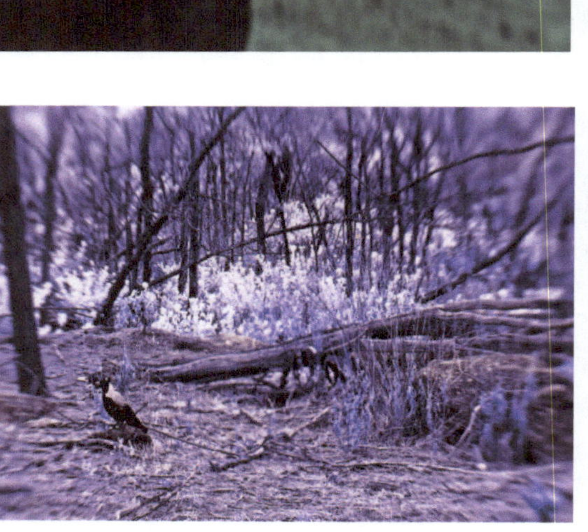

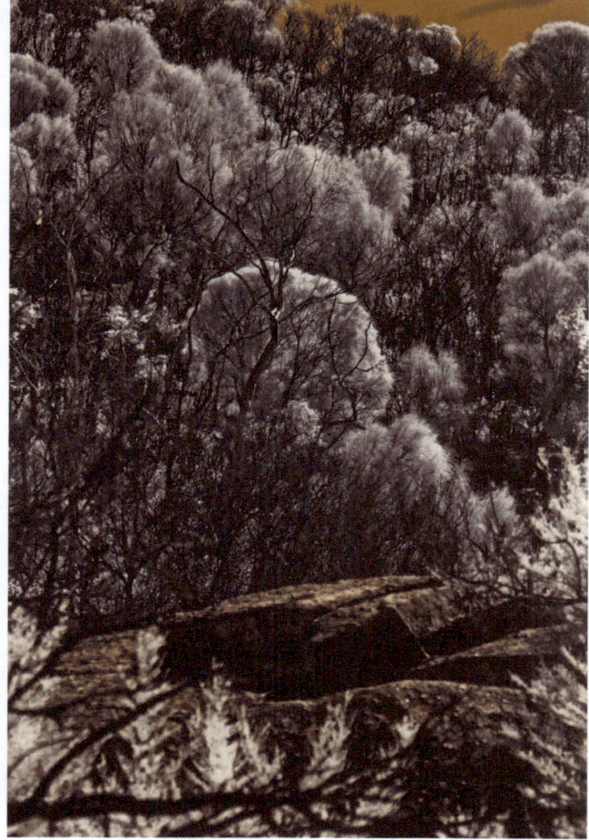

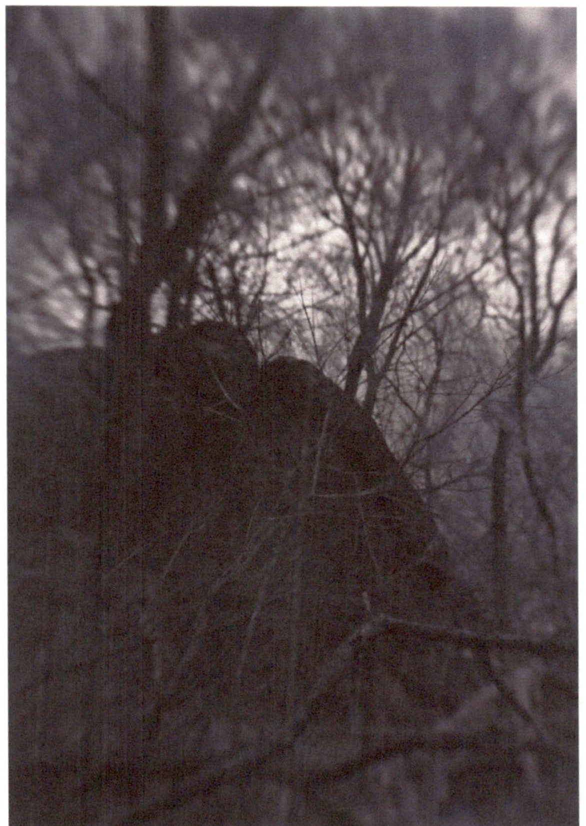

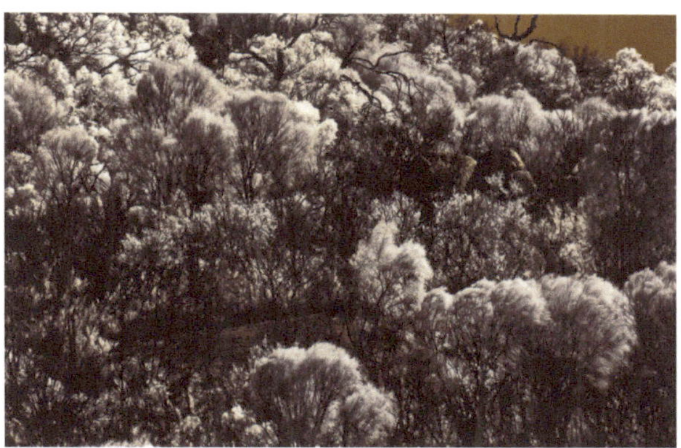

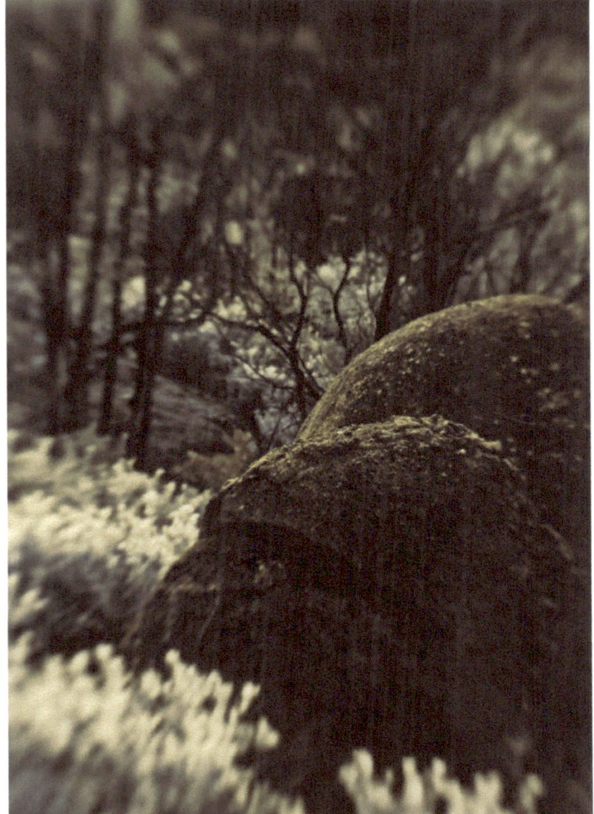

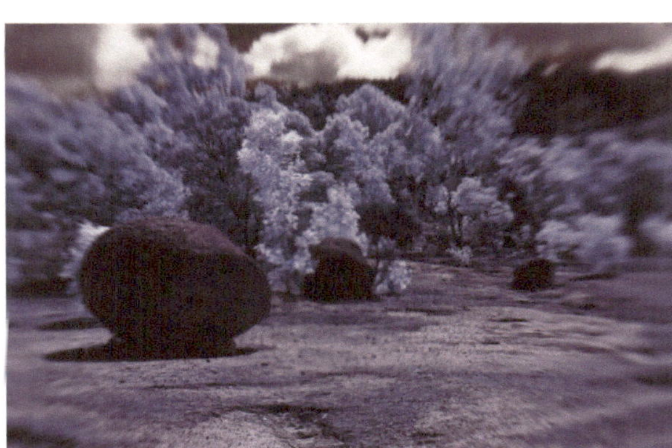

48. Set Assignments

Assignments are not only something you did at school. Setting yourself assignments is a great way to focus the attention and force yourself to extend your creativity. The other advantage of assignments is that you get practice at building up a body of work that should all work well together in a book, multimedia presentation or exhibition. Assignments can be on anything you like. Here are a few ideas:

- Your home town as only a local would see it
- Your home town as a visitor would see it
- Your back yard
- The world from ground level
- Local flowers of spring
- The cold
- Anger
- Solitude
- The changing world

An assignment can really be on anything that catches your attention. The benefit comes from limiting your choices whilst also focusing your attention

Activity

Practice acts of random photography. When you are going through a dry spell (we all do), pick a photography book off the bookshelf, open it at random and set yourself an assignment based on what is on that page. If it is discussing one of the 'rules', then set yourself an assignment to follow and explore that rule for a week. Then do a follow-up assignment to break that rule for a week. If it illustrates a technique, try it. If it shows a photographer's work, try for a week to replicate their style or approach.

At other times set better considered self-assignments. These can have as sim-

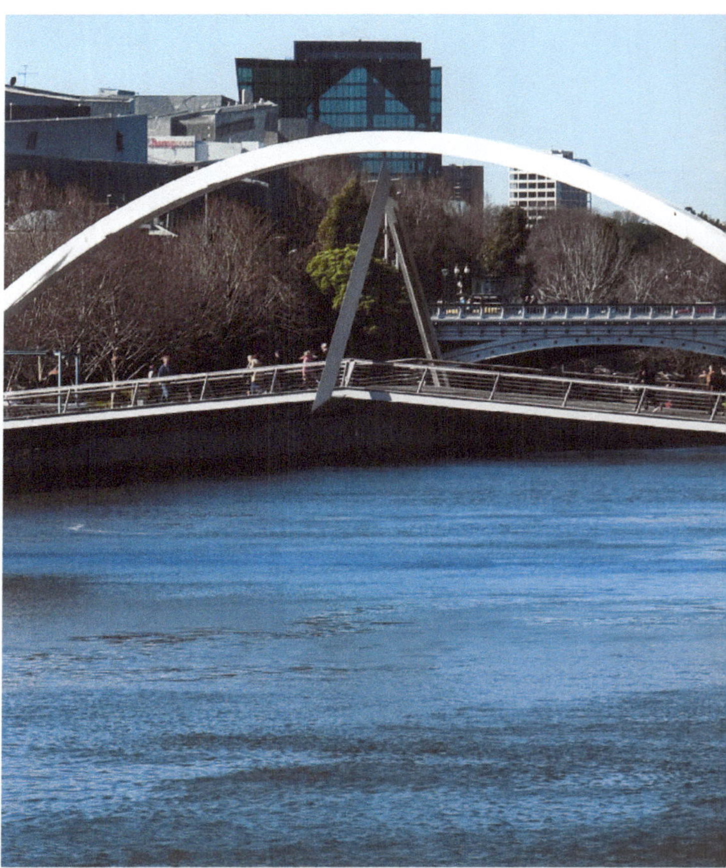

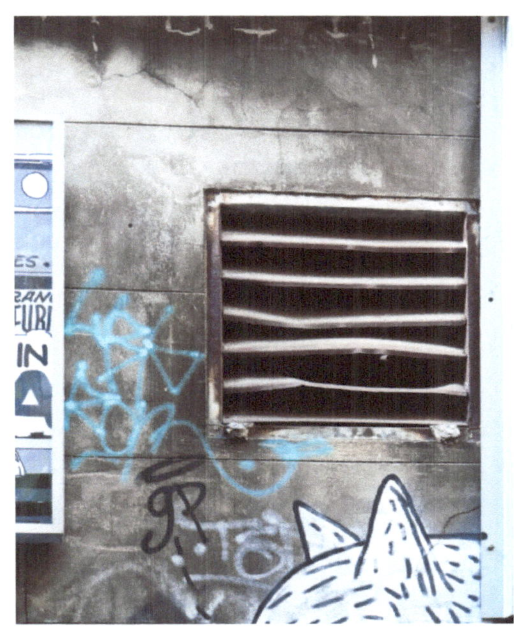

ple or as complex a statement of what the assignment is, as you want. So you could 'shoot the world as a four year old child would' or shoot 'loneliness', both are good. Try shooting your location from the viewpoint of a tourist, only shoot from ground level for a week or month, only shoot images that contain triangles, shoot everything at f1.8 or 1/10 of a second.

Set time limits for an assignment and also push yourself with a set minimum number of strong images to be produced.

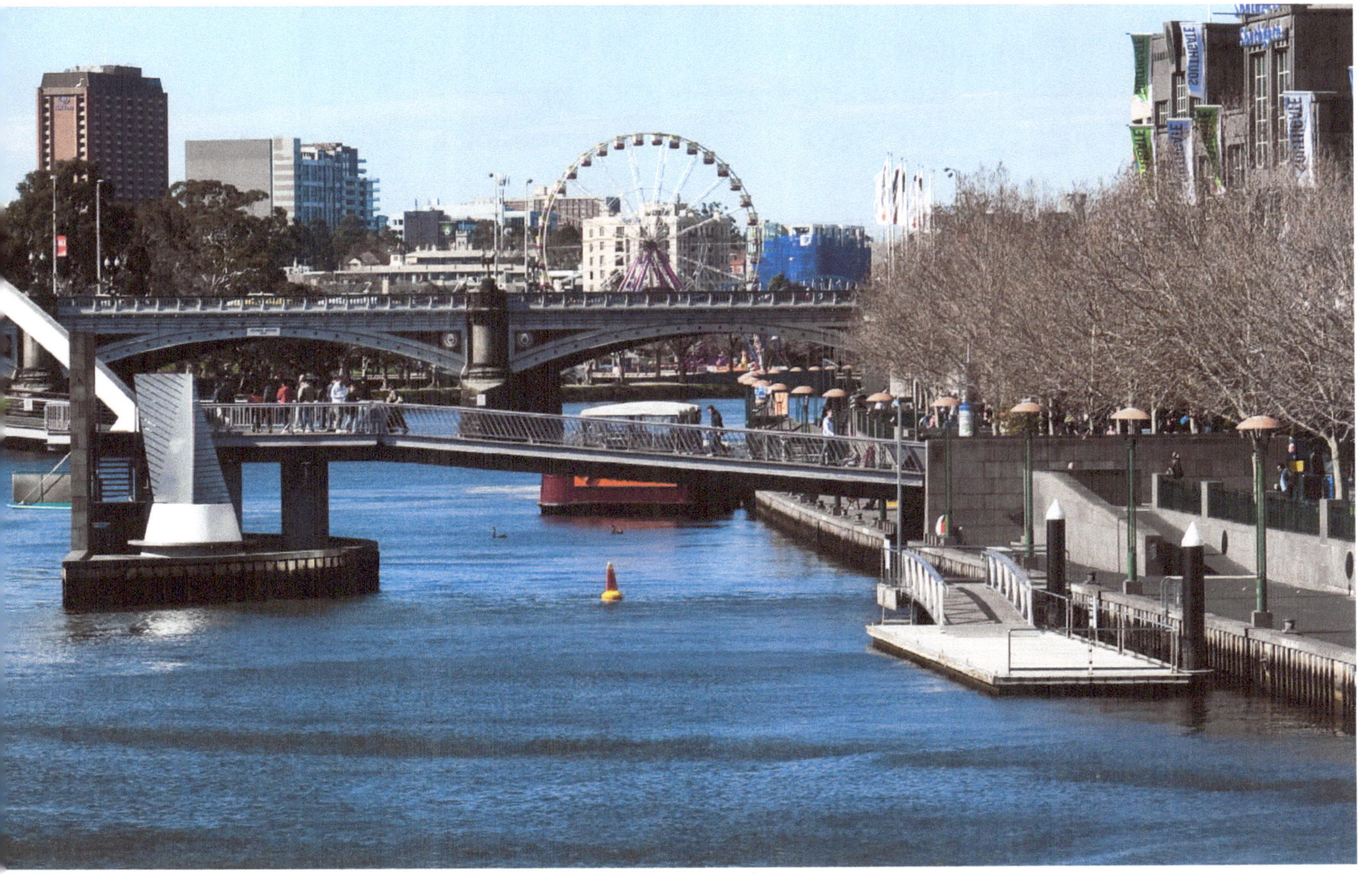

49. Enter Competitions

Testing oneself in comparison to others is an important part of developing any skill set, whether in sport or the arts. It gains you exposure and items on a developing CV (curriculum vitae), but more importantly it also allows you the important opportunity to directly compare your work against others. It will at least give you some basis to compare your work against others. Now one has to be careful not to enter into competitions so far above your present state of thinking about the art form. If you do, then when you are rejected and some work wins that you can not conceive of how it is even decent photography, let alone a winner, you will become so disillusioned that you walk away from the whole experience and learn nothing except that 'contemporary photography makes no sense'. Before entering, look at previous winners and short listed entries and try to figure out if your own work is in the same league as that which is being selected. If not, keep looking.

Competitions range from the free to enter online variety to the major ones where the prizes are huge, there are substantial entry fees and you must ship physical work around. There are competitions on the Internet, competitions organized by the local community or its organizations, and big national and international competitions run by major corporations or institutions. There are general competitions and highly specific ones. Just read the small print. No legitimate competition is going to want you to sign over the rights to your images. In fact no legitimate competition will want any rights over your images at all except those required to use your images for display and to promote the exhibition itself. Anything else is exploitative. The same holds for exhibitions.

Activity

Make a scrapbook or diary and put in there not only upcoming competitions and exhibitions but also articles, etc about previous winners.

Put into your main diary details of upcoming competitions and exhibitions well ahead of time.

Join up to any competition mailing lists so that you will always know when the next call for entries happens.

After some period of research, choose a competition where you believe (after careful consideration) that your work is at least as strong as that which is winning. Enter it. You may have to enter several times before you get a real feeling about whether you have a chance.

Do not let a failure or rejection put you off the whole thing. They say the difference between a successful businessman and a failure is not how many mistakes they make, but what they learn from them. Where possible, ask for feedback. Where not, compare your work against what wins and try to figure it out.

These are three images from a portfolio of ten that won me an award in the Panasonic Lumix Life Photography Competition in 2009. You never know what will come out of entering competitions. The exposure can be good, an award can be leveraged in your career or just provide a nice piece of encouragement when you hit one of those 'Long Darkroom Nights of the Soul' that happen to all photographers. You gain insight into your work even from the selection process you go through in choosing what images to enter.

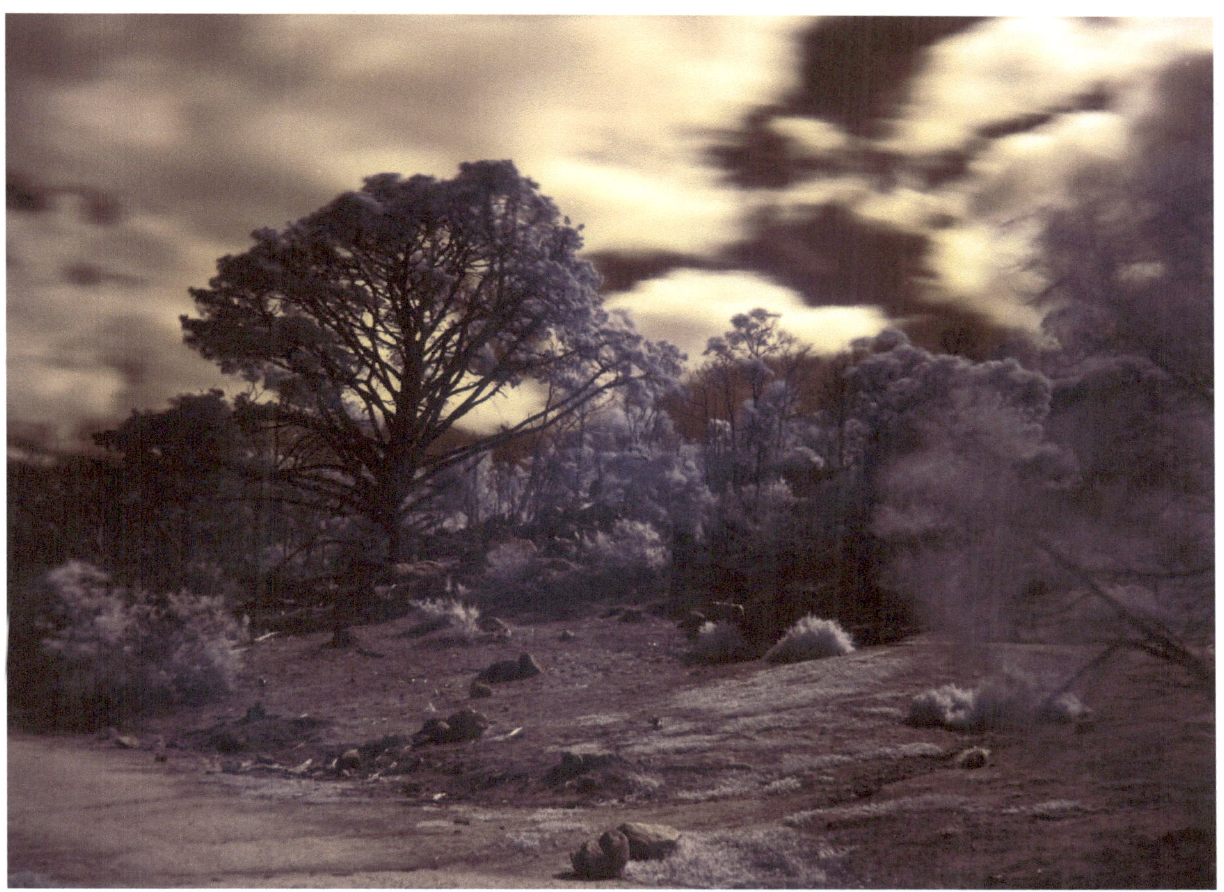

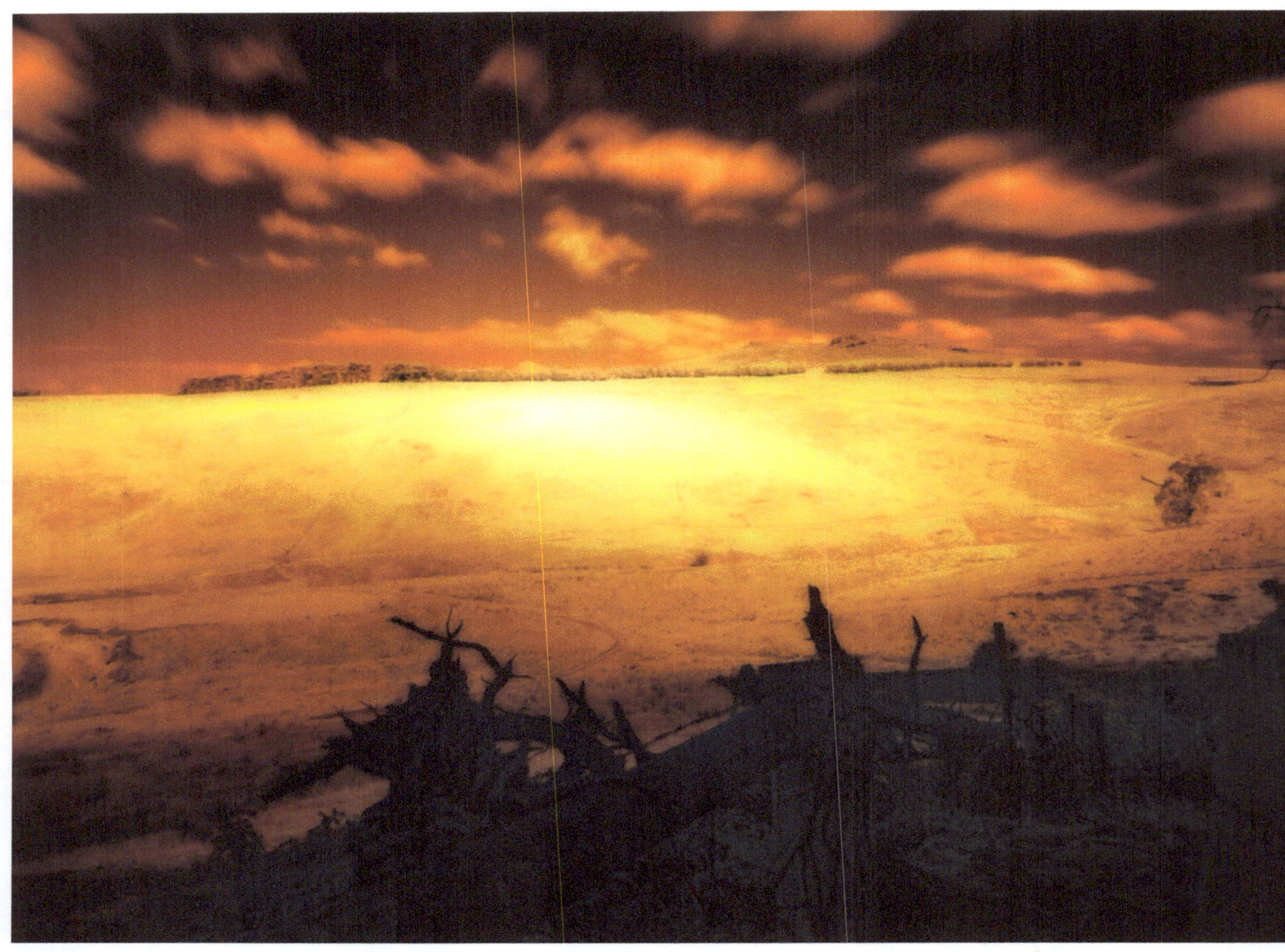

Style

It is very important to find your own look or style. While many do not like it, I have fallen in love with the false colour I produce from processing infrared shots. It doesn't matter what your look is, so long as you find one. This might be very subtle colour in what looks like a BW image, strongly saturated colour, blurred clouds, a strong graphic element always in one corner or whatever.

Once you think you are finding something you love you need to push it to extremes to determine exactly what degree of it you want. In art terms this is often discussed as pushing your work to the point of destroying it and this is a key part of the development of an artist: art destruction. Same with photography. If you are not courageous enough to push your work to real extremes you will never find the exact point that you can be passionate about. Cautious people stop at nice, brave people push it to extremes in the hope of creating amazing. Which are you?

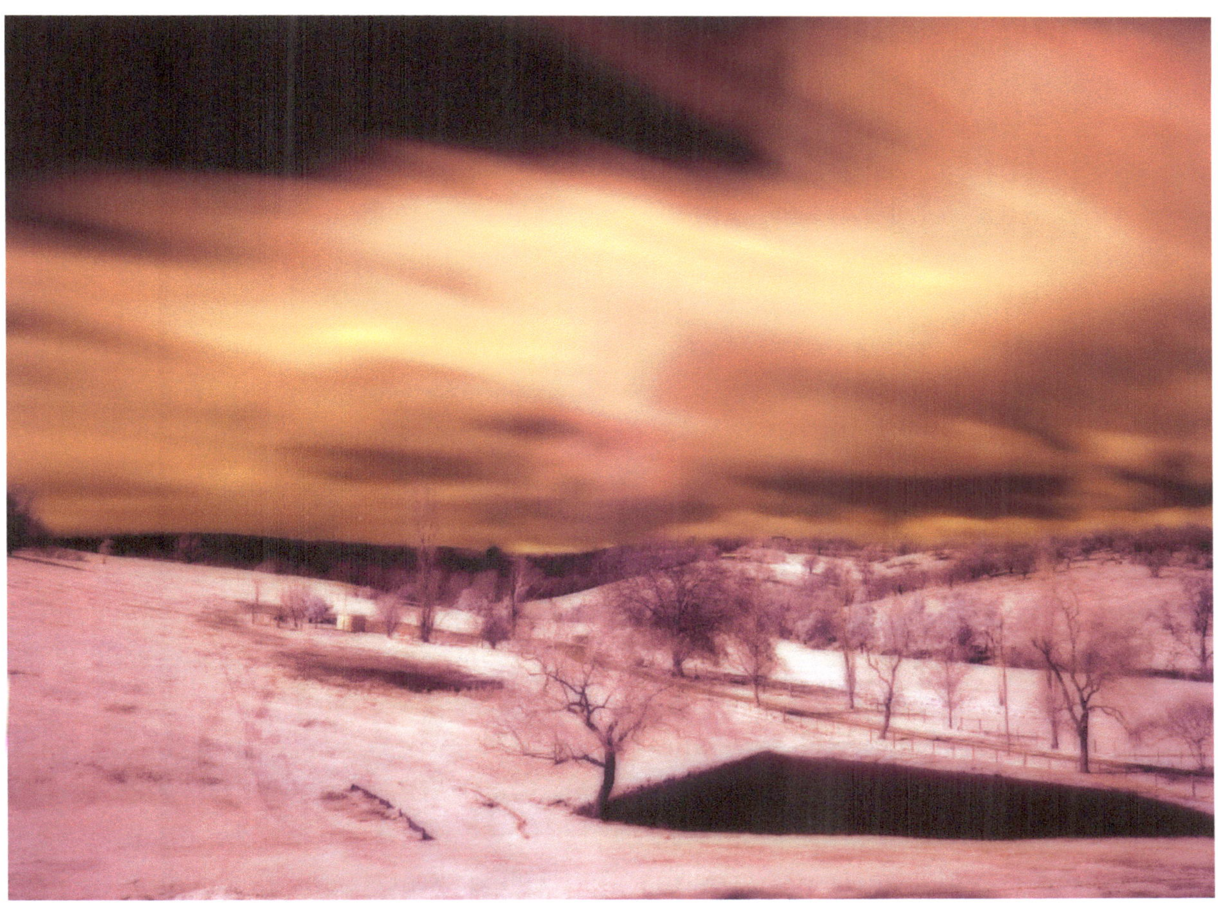

50. Exhibitions

Exhibitions have many benefits beyond the obvious of selling your work. You could summarize these benefits as:

- Careful analysis of your own work
- Immediate sales at the exhibition
- Building brand awareness of yourself and your work
- Chance to meet and network with other photographers and artists
- Creation of business leads

The preparation for an exhibition is of huge value in itself. You need to go through your work with a cold, harsh eye, assessing quality and also discovering the ways in which your work can strengthen or weaken each other when placed together. A exhibition is not just a collection of individual works. You need to find works than sit well together on the walls, that reinforce each other and perhaps that elaborate a concept or theme as you move through the exhibition.

Exhibition sales are an obvious benefit, but they perhaps should not be your main focus unless fine art or art photography is your main gig. Sales can vary hugely depending on the venue, audience suitability and the general state of the economy.

Doing business, and this includes art, is about brand awareness, you and your work forming the brand. An exhibition provides the opportunity for exposure, publicity in local and national papers and magazines, television or radio interviews, direct marketing and more. This is where many exhibitors fall down. The gallery will not do it all for you. You need to seize the day and go for it.

An exhibition will draw to it people interested in the type of work being shown. So you will not only, and hopefully, have an audience of art and photography collectors, but you will also get other photographers and artists along. The fact that they have chosen to come to see your work means they have effectively preselected themselves to have some common interests. Make sure you get around on the night and connect to as many people as possible, grabbing contact details or at least making sure they have yours. Out of such meetings can develop friendships and collaborative arrangements, future joint or group exhibitions and much more.

Other people attend openings and the gallery during the run of the exhibition, such as local business people. This can present you with the opportunity to make connections that can lead to photographic or other work commissions, now or in the future. If you are in a smallish town or city be sure to follow-up the exposure some time later with flyers, brochures, etc if you do other than pure art photography. It will jog peoples' memories of your exhibition and continue building awareness of you and your services.

If your focus is on the serious art world you need to be careful about where you exhibit. Some exhibition opportunities will not help you on the CV and may even hold you back from being given a chance by a serious gallery. Building a serious art career requires careful planning.

Exhibitions are a core part of every photographer's journey. They cause you to look at your work differently, expose you to different ways of interpreting your work and generally shake you out of a stuck state. You should take every opportunity to exhibit your work, and different work each time, so it pushes you to constantly create new and better work. Make sure you also allocate plenty of time to hang out at the exhibition, talk to visitors and listen carefully. That way you will gain the most.

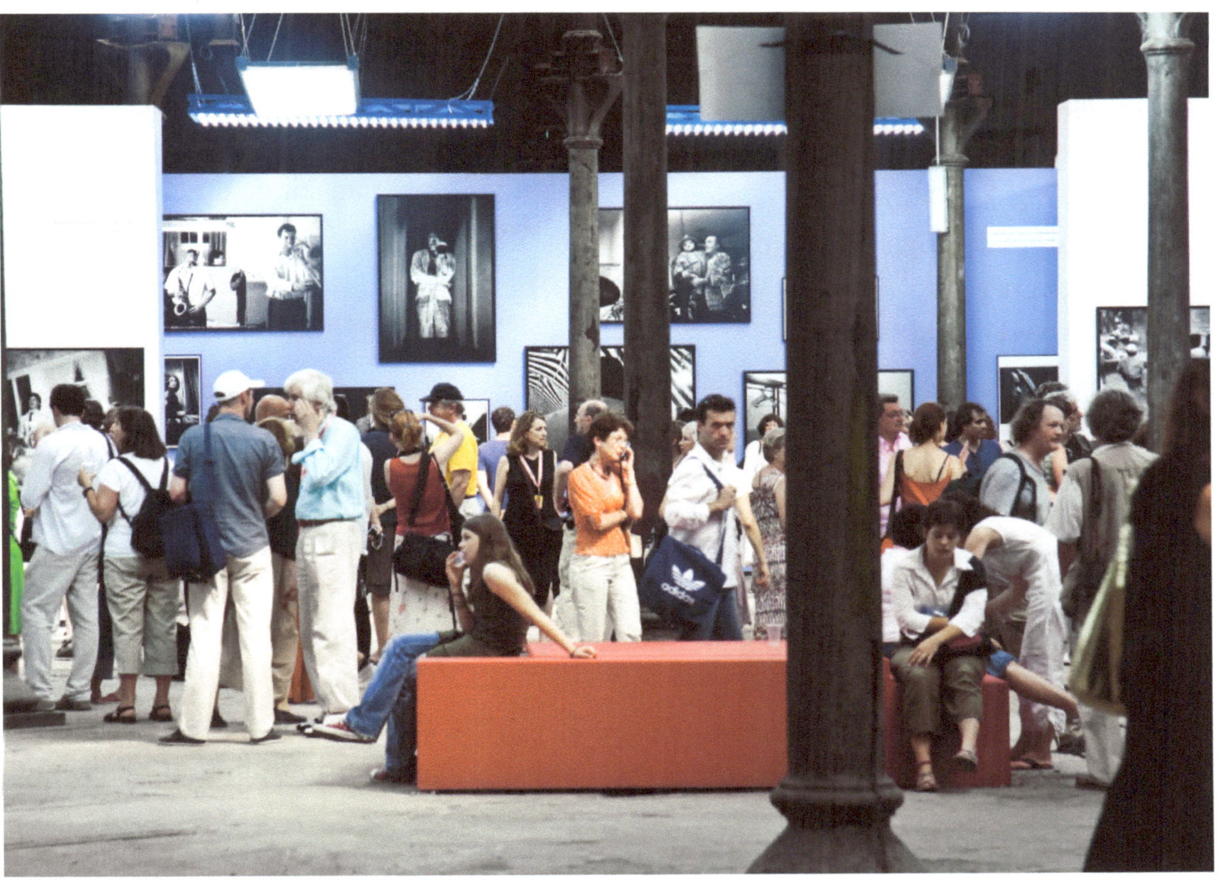

Resources

In advancing your photography you will benefit greatly from looking at a lot of photography. This means exhibitions, books and magazines. Checkout your local library to see what their photography section is like. Then venture further afield. Here are some resources I would recommend.

Magazines

Silvershotz - The International Journal of Fine Art Photography, is a great magazine that is put together in the Uk and Australia but showcases work from an international range of photographers. Great magazine.

- www.silvershotz.com

LensWorks - A great magazine that contains portfolios of photographers and great articles.

- www.lenswork.com

View Camera - while aimed at view camera users, obviously, it contains great photography that someone using any format could benefit from examining.

- www.viewcamera.com

Aperture - This is a great magazine, though a challenging one for many photographers to deal with because of its truly contemporary art photography orientation. It thus seems weird to many photographers.

- www.aperture.org

Focus - is a great magazine for fine art photography. While they took a break during the global financial crisis they are still there and new issues are coming out.

- www.focusmag.info

Eyemazing - is a contemporary art photography magazine somewhat similar to Aperture. Excellent read and great images.

- www.eyemazing.com

Black and White - Also known as B&W, it is an excellent magazine on monochrome photography.

- www.bandwmag.com

Outdoor Photographer - is an excellent US magazine on outdoor photography, naturally enough.

- www.outdoorphotographer.com

The back issues of these magazines are well worth seeking out, either in libraries or from the publisher. Since the emphasis is not on the technology but on the art, they do not date the way the technology oriented photography magazines do. If you are struggling to find some of these check out the library of a local college or university with a strong photography focus.

Websites

www.dimagemaker.com - Yes, this is one of my websites but it does contain a lot of tutorials that you can benefit from.

www.the37thframe.org - Photo-journalism focus.

www.positive-magazine.com - online magazine with strong reportage orientation.

www.boston.com/bigpicture - news stories through pictures.

www.flakphoto.com - daily photography magazine with an arts focus.

www.socialdocumentary.net - uses photo-journalism to address social issues.

www.fstopmagazine.com - contemporary photography online magazine.

http://vewd.org/ - documentary photography magazine.

www.chambrenoire.com - French photography magazine with portfolios of great work.

www.lensculture.com - contemporary art photography.

www.filemagazine.com - a great website of unexpected photography.

www.zonezero.com - Pedro Meyer's site with great portfolios and articles.

www.coloursmag.com - Colour's Magazine covers international photography with great articles.

deepsleep.org.uk - an online photography magazine out of the UK.

www.seesawmagazine.com - Interesting photography articles in a magazine form.

www.purpose.fr - French photography magazine.

www.fractionmagazine.com - US photography online magazine.

www.photoeye.com/magazine - photo book oriented site.

Books

There are too many great books out there to give you a sensible list. What you particularly want to look at are monographs of photographers' work, books that discuss the thought processes of great photographers and books that cover composition, colour theory and more.

Organisations

The National Association of Photoshop Professionals is a good organisation for those wanting to push their Photoshop skills.

- www.photoshopuser.com

Aardenburg Imaging & Archives is an organisation focused on addressing the archival qualities of digital imaging materials through international and independent testing standards

- www.aardenburg-imaging.com

Amien is an organisation oriented around the qualities of artists materials, so many of which photographers use. Great information is in their forums.

- www.amien.org

Local professional photography organisations exist in all countries. Many allow affiliate membership to people who are not fully professional photographers. Join up, go to their events, and learn from the pros.

Similarly there are art organisations in all countries and these are often worth engaging with for lists of exhibition opportunities, competitions and awards and much more.

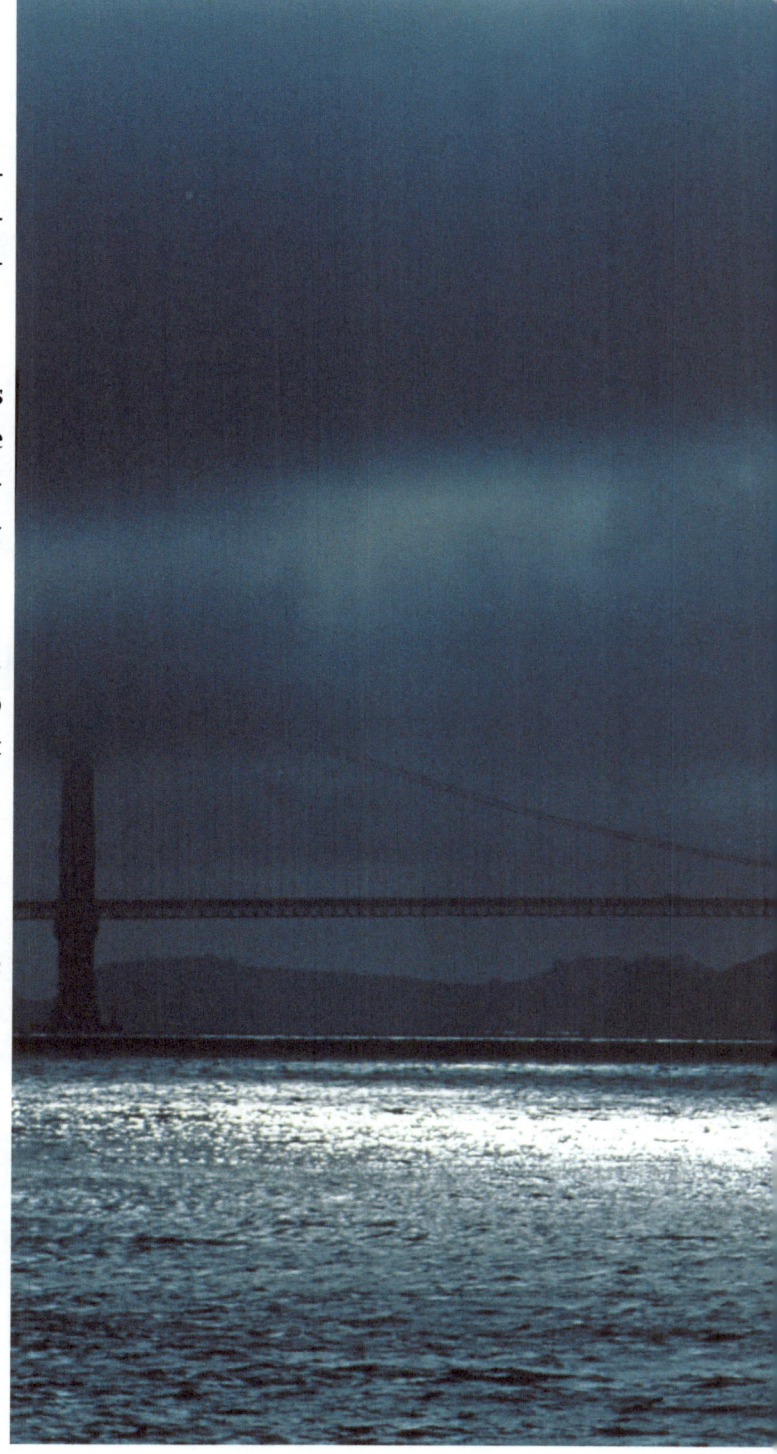

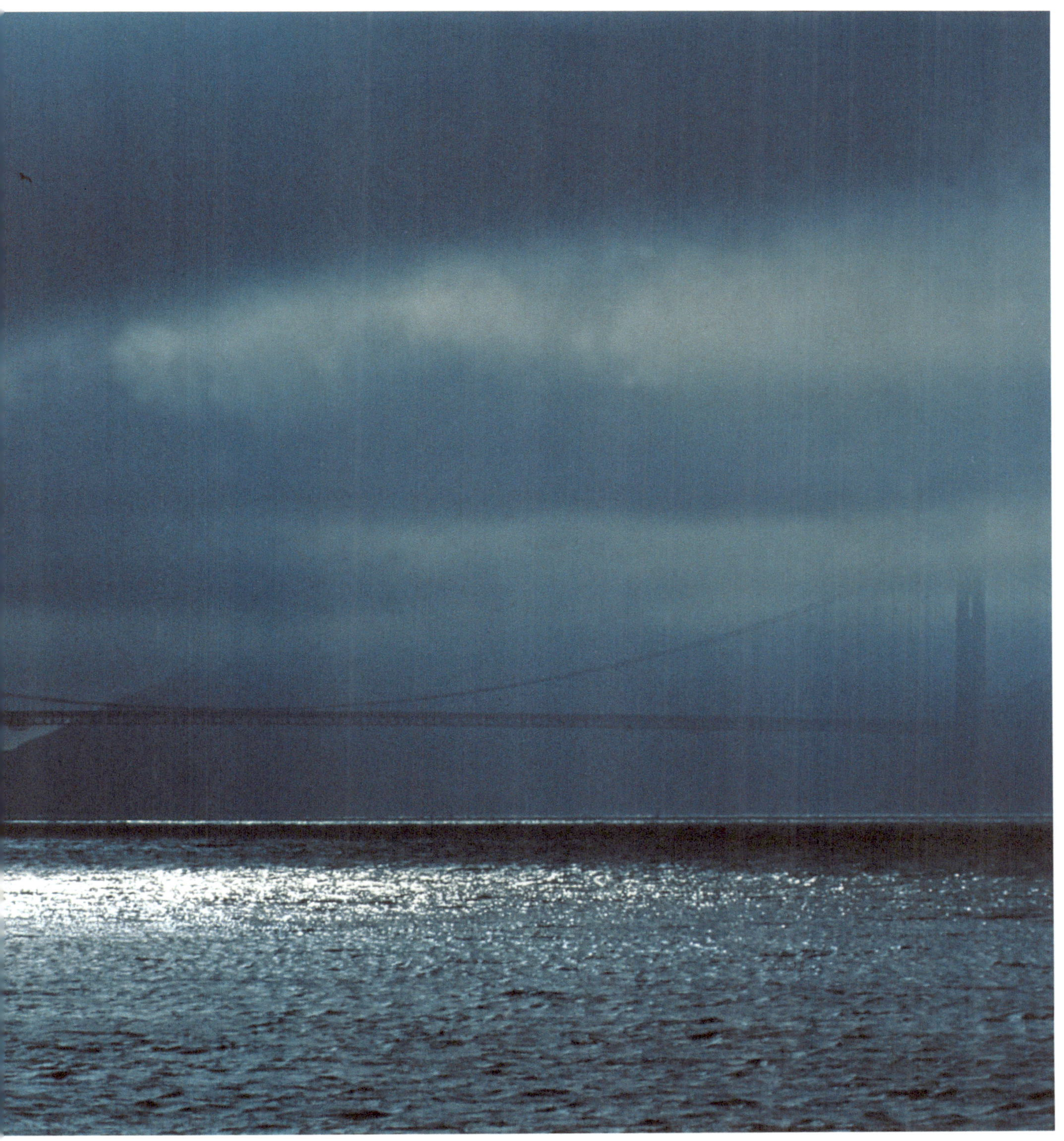

Index

www.ingramcontent.com/pod-product-compliance
Lightning Source LLC
Chambersburg PA
CBHW050713180526
45159CB00003B/1014